*Studies in International Political Economy*
Stephen D. Krasner, Editor
Ernst B. Haas, Consulting Editor

The Problems of Plenty: *Energy Policy and International Politics*,
   by Peter F. Cowhey

Standing Guard: *Protecting Foreign Capital in the Nineteenth and Twentieth Centuries*,
   by Charles Lipson

Structural Conflict: *The Third World Against Global Liberalism*,
   by Stephen D. Krasner

Liberal Protectionism: *The International Politics of Organized Textile Trade*,
   by Vinod K. Aggarwal

The following volumes will appear in the series in 1986:

The Power of Ideology: *The Quest for Technological Autonomy in Argentina and Brazil*,
   by Emanuel Adler

The Politicized Market Economy: *Alcohol in Brazil's Energy Strategy*,
   by Michael Barzelay

Ruling the Waves: *The Political Economy of International Shipping, 1945– 1985*,
   by Alan Cafruny

Banker to the Third World: *Latin America and U.S. Capital Markets, 1900–1980*,
   by Barbara Stallings

From Marshall Plan to Debt Crisis: *Foreign Aid and Development Choices in the World Economy*,
   by Robert Wood

# The Politicized Market Economy

MICHAEL BARZELAY

# The
# Politicized
# Market Economy

*Alcohol in Brazil's
Energy Strategy*

University of California Press

Berkeley / Los Angeles / London

University of California Press
Berkeley and Los Angeles, California

University of California Press, Ltd.
London, England
© 1986 by The Regents of the University of California

Printed in the United States of America

1 2 3 4 5 6 7 8 9

**Library of Congress Cataloging in Publication Data**
Barzelay, Michael.
　The politicized market economy.

　(Studies in international political economy)
　Bibliography: p.
　Includes index.
　1. Alcohol fuel industry—Brazil. 2. Energy
policy—Brazil. 3. Brazil—Economic policy. I. Title.
II. Series.
HD9502.5.A433B6244　　1986　　338.4'7662669　　85-8612
ISBN 0-520-05382-6 (alk. paper)

*For My Parents*

# Contents

# Foreword

*by Albert Fishlow*

The study of political economy is experiencing a renaissance. After several decades of specialization, intermittently challenged by the insights of bold and independent scholars, the need to relate fundamental propositions of governance and resource allocation in ways that cross disciplinary boundaries is more widely appreciated.

The new approaches to political economy are varied. One important strand, central to dependency and world system views, insists on the relevance of the position of national states in an international hierarchy. Another reexamines the role of the state and its autonomous capabilities. Still a third emphasizes the reciprocal interaction of political and economic decisions in mixed economy settings.

Michael Barzelay's book is an important contribution that significantly advances the way such political-economic interactions can be conceptualized and modeled. It is distinctive for interpreting within a political framework the behavior of economic agents and the resulting market consequences. But the state is no black box. It is peopled by real decision makers and conflicting bureaucratic interests that emit multiple and changing political signals and are constrained by civil society and economic performance. In Barzelay's politicized market economy, private and public interests contend not at random but in a predictable fashion. Understanding that predictability should be the goal of studying political economy. Barzelay confronts this central issue in novel and insightful ways, which is why the book is not only an exemplar of the new political economy but a path-breaking contribution that extends its range.

The reader will find a skilled and sophisticated command of economics and respect for the power of the market mechanism in allocating resources. The reader will also find a subtle treatment of the developmental bureaucratic state, and the machinations and manipulations of public agencies struggling for control not merely to advance narrow concerns but in pursuit of the national interest. In the politicized market economy, the separate impulses come together. There are no private investment decisions, except in far-off corners, that can ignore politics, and no politics that is unshaped by the responses of significant economic actors.

Although there is a merited emphasis on formal and precise statement, this is no theoretical treatise. Barzelay's model is persuasive because it successfully explains the complicated evolution of the alcohol program in Brazil during its first decade. It analyzes Brazilian development policy at a critical moment, a time not only of changing international price signals but also of relaxing authoritarian control. It focuses on a sector that was central to the overall import substitution adjustment strategy followed by the state. Without the idea of the politicized market economy, the history of the alcohol program is puzzling and confused. Economics and political science taken independently ask the wrong questions and provide only partial answers. Barzelay's analysis points in the right direction of moving policy discussions beyond mechanical advocacy of simply getting prices right as the solution to economic imbalance.

His contribution is all the more impressive because it is a first book. He whets our appetite for more. For with a deft hand, and a wisdom befitting a mature scholar, he has demonstrated the advantages of an interdisciplinary approach applicable to other problems in other countries. Not least, Barzelay has communicated these complex ideas in a clear and straightforward prose and with a narrative power that does justice to the drama of the Brazilian alcohol program.

It is a great personal and professional satisfaction to commend this book to a broad readership.

# Acknowledgments

In writing this book, it has become clear to me that almost everything one learns influences what is later observed and how it is evaluated. Since I have learned most from my parents, Ross and Jean Barzelay, it follows that they have shaped this work more than anyone else. Their views of how the world works, what drives the behavior of individuals, and how those motivations get transformed in organizational and market settings have shaped my views fundamentally.

This book is also the product of a constant interplay between abstract theory and concrete problem solving as well as between political science and economics. This interplay directly reflects the stimulation, guidance, and ceaseless encouragement provided by several scholars whom I am proud to call my teachers.

My interest in the energy crisis and in the linkages between its technological and economic aspects was first sparked almost a decade ago at Stanford University by George B. Dantzig and Nathan Buras. It is largely because these remarkable men spent hours upon hours with me during my freshman year that I came to appreciate the use of models in analyzing complex systems.

Three years later, when I proposed to study the politics of Brazil's alcohol program for a senior thesis, Scott R. Pearson strongly urged me first "to get the economics straight." Among other contributions, Pearson's six-year collaboration made possible the economic efficiency analysis of alcohol production I offer in Chapter 2.

After my initial round of field research in 1979, Robert O. Keohane suggested that I examine the case study in light of the emerging literature on how different national political structures facilitate or impair the adjustment of market economies to changes in the international environment. Keohane's special passion for using a wide range of theoretical traditions to understand politico-economic systems is largely responsible for the way in which this study unfolded. Also at Stanford, Robert A. Packenham and Richard R. Fagen offered extremely valuable advice which kept the study on track.

I later had the great fortune to study economics at Yale. My exposure there to Martin Shubik led me to focus more explicitly on the problem of control in economic systems as well as on the microeconomic incentives that arise when investors are playing a "game of strategy" against the state. I hasten to add that this book might not have been completed without Shubik's insistence, three years ago, that it was worth pursuing.

My use of a somewhat formal model to analyze the politicized market economy is due to Carl Alan Batlin, who introduced me to the relevant literature in the theory of finance. Though he faced an uphill battle, Batlin did more than anyone else to convince me of the merits of careful microeconomic analysis.

Over the last two years, I have also had the great privilege of working closely with one of the foremost theorists of politico-economic systems, Charles E. Lindblom. Lindblom not only helped me clarify the conceptual discussion of the policy-making process and the mutual adjustment of investors and state officials; he also went to extraordinary lengths in teaching me how to write effectively. This book matured greatly at his hands.

There is no doubt, however, that Albert Fishlow is the person most responsible for the development of this work from a focused case study to a general analysis of resource allocation processes in steered economies. Fishlow's range continually spurred new lines of inquiry, opening my eyes to new connections between economy and society. While confidently expressing his enthusiasm for the study, Fishlow never failed to encourage me to push harder and reach further. Though it was occasionally disconcerting, he always seemed to keep three steps ahead of me—even in discussing the intricacies of the case study itself. It is impossible to express my appreciation and admiration for this scholar and dear friend in just a few lines.

To Catherine Moukheibir, I am greatly indebted for the substantive criticism and perceptive editorial advice provided throughout the last five years. Of all the other friends who contributed to this project, only a few can be mentioned here. In Brazil, these included Leo Bick, Ernesto Lozardo, Rosa Guilger Gruppo, Antonia Guilger, Sonia Guilger, Helio Mattar, Joubert de Oliveira Brizida, and Carlos Eduardo de Souza e Silva. Back home, those who went to great lengths to help included William Adkinson, Vinod Aggarwal, Don Barth, Albert Chu, Carlos Diaz-Alejandro, Peter Evans, Justin Frankel, Richard Smithey, Lee R. Thomas, Joseph Vadapalas, Albert Vourvoulias, and Sidney Winter.

The field research for this project was initially carried out in mid-1979 under a grant from the Center for Latin American Studies, Stanford University. An opportunity to return to Brazil in mid-1981 was made possible by a grant from the Tinker Foundation and the Center for International and Area Studies, Yale University. The willingness of these institutions to fund an untested student is gratefully acknowledged. For the remarkable flexibility and encouragement provided me over the past five years, I am immeasurably indebted to the Department of Political Science and the School of Organization and Management at Yale.

For their perceptive reading of an earlier draft of this book, I would like to thank Ernst B. Haas and two anonymous readers. James H. Clark, Dore Brown, and Barbara Ras of the University of California Press made the publication of this study proceed like clockwork.

The debts I incurred while writing this book are not limited to my advisers and friends. Most of my impressions of the Brazilian political economy are drawn from the insights of the many individuals who were kind enough to offer their time and share their thoughts. Each person cited in the list of interviews in the bibliography thus contributed to this work in a valuable way.

# 1

# Introduction

## Analysis and Comparison
## of Politico-Economic Systems

Social scientists today can draw upon a wide array of elaborate concepts to understand the basic instruments of social coordination. Some of these concepts are the product of centuries of gradual refinement; many are the inventions of the last few decades. Recent advances in the theories of finance, public goods, information, and general equilibrium, for example, help clarify what the price system can and cannot achieve. Organization theory, another recent innovation, has similarly sharpened our knowledge of the gains that can be attained by coordinating individual efforts through formal hierarchies. A vast assortment of other related concepts aid our inquiry into the variety of complex social processes by which citizens can potentially control their governments. And the modeling techniques as well as solution concepts developed by the theory of games have significantly deepened our understanding of mutual adjustment processes generally and bargaining in particular.[1]

Specialization in the production of professional knowledge about the social world is surely one reason why these out-standing analytic advances have been made. This same special-ization, however, has impaired progress in the analysis of politico-economic systems. Few scholars have transcended disciplinary lines and formulated novel conceptions of the many linkages among the instruments of social coordination.[2] Progress along these lines is also impeded by the sheer complexity of politico-economic interactions. The notably limited human capacity for visualizing the shape of radical social change is testimony to the difficulty of comprehending the "system-wide behavior" of new combinations of the basic instruments of social calculation and control.[3] For these reasons, among others, knowledge of alternative politico-economic systems derives largely from the work of scholars who have explored the variety of institutions and practices in

---

[1]Some of the more accessible and synthetic contributions to these areas are: Kenneth J. Arrow, *The Limits of Organization* (New York: Norton, 1974); Frank Hahn, "Reflections on the Invisible Hand," *Lloyds Bank Review* (April 1982):1–21; Amartya Sen, "The Profit Motive," *Lloyds Bank Review* (January 1983):1–20; Oliver L. Williamson, *Markets and Hierarchies: Analysis and Antitrust Implications* (New York: Free Press, 1975); Charles E. Lindblom, *Politics and Markets: The World's Political-Economic Systems* (New York: Basic Books, 1977); Lindblom, *The Policy-Making Process*, 2d ed. (Englewood Cliffs, N.J.: Prentice-Hall, 1980); Robert A. Dahl, *Dilemmas of Pluralist Democracy* (New Haven: Yale University Press, 1982); and Martin Shubik, *Game Theory in the Social Sciences: Concepts and Solutions* (Cambridge, Mass.: M.I.T. Press, 1982). The classic study on the fundamental instruments of social coordina-tion (specifically, the price system, hierarchy, polyarchy, and bargaining) and politico-economic systems is Robert A. Dahl and Charles E. Lindblom, *Politics, Economics, and Welfare* (Chicago: University of Chicago Press, 1976).

[2]First among these are Charles E. Lindblom and Albert O. Hirschman, who have both made significant contributions to the analysis of politico-economic systems for forty years.

[3]A point stressed in Hirschman, *Journeys Toward Progress* (New York: Norton, 1973), pp. 254–55.

countries around the world. At a minimum, these studies collectively provide a descriptive inventory of the combinations of techniques that are used to solve complex social problems, such as marshaling human and material resources and putting them to productive use.

The institutional variation among these systems is so enormous that broadly comparative work, just like less contextual analysis, usually founders on the complexity of the subject matter. One notable exception is Charles E. Lindblom's *Politics and Markets*. But the fundamental comparisons among market, authority, and preceptoral systems that Lindblom makes in this work lead him to underemphasize the variety of distinct institutional arrangements *within* the category of actual market systems. Broadly comparative analyses of market-oriented systems are still in short supply.

Perhaps the classic attempt to forge useful inventories and generalizations across market-oriented systems was Andrew Shonfield's *Modern Capitalism*.[4] Among other contributions, Shonfield described the "instruments" of state economic policy-making used during the 1950s and early 1960s in Britain, France, Germany, and Italy to shape their respective patterns of private investment. Following in this tradition, Peter Katzenstein and several colleagues have broadened the empirical frame of reference and asked how the varied policy-making institutions and political structures of advanced industrialized countries, including the United States and Japan, have contributed to their distinctive international economic strategies.[5] This highly ambitious collective undertaking has yielded a number of important implications. For example, Katzenstein's comparative analysis implies that Japan, because of the wide range of sector-specific policy-making instruments available to state officials, can compete more effectively than other coun-

[4]Shonfield, *Modern Capitalism: The Changing Balance of Public and Private Power* (London: Oxford University Press, 1965).

[5]Peter J. Katzenstein, ed., *Between Power and Plenty: Foreign Economic Policies of Advanced Industrial States* (Madison: University of Wisconsin Press, 1978).

tries in world markets. By implication, the United States and Britain are seen to be at a competitive disadvantage relative to countries in which the state is a more integral participant in the microeconomic process.

The possibility of greater state microeconomic intervention is currently one of the most salient politico-economic issues in countries, such as the United States, which rely heavily on the price system to allocate resources between productive activities. On the other hand, authorities in many countries where the state has taken substantial responsibility for shaping resource flows are tentatively delegating more of this task to producers and consumers interacting through the price system. Is greater use of either the price system or sector-specific policies to allocate resources likely to increase economic welfare in these countries? Even if agreement could be reached on the meaning and measurement of economic welfare, as social scientists we cannot yet claim to have formulated an adequate answer to this complex and pressing question. Our knowledge of how resource allocation patterns are determined in systems where state officials attempt to steer private investment decisions is still highly fragmentary. Until we know what drives the allocation of resources in these systems, we cannot begin to determine the welfare effects of shifts toward or away from extensive state microeconomic intervention.

One route to greater understanding of this question is to build politico-economic models of the resource allocation process that can account for both government policies and resource flows. Such a clearly articulated theoretical structure is needed to guide and connect research on the effects of sector-specific policy-making in a wide variety of political and economic contexts.[6]

---

[6]On the importance of model building, see Richard R. Nelson and Sidney G. Winter, Jr., *An Evolutionary Theory of Economic Change* (Cambridge, Mass.: Harvard University Press, 1982), pp. 3–48.

# The Politicized Market Economy

*Modeling Mutual Adjustment*

With this research strategy in mind, I pursue two interwoven projects in the present study. One is to develop a model of the resource allocation process in politicized market economies. In these systems state officials, pursuing a variety of political and other objectives, attempt to use sector-specific policies to determine what the private sector produces, consumes, and owns. The specific formulation of the model of the politicized market economy provided here is less important than the general style of analysis. The essential feature of this model is that both sector-specific policies and private investment decisions are treated as endogenous variables. This feature of the analysis reflects the fact that both policy actions and investment flows are in reality products of complex mutual adjustment processes.

In politicized market economies, state officials pervasively employ sector-specific policies to induce private investors to purchase and operate capital assets in selected economic activities. But investors will presumably make these commitments only if this use of funds is expected to be privately profitable given the opportunity cost of passing up alternative investments. What makes this interaction especially complex is the inescapable fact that capital investments are long-lived whereas most sector-specific policies may not be. Due to this asymmetry, we cannot account for capital budgeting decisions in politicized market economies unless we explain how investors form their expectations of future sector-specific policies. Since these expectations are rationally based on incisive political analysis, purely economic models of resource allocation in this kind of system are inherently insufficient. Purely political models of the resource allocation process are equally incomplete because they are not sensitive to the variety of other factors that influence rational investment decisions in a market system. The politico-economic model developed here is one

attempt to explain how policy, expectations, and private resource flows are mutually determined as state officials and
investors adjust to each other.

### Analyzing Brazil's Steered Economy

The second project undertaken here is to understand how the
resource allocation process works in one of the world's most
politicized market economies. For a variety of complex
historical reasons, many relating to the effects of the Great
Depression, the Brazilian state first became the engine of
economic growth in the 1930s.[7] Through exchange rate policy,
public investment, the creation of state-owned enterprises,
inflationary finance, trade protection, and numerous less
important measures, state officials have since tried to cultivate
a pattern of production and consumption that reflects their
image of an economically developed society.[8]

One consequence of this fifty-year process is that each sector
of the Brazilian economy has developed its own special
political characteristics. Often a sector is the focus of state
promotion or regulation because the commodity produced,
such as steel, automobiles, petrochemicals, or capital goods, is
thought essential to a developed economy. Sometimes a sector

---

[7]See Peter Flynn, *Brazil: A Political Analysis* (Boulder, Colo.: Westview
Press, 1978), pp. 59–131. Brazil's earlier industrialization, ushered in by
fortuitous events in the 1880s, contributed to the country's relatively smooth
economic adjustment to the Great Depression. See Albert Fishlow, "Origins
and Consequences of Import Substitution in Brazil," in *International
Economics and Development: Essays in Honor of Raul Prebisch*, ed. L. E. DiMarco
(New York: Academic Press, 1972), pp. 316–419.

[8]For a useful general discussion of these policies and their effects, see
Werner Baer, *The Brazilian Economy: Its Growth and Development* (Columbus,
Ohio: Grid Publishing, 1979). For a discussion of the ideas that encouraged
state-led industrialization, see Albert O. Hirschman, "Ideologies of Devel-
opment in Latin America," in his *A Bias for Hope: Essays on Development and
Latin America* (New Haven: Yale University Press, 1971), pp. 270–311; and
Hirschman, "The Rise and Decline of Development Economics," in his
*Essays in Trespassing: Economics to Politics and Beyond* (Cambridge: Cambridge
University Press, 1981), pp. 10–15.

is politically important because the producers are key supporters of the regime. Or regulation is undertaken to protect local private capitalists in a certain line of business from having to compete with state or multinational enterprises.[9] Some sectors receive privileged attention for a variety of reasons. For example, state officials began to promote the development of the capital goods industry at a staggering pace after 1974—partly to substitute for imports, partly to create a more advanced economic structure, and partly to rekindle political support from Brazilian capital goods producers and local private capitalists in general.[10]

Owing to a variety of complex historical processes, sector-specific policies have become core elements of Brazil's political as well as economic systems. Although the centrality of sector-specific policy-making in Brazilian politics is largely a by-product of the country's late-late industrialization, this position was further accentuated by the particular kind of regime that ruled Brazil from April 1964 to March 1985.[11] Breaking with the long-standing tradition of frequent but short interventions in national politics, the military seized power in 1964

[9]This characterization of the Brazilian politico-economic system owes much to the highly innovative sociology of Peter Evans. See his comparative analysis of the textile, pharmaceutical, and petrochemical industries in *Dependent Development: The Alliance of Multinational, State, and Local Capital in Brazil* (Princeton: Princeton University Press, 1979). Another essential Evans contribution, which compares the petrochemical and capital goods sectors, is "Reinventing the Bourgeoisie: State Entrepreneurship and Class Formation in Dependent Capitalist Development," in *Marxist Inquiries*, ed. M. Burawoy and T. Skocpol (Chicago: University of Chicago Press, 1982), pp. S210–47.

[10]On state promotion of the capital goods industry in Brazil, see José Serra, "Three Mistaken Theses Regarding the Connection Between Industrialization and Authoritarian Regimes," in *The New Authoritarianism in Latin America*, ed. D. Collier (Princeton: Princeton University Press, 1979), pp. 99–163. As we will see, these same motives also propelled forward the National Alcohol Program.

[11]For a comparison of "late" and "late-late" development, see Albert O. Hirschman, "The Political Economy of Import-Substituting Industrialization in Latin America," in *A Bias for Hope*, pp. 85–123.

and began to rule.[12] Proclaiming that politics would be removed from government, the military regime dispensed with
such modern organizational links to society as political parties
and other forms of alliances with broad social groups.[13] In
claiming authority to rule, the military instead propounded an
elaborate doctrine of national security that had evolved in
response to several perceived threats, including an economic
crisis and the Cuban Revolution. The military's apparent mission in coming to power was to restructure Brazil's political
and economic systems in a way that would eliminate these
perceived threats.

The regime intensified the use of sector-specific policy instruments such as taxes, subsidies, trade protection, credit
provision, public investment, price controls, and direct regulation. Sector-specific policies were designed to achieve rapid
economic growth and thereby enhance general public support
for the regime.[14] Complementing this aggregate strategy, sector-specific policies were also employed to cultivate the support of certain social groups, including the middle class and
local private capitalists in both industry and agriculture.[15]

In light of the inherited features of Brazilian development—
the shape of its late-late industrialization, the dominance of
state and multinational enterprises in many eonomic sectors,

[12]On the breakdown of the "moderating pattern" of civil-military
relations, see Alfred Stepan, *The Military in Politics: Changing Patterns in Brazil*
(Princeton: Princeton University Press, 1971).

[13]See Fernando Henrique Cardoso, "On the Characterization of Authoritarian Regimes in Latin America," in Collier, *The New Authoritarianism*, pp.
33–57.

[14]Economic growth, always an element, eventually became the keystone of
the military's "legitimacy formula." For a telling indication, see the
government's *II National Development Plan, 1975–79* (Brasilia, 1974).

[15]On class alliances under authoritarian rule in Latin America, see Alfred
Stepan, *The State and Society: Peru in Comparative Perspective* (Princeton:
Princeton University Press, 1978), pp. 73–113. According to Fernando
Henrique Cardoso, sector-specific policy-making helped link the regime
with civil society. The links *partially* substituted for corporative arrangements
with class organizations or political parties. See Cardoso, "The Characterization of Authoritarian Regimes," pp. 35–44.

the weakness of political institutions linking social groups, political elites, bureaucrats, and managers of state enterprises, as well as the political mission and strategy of the now displaced military regime—it should not be surprising if the pattern of microeconomic intervention and outcomes in Brazil differs from that found in other politicized market economies. Comparing the Brazilian system with these others is a complex project that lies beyond the scope of the present study. I instead examine Brazil's steered economy in a way that suggests its importance for comparative analysis.[16]

## Obstacles to Policy Effectiveness

Developing a model of the politicized market economy is the primary vehicle by which I investigate the logical consequences of specific politico-economic structures for resource allocation patterns.[17] These structures are represented in my model by two parameters: the overall goals pursued by top authorities and the dispersion of authority over sector-specific policy-making.[18] In elaborating the model, I draw heavily on modern finance and organization theory to show how these and other parameters shape the policy-making process and private investments in this kind of market system. For example, I identify the conditions under which top authorities will likely fail to achieve their sector-specific objectives—despite the wide array of policy instruments formally under their control. I argue that policy ineffectiveness, so defined, is more likely to occur when

[16]One preliminary way to widen the scope of inquiry along the lines established in the Katzenstein volume would be to compare the politico-economic structures and policy-making processes in Brazil and Japan. The presence of a hegemonic political party, the consistent priority granted the promotion of exports, and the prodigious political and economic strength of local private capital are certainly among the important domestic factors that distinguish the Japanese case from the Brazilian one.

[17]Such structures generally change slowly as new political and economic commitments are made. But the pace of change could become rapid in Brazil during the first years of democratic rule.

[18]In Chapter 4 I explain why these parameters were selected.

top authorities pursue intensely contradictory regime goals and systematically delegate policy-making authority over each sector to many competing state agencies. This tendency, however, can be offset by a variety of contextual factors. For instance, a highly threatening international environment can mitigate some of the contradictions among a regime's objectives. Many other situation-specific factors can also offset the effects of intensely contradictory regime goals and a segmented policy-making apparatus; several of these factors are identified in the model.

Recent analyses of Brazil's politico-economic system, in one way or another, have elucidated many contradictions among the goals that the military regime tried to pursue during its last decade of rule.[19] One of the most severe contradictions has been that between achieving macroeconomic stability and strengthening the politico-economic position of local private capitalists. There also have been contradictions between the goal of maintaining access to world credit markets and countless macropolitical objectives. In recent years, moreover, the objective of achieving macroeconomic stability—controlled inflation, aggregate growth, and external balance—has become internally contradictory due to the oil shocks, the world recession, the crisis in international credit markets, policy blunders, and certain economic relationships in Brazil.[20]

[19]Two of the most explicit discussions can be found in Evans, *Dependent Development*, pp. 274–97, and in Serra, "Three Mistaken Theses," pp. 148–63.

[20]For insights into the development of the economic contradictions in the Brazilian model, see Edmar L. Bacha, "Issues and Evidence on Recent Brazilian Economic Growth," *World Development* (January/February 1977): 47–67; Bacha, "Selected Issues in Post-1964 Brazilian Economic Growth," in *Models of Growth and Distribution for Brazil*, ed. L. Taylor et al. (New York: Oxford University Press, 1980), pp. 17–45; and Bacha, "Vicissitudes of Recent Stabilization Attempts in Brazil and the IMF Alternative," in *IMF Conditionality*, ed. J. Williamson (Cambridge, Mass.: M.I.T. Press for the Institute for International Economics, 1983), pp. 283–340. For a qualitative discussion of behavioral relationships in the Brazilian economy, see Alejandro Foxley, "Stabilization Policies and Their Effects on Employment and Income Distribution: A Latin American Perspective," in *Economic Stabilization in Developing Countries*, ed. W. R. Cline and S. Weintraub (Washington, D.C.: Brookings Institution, 1981), pp. 191–233.

In examining the history of the National Alcohol Program, we will see how these contradictions and the notorious segmentation of the Brazilian state have impaired central control over the policy-making process and the behavior of private investors. We will also see how these tendencies have sometimes been overwhelmed by various situational factors.

## Alcohol Energy in Brazil

The Brazilian National Alcohol Program (*Proálcool*) is among the world's most ambitious efforts to produce a renewable fuel as a petroleum substitute. More than 10 billion liters of alcohol are currently produced each year from roughly 300 privately owned distilleries. Most of this enormous output is consumed in 2 million passenger cars whose engines can burn only pure alcohol fuel. Those who have committed their resources to alcohol production and consumption include large sugarcane producers, small agricultural producers organized through cooperatives, individual owners of alcohol-powered cars, multinational automobile companies, the state-owned Banco do Brasil, and the World Bank. By virtue of the impressive investments made by such a wide range of important domestic and foreign actors, alcohol is now a significant institutionalized commodity in Brazilian agriculture and a key element in the country's transportation and energy systems.

### *Mutual Adjustment in State Politics*

This transformation of the Brazilian economy did not result from a smooth process in which the state easily induced private investors to undertake the necessary capital projects—building distilleries, expanding sugarcane production, retooling automobile plants, buying alcohol-powered cars, and the like. From mid-1975, when President Ernesto Geisel first suggested that policy be used to stimulate the conversion of sugarcane into alcohol fuel, until late 1979, the prospect of a rapid expansion in alcohol production generated a tremendous struggle between top authorities and certain state agencies.

Although it was imprudent for state officials to oppose the *idea* of converting sugarcane into alcohol, the specific formulation of the program left the door wide open for some agencies to undermine *Proálcool* during its implementation.[21]

The great obstacles in the path of the alcohol program were created by the state financial apparatus and the state oil monopoly, Petrobrás. The former, which included the Central Bank, the Banco do Brasil, and the Ministry of Finance, controlled the disbursement of subsidized credit to those sugar producers who wished to expand their alcohol distilleries. Accommodating the policy preferences of President Geisel took a back seat to the objective of attaining macroeconomic stability and other institutional goals. Apparently aware of the high cost of producing alcohol relative to the value of this gasoline substitute, top policymakers in the financial bureaucracy were extremely reluctant to underwrite a major new commitment to such an economically inefficient activity. Project approvals were delayed for months or years, despite the continual prodding of the state credit agencies by the highly respected President Geisel.

Meanwhile, Petrobrás officials were busy devising some ingenious schemes to defuse the threat to their monopoly posed by the alcohol program. Taking advantage of a loophole in the 1975 *Proálcool* decree, Petrobrás indicated its intention of keeping as much control of the liquid fuels sector as possible by announcing plans to produce alcohol from

[21]In the late 1960s and early 1970s, the government's Institute of Sugar and Alcohol launched an ambitious program to modernize and expand Brazil's capacity to export sugar. That program was carried out zealously during 1973–75 with revenues generated by a temporary tenfold increase in world sugar prices. By late 1975, however, world prices fell back to their former low levels and short-term prospects for exporting sugar at favorable prices began to look bleak. Producing alcohol from surplus sugarcane was a measure often employed by the government to aid the sugar industry at such times. The political appeal of alcohol production was enhanced by the first large increase in oil prices by OPEC in 1973–74, which made an indelible mark on Brazil's external balance. More than 80 percent of the country's petroleum was imported at the time.

manioc (cassava). At the same time, Petrobrás officials tried to keep alcohol production identified solely with reducing excess capacity in the sugar industry. Locked in a more general struggle to defend its public enterprise property rights, Petrobrás gained a reputation as Enemy Number One of alcohol production in Brazil.

How did these government entities get away with their open defiance of central decision makers' efforts to lure resources into alcohol production?[22] Most organization theorists would begin to explain such a pattern by pointing out that agencies are generally established by central decision makers in order to deal with a pressing problem of the time. Since organizations tend to become ends in themselves, the mission of an established agency could easily conflict with what central decision makers perceive to be the priorities of the *present* time. An agency might not fear that its organizational integrity would be jeopardized by its current opposition to central decision makers' policy wishes because grants of authority, in time, take on their own legitimacy. This aura of legitimacy is to some extent the moral embellishment of an agency's specialized technical competence, autonomous financial resources, support of key social groups, or some combination of the three. It would therefore seem perfectly rational for a highly capable agency, secure in its policy-making authority, to ignore the requests of central decision makers if these requests run counter to the agency's organizational interests.

But if this line of reasoning is swallowed whole, the post-1979 period of the National Alcohol Program becomes extremely puzzling. During this important period, the alcohol program's earlier opponents behaved as if they were its best friends. Petrobrás contributed to the appearance of support by canceling its media campaign against the expansion of the

[22]The term *central decision makers*, used throughout this study, refers generally to the individuals and roles located closest to the center of political power in a state or regime. In authoritarian Brazil, these included the president of the republic, top military officials, and a few key civilian technocrats.

program and by importing heavier crudes to accommodate the rise in alcohol consumption. Help also came from the financial bureaucracy. After spending years restricting project approvals, the Central Bank and the Banco do Brasil began to disburse nearly all the subsidized credits requested by those willing to invest in alcohol distilleries. Furthermore, the previously aloof National Petroleum Council stepped in to assure that the alcohol marketing chain would link production to consumption.

If it was rational for some state agencies to oppose central decision makers in the early phases of the alcohol program, why was it also rational for these same agencies to give their utmost to the alcohol program after 1979? In stark contrast to their behavior in the 1975–79 period, the early opponents of the alcohol program were apparently *constrained* by central decision makers when they selected their policy actions in 1980 and beyond. In devising the model of policy-making in Chapter 4 and in interpreting this episode of the National Alcohol Program in Part II, one of my tasks will be to identify the conditions under which these constraints are likely to arise. By identifying these conditions, we can more confidently predict when policies toward a given economic sector are likely to be consistently favorable.

### Mutual Adjustment Between "State" and "Market"

The sharp unresolved conflicts between state officials during the 1975–79 period did not block the expansion of alcohol production. From a low base of 600 million liters per year, alcohol production approached 3 billion liters per year by 1979. To unravel this puzzle, it is useful to ask why existing sugar producers commited some of their resources to alcohol-specific assets. This question, in turn, raises a variety of fundamental issues about the way wealth-seeking investors budget their capital in politicized market economies. In these systems, the cash flows generated by many investment projects depend primarily on uncertain future sector-specific policies. (Alcohol distilleries are perfect examples.) By investing in this kind of project, cash flows can be insulated from marketplace eventualities. In doing so, however, investors increase their exposure to shifts in policy.

For many investors, uncertainty over policy and uncertainty over marketplace outcomes are qualitatively different. Privileged investors, who might occupy a strategic position in the economic system or who for other reasons might be able to influence the relevant policy decisions, are likely to prefer to invest in assets specific to a commodity like alcohol (with its high exposure to policy shifts) rather than in another project whose cash flows are exposed to the vagaries of the marketplace. These investors would likely prefer to bear *strategic* rather than *exogenous* uncertainty, to use the language of game theory. Strategic uncertainty arises when each player must take each other player's capabilities and goals into consideration when making decisions. Each player therefore exercises some indirect control over the others, and they all engage in mutual adjustment. Faced with exogenous uncertainty, or the possibility of events over which one cannot exercise any degree of control, a player must simply adapt. This second kind of uncertainty is the only one that enters most models of capital budgeting in market economies. To value projects in a politicized market economy, it is necessary to elaborate upon this framework. For these reasons, I begin the model-building exercise by asking how a rational investor would choose among alternative projects in an environment of strategic and market (exogenous) uncertainty.

In applying the model to the alcohol case, I will show why sugar producers were willing to invest in alcohol-specific assets despite the ongoing policy battles. I will also use this rational choice framework to explain why the automobile industry decided to produce alcohol-powered cars in 1979; why landowners initially outside the sugar sector were unwilling to make alcohol-specific investments until early 1980; and why after September 1980 consumers began to buy thousands of alcohol-powered cars each month. By analyzing the political and economic basis for these decisions, I will show how the first alcohol boom undermined itself and collapsed by June 1981. And I will explain why in September 1982, despite the ongoing slide in world oil prices, consumers triggered a second alcohol boom by purchasing record numbers of alcohol-powered cars. Explaining why Brazil's National Alcohol Program fluctuated between these extremes, I submit, brings us many steps closer to an understanding of the resource allocation process in a politicized market economy.

# Efficiency, Incentives, and a Politico-Economic Model of Resource Allocation

# The Economic
# Efficiency of Alcohol Production:
# Analysis and Implications

In the early days of *Proálcool*, Brazilian sugar producers were in an excellent position to persuade proximate decision makers and the informed public that the production of alcohol from sugarcane furthered the national interest. Such an equation of group and national interests was made plausible by a deceptively simple line of reasoning.

World oil prices had quadrupled.

Current account deficits and inflation were higher and income growth was slower.

Alcohol production would ultimately reduce petroleum imports.

Alcohol production would therefore help Brazil adjust to

the OPEC oil shock by saving foreign exchange, reducing inflation, and enhancing income growth.

This rationale for the alcohol program was often embellished with other, more emotive arguments. Many proponents stressed, for example, that the use of nationally developed technology to produce this form of renewable energy would represent a unique Brazilian response to the OPEC challenge. But the most generally compelling defense for *Proálcool* was the claim that alcohol production would save foreign exchange for Brazil.

When economists evaluate the foreign exchange savings that could be achieved by substituting domestically produced goods for imports, they usually weigh these savings against the costs of generating them. If the cost to the country of saving a certain amount of foreign exchange through import substitution is greater than the value to the country of the increment in foreign exchange savings, most economists would say that producing the import substitute is economically *inefficient*. In strict economic efficiency terms, then, it is not necessarily true that producing an import substitute, like alcohol, saves foreign exchange.

To appraise the claim that alcohol saves foreign exchange in this more precise sense, we must investigate whether the opportunity costs of producing alcohol are exceeded by the value of alcohol as a petroleum substitute. Opportunity costs arise from the fact that sugarcane cultivation, harvesting, and milling as well as alcohol distillation divert scarce domestic resources such as land, labor, and capital from alternative activities.[1] The value of alcohol fuel depends on how much

---

[1] The opportunity cost of using domestic resources for alcohol production is measured by their value in the most profitable alternative activities. For a discussion of the "alternative cost" principle by one of its most devoted advocates, see Frank H. Knight, "Economics," in Knight, *On the History and Method of Economics: Selected Essays* (Chicago: University of Chicago Press, 1956), pp. 3–33, or Knight, *The Economic Organization* (New York: A. M. Kelley, 1967).

gasoline consumption declines per unit of alcohol produced, on how much petroleum imports fall per unit of diminished gasoline consumption, and on world oil prices.

Estimating opportunity costs and returns requires us to analyze a wide array of factors, including domestic resource costs, changes in world sugar and oil prices, the fuel efficiency of alcohol-powered cars, the flexibility of petroleum refinery cracking ratios, and movements in the fundamental equilibrium exchange rate between the cruzeiro (the Brazilian currency) and the dollar. In this chapter, I investigate these and other determinants of the economic efficiency of producing alcohol at Brazil's most technically efficient plantations, mills, and distilleries, which are located in the Center-South region. This analysis yields the most likely estimate of Brazil's net economic returns from alcohol production and consumption. The methodological discussion also provides an appreciation for the uncertainty that necessarily attaches to estimates of costs and returns in an imperfect and turbulent world.[2]

## Assessing Phase One: 1975–79

*Initial Conditions and Upward Potential*

Due to the confluence of declining sugar export volumes and the maturation of huge new state-financed investments in the sugar sector, a serious problem of surplus sugarcane production and processing capacity began to appear in 1975.[3] Faced

[2]I am deeply indebted to Professor Scott R. Pearson of the Food Research Institute at Stanford University for his instigation of and collaboration on the social benefit-cost analysis discussed in this chapter. Some of the analysis has previously appeared in Barzelay and Pearson, "The Efficiency of Producing Alcohol for Energy in Brazil," *Economic Development and Cultural Change* (October 1982):121–44, and in a reply to a comment on this paper in the July 1985 issue, pp. 857–63. I would like to thank the University of Chicago Press for permission to reprint material from these publications.

[3]Sugar exports reached 3.0 million tons in 1973 and then declined to 2.5 million in 1974, 1.7 million in 1975, and 1.2 million in 1976 (from Central Bank of Brazil, *Annual Report, 1981*). During this same period, the Brazilian state loaned the sugar sector $US 4.3 billion (in 1981 prices) for capital

with this threat, private sugar producers (*usineiros*) and the government Institute for Sugar and Alcohol (IAA) sought alternative uses for the surplus cane. The search for alternatives did not require exceptional imagination since, by 1975, Brazil had nearly fifty years experience producing anhydrous alcohol from sugarcane and mixing this fuel with gasoline. This long experience demonstrated that conventional gasoline engines could operate efficiently so long as alcohol did not exceed 20 percent of these engines' intake of fuel. For this 20 percent limit to be reached, alcohol production would have to expand from roughly 600,000 liters in 1975 to 3 billion liters per year.[4] The production of 3 billion liters would generate a demand for about 50 million metric tons of sugarcane. Even a fraction of this potential demand would be welcomed by the *usineiros*.[5]

Because excess sugarcane production and milling capacity was available, alcohol production could increase substantially if distilleries were expanded at existing sugar mills and if producers were permitted to convert a larger portion of their sugarcane crop into alcohol fuel. Government policies during Phase One of *Proálcool* facilitated both distillery expansions and higher conversion rates.

### Methodology and Data Sources

*Social and private prices.* To evaluate the economic efficiency of alcohol production and consumption, we must first estimate the opportunities forgone by Brazil as the result of diverting scarce resources into this activity. We could con-

---

investment. See Salmão L. Quadros da Silva, "O crescimento da lavoura canavieira na Brasil na década de 70," *Revista Brasileira de Economia* (January/ March 1983):39–54. For a longer historical perspective on the origins of the alcohol program, see Chapter 5.

[4]In 1975, gasoline consumption was about 14.5 billion liters (from Conselho Nacional de Petróleo, *Anuário Estatístico, 1982*).

[5]The 1.5 million ton decline in sugar exports between 1973 and 1975 was approximately equivalent to a 25 million metric ton decrement in sugarcane production.

ceivably assume that the prices producers actually pay for their inputs, known as private prices, are equivalent to the value of these resources in their best alternative activities. This assumption would rest on one of the bedrock propositions of modern welfare economics—namely, that market prices measure social costs and benefits when transactions are costless and when markets are free of government intervention.[6] These theoretical conditions, however, never obtain in the real world. We must therefore adjust the available data for the effects of market imperfections, externalities, and government incentives. The adjusted data are estimates of social costs, which can diverge substantially from the private costs actually experienced by producers and consumers.[7]

*Quality of the data.* The only extensive and detailed study of costs in the Brazilian sugar industry is performed annually by Copersucar, the cooperative of private sugar and alcohol producers in the Center-South states of São Paulo and Paraná. The Copersucar annual reports contain the best data available for analyzing the costs of producing alcohol fuel in Brazil. Because of inadequate data, Northeastern Brazil, the country's second most important sugarcane-producing region, unfortunately must be excluded from the analysis.[8] The social costs of production are said to be substantially greater in the North-

[6]See Ronald Coase, "The Problem of Social Cost," *Journal of Law and Economics* (October 1960):1–44. For useful discussions, see Eugene Silberberg, *The Structure of Economics* (New York: McGraw-Hill, 1978), pp. 494–97, and Guido Calabresi and A. Douglas Melamed, "Property Rules, Liability Rules, and Inalienability: One View of the Cathedral," *Harvard Law Review* (April 1972):1089–1127.

[7]The distinction between private and social costs and returns is central to W. M. Corden's theory of domestic divergences and to a long literature on social benefit-cost analysis; see Corden, *Trade Policy and Economic Welfare* (Oxford: Clarendon Press, 1974). For an eminently accessible presentation of these concepts and benefit-cost analysis generally, see C. Peter Timmer, Walter P. Falcon, and Scott R. Pearson, *Food Policy Analysis* (Baltimore: Johns Hopkins University Press, 1983).

[8]São Paulo and Paraná, however, account for about 75 percent of Brazil's alcohol production.

east, where plantations and mills are less modern than in the Center-South. The estimates of alcohol production costs presented here, therefore, probably understate the national average.

A second problem with relying exclusively on Copersucar data is that these costs might be tinged with some degree of strategic misrepresentation. Although Copersucar *usineiros* are proud of their modern and efficient facilities, they are also interested in obtaining lucrative prices for their products. Their annual survey of costs is conducted, in part, to influence the prices the IAA will guarantee producers in the coming year. Here we are in the difficult position of making a judgment about "impacted" information.[9] Having conducted interviews with Copersucar officials who claimed that their data are representative of productive units that are somewhat less efficient than the average for the region, I will assume that average costs in São Paulo and Paraná are 80 percent of the reported levels.

The data used here are taken from the survey for the 1978–79 harvest year.[10] This was the final complete harvest year of Phase One. Detailed production costs are reproduced in Appendix 1 (for sugarcane) and Appendix 2 (for alcohol). Our task now is to adjust these data for estimated divergences between private and social prices.

### Estimation of Social Costs in the Base Period: 1978–79

*Market imperfections.* Since the markets for land and labor in the relatively developed Center-South region are generally considered to be well integrated and competitive, we can assume that market land rental and wage rates are good indicators of the social costs of land and labor, respectively.[11]

[9]Oliver Williamson, *Markets and Hierarchies: Analysis and Antitrust Implications* (New York: Free Press, 1975).

[10]Copersucar, *Aspectos econômicos da produção de cana, açúcar e álcool: período 1978/80* (São Paulo: Copersucar, 1980).

[11]Land rental rates are not distorted by the premium paid by landowners who buy real estate to protect their wealth against inflation.

Capital markets, however, are highly regulated by the state.[12] Consequently, the social cost of capital cannot be estimated by prevailing interest rates or by any other simple empirical method. As a point of reference, the scarcity value employed by economists during the Brazilian economic miracle (1968–73) was usually in the range of 12 to 18 percent per year. But since then real growth rates have diminished. For purposes of analysis, I therefore assume that the social cost of capital is at the lower bound of this range.

*Subsidies and Taxes.* The most important subsidy to the alcohol program comes in the form of cheap credit. Brazilian monetary authorities have offered credit for agricultural and industrial investments in alcohol production at interest rates well below the rate of inflation. Other features of the credit contract, including a sizable grace period, made the implicit subsidy to capital even greater. Because of the complexity of these contracts and the variability of their terms, it is extremely difficult to gauge the realized private costs of capital for alcohol production. Fortunately, we need not adjust reported capital costs since Copersucar imputes a 12 percent opportunity cost of capital, which excludes the effects of the capital subsidy. Capital costs must be adjusted, however, for the 8 percent tax on industrial products (IPI). A more significant tax falls on the fuel used in sugarcane and alcohol production. During 1978–79, these taxes represented about 40 percent of the purchase price of fuel.[13] The costs of "tradable inputs" is adjusted accordingly.

---

[12]State intervention in credit markets and direct provision of subsidized finance are especially pronounced in the agricultural sector. For two perspectives on this aspect of Brazil's steered economy, see João do Carmo Oliveira and Roberto Marcos da Silva Montezano, "Os limites das fontes de financiamento à agricultura no Brasil," *Estudos Econômicos* (August 1982):pp. 139–59; and Milton da Mata, "Crédito rural: caracterização do sistema e estimativas dos subsídios implícitos," *Revista Brasileira de Economia* (July/ September 1982):215–45.

[13]Calculated from Conselho Nacional de Petróleo, *Anuário Estatístico, 1980.*

*Externalities.* There are two principal ways in which the externalities of alcohol production and consumption could drive a wedge between private and social costs. First, the combustion of alcohol is said to cause less pollution than that of gasoline. A decrease in pollution would increase the social profitability of alcohol production. Second, the liquid residue of the distillation process, known as *vinhoto*, is a potential pollutant unless properly treated. The possible magnitudes of these opposing effects are the subject of continuing debate in Brazil. In the absence of reliable data on the social costs and benefits of these effects, no attempt can be made here to deal quantitatively with either externality.

*Total social costs.* Taking these factors into consideration, total social costs in the base period (measured in September 1978 prices) were Cr$ 4.47 per liter.[14] The breakdown of these costs between stages of production and type of factor input is shown in Table 1. Now we must convert these cruzeiro costs into their dollar equivalents so that they may be compared with the social returns that accrue from alcohol production.

*The shadow price of foreign exchange.* In September 1978, the Brazilian Central Bank exchanged 19 cruzeiros per U.S. dollar. If this exchange rate measured the marginal value of a dollar to the Brazilian economy, the total social costs of alcohol production would have been $US 0.23 per liter. However, we cannot be sure that the prevailing exchange rate actually reflected the *fundamental value* of the cruzeiro in relation to the dollar. The prevailing exchange rate was affected not only by the Central Bank's macroeconomic policy but also by the structure of trade protection. If tariffs and restrictions on imports were eliminated, for example, the increased demand for foreign goods would almost certainly cause the exchange rate to depreciate. The resulting hypothetical exchange rate, according to most economists, would be a better measure of

[14]This figure is adjusted for the possible overestimation of costs by Copersucar.

TABLE 1. *Social Costs of Alcohol Production: 1978–79[a]*

| Process Stage | Labor | Capital | Land | Tradable Inputs[b] | Total Social Costs |
|---|---|---|---|---|---|
| Sugarcane Production, Collection, and Transport | | | | | |
| Cr$/mt | 36.82 | 46.04 | 29.20 | 63.26 | 175.32 |
| Cr$/liter[c] | 0.53 | 0.66 | 0.42 | 0.90 | 2.51 |
| Milling and Distilling | | | | | |
| Cr$/liter | 0.48 | 0.94 | — | 0.54 | 1.96 |
| Total Social Costs | | | | | |
| Cr$/liter | 1.01 | 1.60 | 0.42 | 1.44 | 4.47 |

[a]September 1978 prices adjusted for possible 20 percent overestimation by Copersucar.

[b]Not adjusted for cruzeiro overvaluation in base period.

[c]Based on an industrial yield of 70 liters per metric ton of sugarcane, as reported by Copersucar.

the social value of foreign exchange than the prevailing rate.[15] Since the estimation of the shadow exchange rate requires this kind of thought experiment, the extent to which the cruzeiro was overvalued at any given time is subject to a high degree of uncertainty.[16] With the appropriate caveats, I adopt the following approach to estimate the shadow exchange rate in the base period (1978–79).

In a recent paper, Edmar Bacha argues that the cruzeiro was substantially overvalued in terms of the dollar in 1968, when Brazil introduced its well-known system of frequent mini-devaluations.[17] In the 1968–76 period, according to Bacha,

[15]See Edmar L. Bacha and Lance Taylor, "Foreign Exchange Shadow Prices: A Critical Review of Current Theories," *Quarterly Journal of Economics* (May 1971):197–224.

[16]For a sense of the controversy, see Robert Fendt, Jr., "The Crawling Peg: Brazil," in *Exchange Rate Rules*, ed. J. Williamson (New York: St. Martin's Press, 1981), pp. 140–51.

[17]Edmar L. Bacha, "Notes on the Brazilian Experience with Minidevaluations, 1968–1976," *Journal of Development Economics* (December 1979):463–81.

these exchange rate adjustments approximately corrected for the difference between Brazil's inflation and that of its main trading partners. Assuming that the cruzeiro was 20 percent overvalued in 1968, this degree of overvaluation appears to have persisted over the period Bacha analyzed.[18]

Between December 1976 and December 1978, the cruzeiro appreciated against the dollar in real terms (that is, adjusting for differential inflation) by roughly 10 percent.[19] But this appreciation of the cruzeiro occurred when the Carter administration was "talking down" the dollar in order to achieve certain macroeconomic objectives.[20] John Williamson estimates that during these two years the real effective exchange rate for the dollar depreciated about 10 percent relative to its fundamental equilibrium level.[21] These estimates of the cruzeiro's appreciation and the dollar's depreciation imply that the initially overvalued cruzeiro neither appreciated nor depreciated with respect to the fundamental value of the dollar during 1977 and 1978. My basic analysis will assume, therefore, that the prevailing exchange rate remained 20 percent overvalued in the base period (1978–79).[22]

One consequence of the cruzeiro's overvaluation at the time is that the domestic prices of tradable inputs, such as fuel, fertilizer, and pesticides, understated their true opportunity

[18]In one study, Bergsman concludes that in 1967 the exchange rate was approximately 20 percent overvalued with respect to the equilibrium rate that would arise in the absence of protection for the economy as a whole; see Joel Bergsman, *Brazil: Industrialization and Trade Policies* (London: Oxford University Press, 1970), p. 45. In "Brazilian Experience with Minidevaluations," Bacha also cites evidence that is roughly consistent with this result.

[19]IMF, *International Financial Statistics*, various issues.

[20]For background and analysis, see Robert O. Keohane, "U.S. Foreign Economic Policy Toward Other Advanced Capitalist States: The Struggle to Make Others Adjust," in *Eagle Entangled: U.S. Foreign Policy in a Complex World*, ed. K. Oye, D. Rothchild, and R. J. Lieber (New York and London: Longman, 1979), pp. 91–122.

[21]John Williamson, *The Exchange Rate System* (Cambridge, Mass.: M.I.T. Press for the Institute for International Economics, 1983).

[22]The assumed shadow exchange rate in the base period is therefore Cr$ 23 per dollar instead of the prevailing exchange rate of Cr$ 19 per dollar.

costs by 20 percent.[23] In the base period, the social cost of tradables was therefore Cr$ 1.73 rather than Cr$ 1.44. But the total social cost of alcohol was only $US 0.21 per liter when these costs are converted into dollars at the shadow exchange rate (instead of $US 0.23 without this adjustment).

### Social Profitability: 1978–79

*Social returns.* In estimating the value of alcohol production, it is necessary to know what social returns accrue from reducing gasoline consumption. If the production of 1 liter of alcohol in the base year permitted petroleum imports to decline by 1 liter, the dollar value of alcohol would have equaled the world price of petroleum plus the refining costs otherwise incurred in converting crude oil into a liter of gasoline.[24]

It is likely that the assumption of a one-for-one substitution between alcohol and petroleum was realistic in 1978–79. First, Petrobrás apparently could adjust its refinery operations at that time to accommodate the relatively small impact of alcohol production on the *relative* demand for petroleum derivatives. Since the production of nongasoline derivatives

[23]In social benefit-cost analysis, the cost of tradable inputs is measured in world prices, even if these goods are produced domestically. This is because world prices represent the forgone export values of domestically produced tradables as well as the social cost of expenditures on imported inputs.

[24]Since no detailed information is available on the characteristics of Brazilian refineries, refining costs were estimated in the following way. Energy costs in refining are taken to be 9 percent of the price of petroleum (since energy requirements equal 7 to 12 percent by volume of crude oil intake according to U.S. Department of Energy, *The Potential for Energy Conservation in Nine Selected Industries*, vol. 2). It is assumed that nonenergy costs, mainly capital costs, remain constant. These costs were approximately $US 0.043 per gallon in 1979. For any year, refining costs in Brazil are taken to be $US 0.043 plus 9 percent of the world price of crude (all in per gallon terms). The formula for converting world crude oil prices per barrel into gasoline or alcohol-equivalent values in liters is: $[\$US\ 0.043 + (1.09 \times P_0/42)] \times 1/3.785$, where $P_0$ refers to the world price of crude oil per barrel (in dollars).

per barrel could be increased, petroleum imports were able to decline in step with increased alcohol consumption. Second, anhydrous alcohol could be consumed in ordinary engines as efficiently as gasoline, so long as alcohol did not constitute more than 20 percent of the motor fuel intake.

*Net social losses.* The anhydrous alcohol produced during the 1978–79 harvest year was consumed in calendar year 1979, when Brazil imported petroleum for $US 17.25 per barrel.[25] Adjusting for petroleum refining costs, the social return to alcohol production was therefore $US 0.13 per liter. Since the social cost of alcohol production is estimated to have been $US 0.21, Brazil experienced a net social loss of $US 0.08 per liter. This net social loss is substantial when the size of the period's output is considered. Some 2.5 billion liters were produced in 1979, creating a total social loss of about $US 175 million. In the two previous years, the value of alcohol per liter was about $US 0.02 less than in 1979 (due to lower petroleum prices), but the quantities produced were somewhat smaller as well.

## Implications

These estimated social losses on anhydrous alcohol production in 1978–79 give us some sense of the magnitude of the bailout provided to the sugar industry by the government in the years between the oil shocks. Perhaps it is now clear why the assumption that alcohol production necessarily saves foreign exchange was so critical to the perception that *Proálcool* was good for Brazil in these years.[26] But have we missed an element of the economic rationale? After all, by the time *Proálcool* was created the inordinate investments made in recent years had

[25]Data on petroleum import prices are from Conselho Nacional de Petróleo, *Anuário Estatístico, 1982.*

[26]The political rationale behind the bailout of the sugar industry was actually a great deal more complicated than suggested by the implied notion that foreign exchange is infinitely valuable. For an analysis of the political relationship between the *usineiros* and the state, see Chapter 5.

already become "sunk costs." In order to evaluate the efficiency of alcohol production from these previously existing plantations and mills, we might assume that the opportunity cost of fixed capital, except for new distilleries, was actually zero. In this limiting case, the social cost of alcohol production would have been about 16 cents in the base period, cutting the estimated losses down to only 3 cents per liter. To the extent that these capital investments otherwise would have been idled, the economic justification of alcohol production from facilities in existence before the collapse of world sugar prices was considerably more tenable than suggested above.

## Assessing Phase Two: 1980–83

### *Technological Transformation*

In the early 1980s, the Brazilian government authorized and subsidized the vast expansion of sugarcane production capacity as well as industrial investments in mills and distilleries. By 1983, annual sugarcane production reached 216 million tons, up from 129 million tons in 1978.[27] A sizable percentage of this agricultural output was processed at autonomous distilleries— complexes that cannot produce sugar as an alternative end product. The accelerating expansion of sugarcane cultivation and the construction of autonomous distilleries illustrated the political break between the sugar and alcohol sectors during Phase Two.[28]

This break became even cleaner when the automobile industry began to produce and market alcohol-powered cars. Faced with strong incentives, most consumers selected models equipped with alcohol engines when they purchased automobiles in the six months following the outbreak of the Iran–Iraq War in September 1980 and again after September 1982.

[27]Economist Intelligence Unit, *Quarterly Economic Review of Brazil*, Annual Supplement, 1984, p. 11.

[28]For the political underlay of technological choice in the alcohol program, see Part II of this study.

Once these cars were purchased in large numbers, Brazil became committed—both politically and technologically—to the substitution of gasoline by alcohol. Phase Two represented a bold and essentially irreversible commitment to the production and consumption of alcohol fuel in Brazil.

### Comparative Fuel Efficiency

During Phase Two *anhydrous* alcohol continued to be mixed with gasoline and consumed in ordinary automobile engines, while pure *hydrated* alcohol began to be consumed in factory-made or converted alcohol engines. Although factory-made alcohol cars are significantly more fuel efficient than cars with converted engines, they still consume roughly 15 to 25 percent more alcohol fuel than regular engines operating on gasoline or gasohol. In 1982, for example, the Volkswagen Passat, Ford Belina, and Fiat achieved 16, 23, and 25 percent better mileage when equipped with gasoline engines, respectively.[29] The average ratio of alcohol to gasoline consumption for these three models was 1.2 to 1. I will use this datum to estimate the value of hydrated, relative to anhydrous, alcohol.

### World Oil Prices and Social Returns

As the result of the general tightening of international petroleum markets, the Iranian Revolution, and the Iran–Iraq War, world oil prices reached record levels in 1981. In that year, the average price Brazil paid for its imported oil was over $US 34 per barrel. Since then, however, world recession, conservation, and technological change have driven petroleum demand downward. Unable to coordinate its production and pricing policies in the face of these trends, OPEC was forced to lower its posted prices to $US 29 per barrel. The decline in real oil prices, of course, has been even sharper. The real price of oil in 1983, for example, was $US 22.50, only about 8 percent

[29]The tests were performed by the Brazilian motor car magazine *Quatro Rodas* and the results reported in *Veja* (10 March 1982):105.

TABLE 2. *World Oil Prices and the Social Return to Alcohol Production (in $US)*

| Prices and Returns[a] | 1979 | 1980 | 1981 | 1982 | 1983 |
|---|---|---|---|---|---|
| Nominal Oil Prices (per barrel) | 17.25 | 29.60 | 34.40 | 32.90 | 29.00 |
| Real Oil Prices (per barrel) | 17.25 | 25.96 | 27.65 | 25.90 | 22.53 |
| Real Value of Gasoline (per liter) | 0.13 | 0.19 | 0.20 | 0.19 | 0.17 |
| Real Value of Anhydrous Alcohol (per liter) | 0.13 | 0.19 | 0.20 | 0.19 | 0.17 |
| Real Value of Hydrated Alcohol (per liter) | n.a. | 0.16 | 0.17 | 0.16 | 0.14 |

n.a. = not applicable

[a]Real prices in 1979 dollars.

greater than in 1979.[30] Table 2 displays the series of real and nominal oil prices for the 1979–83 period. The unit value of anhydrous alcohol remains equal to that of gasoline; the unit value of hydrated alcohol is equal to 83 percent of the unit value of gasoline (reflecting the relative fuel inefficiency of alcohol cars).

For purposes of analysis, I will continue to assume that anhydrous alcohol substituted for imported petroleum on a one-for-one basis. However, there is circumstantial evidence that Brazilian refineries were not always sufficiently flexible to permit the output of gasoline per barrel of crude to decline in accordance with increasing alcohol consumption. Gasoline stocks accumulated rapidly in 1980–81 as the demand for gasoline decreased precipitously relative to the demand for other petroleum derivatives. Press reports in those years also rumored that gasoline was being exported to neighboring

---

[30]The U.S. wholesale price index is used here to deflate nominal oil prices into 1979 dollars.

countries at a deep discount. The price obtained by Brazil for these exports represented the marginal value of alcohol production. But since the government's National Petroleum Council keeps export prices confidential, we are in the unenviable position of evaluating this economic activity with purposefully incomplete information.

The assumption that petroleum imports declined at the same rate as gasoline consumption, though unrealistic during 1980–81, may have approximated the actual situation in subsequent years. In 1982, petroleum refined in Brazil yielded, on average, only 18.5 percent gasoline, down from 28 percent in 1978.[31] This trend suggests that refinery cracking ratios were quite flexible, at least over a period of years. Another piece of evidence indicates that the valuation assumption used here is probably realistic. Gasoline exports increased by 1.2 billion liters over the 1980–82 period. These exports, which were worth as much as $US 600 million in 1982 and 1983, may be comparable to the per-unit value of gasoline displayed in Table 2, which is based on world crude oil prices and estimated refining costs.[32]

### Estimated Social Costs

*Fuel and nontraded goods.* Since the analysis is conducted in real terms, we need not consider the effects of inflation. Cruzeiro costs must be adjusted, however, for the rising fuel costs of the 1979–81 period and the declining fuel costs of the 1982–83 period.[33] A second adjustment should be made for the rising cost of nontraded domestic resources such as land and labor, net of productivity gains. In the absence of data on these variables, I assume that productivity improvements in

[31]Conselho Nacional de Petróleo, *Anuário Estatístico*, 1979, 1983.

[32]Petroleum product export data are from Economist Intelligence Unit, *Quarterly Economic Review of Brazil*, no. 2, 1984, p. 23.

[33]In the base period, fuel costs were approximately Cr$ 40 per liter.

sugarcane and alcohol production offset any increases in factor prices.[34]

*The shadow price of foreign exchange: 1979–83.* The period under review here was an extremely turbulent one for the world and, consequently, Brazilian economies. Beginning in 1979, upward pressure on both world oil prices and interest rates created a $US 10.7 billion deficit on Brazil's current account. Within two years, the world economy was in the depths of a severe recession, contributing to a steep decline in the value of Brazil's exports. By accumulating larger external debts at widening spreads over prime lending rates, Brazil avoided any significant liquidity crunch during these difficult years. But the September 1982 Mexican payments crisis unsettled this precarious equilibrium. As the market for international loan syndications dried up, Brazil had few choices but to turn to the International Monetary Fund for assistance. During 1983, the burden of servicing the $US 90 billion foreign debt continued to keep the current account in deficit ($US 6 billion), despite a severe local recession, real oil price declines, and the moderation in nominal world interest rates.

In converting social costs into their dollar equivalents, we must be sensitive to the effect of these events on the fundamental value of the cruzeiro. As mentioned above, the fundamental value or shadow exchange rate is not an observable variable. Following Williamson, the fundamental exchange rate is defined as the one that would bring about the targeted current account deficit or surplus.[35] Hence, attention will focus on the trade and services accounts; no direct consideration of the capital account will be undertaken.

---

[34]During periods of rapid economic growth, this assumption favors the estimated social profitability of alcohol production; during periods of recession, the same assumption reduces estimated social profits relative to their true values. The period analyzed here included both macroeconomic environments.

[35]Williamson, *The Exchange Rate System*, pp. 26–27.

A common way to measure changes in the shadow exchange rate is to examine movements in the unit value of exports relative to the unit value of imports. Empirical estimates of such movements in the "terms of trade" are, however, imprecise. In the present context, an additional problem is that petroleum price movements must be eliminated from the import price index to avoid double-counting their preponderant impact. (The value of alcohol is directly increased by rising oil prices.)

The effects of the interest rate shock are particularly difficult to estimate since the "real" interest rate is unobservable. If trends in actual interest payments over the period are examined, this crude estimate includes the effects of both higher world interest rates and the doubling of the foreign debt over the period. Nonetheless, the weighted average of changes in the terms of trade and interest payments yields some point of reference to estimate the depreciation of the cruzeiro. This approach suggests that during these crisis years the cruzeiro may have depreciated, relative to the dollar, by 22 percent in real terms.[36]

By the standards of international monetary economics, such a depreciation would be quite extraordinary. This estimate therefore should be tempered by the knowledge that crisis conditions prevailed. Given these considerations, I assume that the fundamental equilibrium exchange rate depreciated by 10 percent in the early 1980s. The true extent of this depreciation is unobservable and just as easily could be less or greater than 10 percent.

To assume, however, that the shadow exchange rate was only 10 percent higher in 1983 than in 1979 overlooks one of the

---

[36]The actual exchange rate, adjusted for differential inflation, depreciated by 15 percent against the dollar over the period. This trend is, however, not an especially valuable measure of changes in the fundamental exchange rate since the prevailing rate varied greatly according to macroeconomic policy objectives. Moreover, the actual exchange rate presumably would have depreciated further if import restrictions had not increased substantially in 1980–82.

most significant international monetary events of this period—
namely, the 40 percent appreciation of the dollar's real
effective exchange rate. How much this appreciation reflects a
movement in the fundamental value of the dollar is a subject
that theorists and forecasters heatedly debate. Once again, I
will rely on the judgment of John Williamson, whose study of
the exchange rate system suggests that a 10 percent appreciation has occurred.[37] If this is true, the fundamental cruzeiro/
dollar exchange rate can be assumed to have risen by 20
percent between 1979 and 1983, reflecting both developments
specific to Brazil as well as the surge in the fundamental value
of the dollar.

Despite the imprecision of these estimates, for purposes of
simplicity I will use a single series of shadow exchange rates to
calculate total social costs of alcohol in dollars:[38]

| Year | 1979 | 1980 | 1981 | 1982 | 1983 |
|------|------|------|------|------|------|
| Cr$/$US | 23 | 25 | 26 | 28 | 28 |

## Social Profitability

Relative to the base period, these shadow exchange rates raise
the social cost of tradable inputs in domestic currency but
lower total social costs in dollars:

| | 1979 | 1980 | 1981 | 1982 | 1983 |
|------|------|------|------|------|------|
| Total social costs (Cr$ per liter) | 4.75 | 5.15 | 5.33 | 5.43 | 5.32 |
| Total social costs ($US per liter) | 0.21 | 0.21 | 0.21 | 0.19 | 0.19 |

[37]Williamson, *The Exchange Rate System*, fig. A7.

[38]This series is a damped version of that calculated on the basis of
weighted movements in the terms of trade and interest payments, assuming
that the cruzeiro was 20 percent overvalued in the base period. Readers who
wish to conduct their own sensitivity analysis on the shadow exchange rate
are reminded that all the estimates considered here, including the shadow
rate for the base period and movements in the dollar vis-à-vis its fundamental equilibrium, could take on a range of values.

Social returns per liter for anhydrous and hydrated alcohol were presented in Table 2. Net social losses in each year, consequently, were as follows:[39]

| Year | 1979 | 1980 | 1981 | 1982 | 1983 |
|---|---|---|---|---|---|
| Net social loss for anhydrous alcohol ($US per liter) | 0.08 | 0.02 | 0.01 | 0.00 | 0.02 |
| Net social loss for hydrated alcohol ($US per liter) | | 0.05 | 0.04 | 0.03 | 0.05 |

Two factors made *anhydrous* alcohol competitive with gasoline in the early 1980s. The second oil price shock drove up the estimated value of anhydrous alcohol to a peak of $0.20 per liter by 1981. If only the oil price shock had affected net returns, alcohol production would have been more inefficient in 1982 than in the preceding year. But the estimated depreciation of the shadow exchange rate in 1982 allowed anhydrous alcohol to break even, in social terms, in that year. The relatively steep subsequent decline in real world oil prices nonetheless signaled that anhydrous alcohol production would become and remain socially unprofitable.[40]

Despite the increases in world oil prices in 1980–81 and the substantial depreciation of the shadow exchange rate over the period, *hydrated* alcohol remained a significantly inefficient substitute for gasoline. Even in 1982, when the imputed exchange rate was Cr$ 28 per dollar and gasoline was valued at 19 cents per liter, hydrated alcohol generated net social losses of an estimated 3 cents per liter. The further decline in real oil prices in 1983 widened the gap between social costs and returns.

[39]Total production of anhydrous alcohol was 2.20 billion liters in 1979, 2.25 in 1980, 1.15 in 1981, and 2.02 in 1982. Comparable data are unavailable for 1983.

[40]If 1982 production levels are used for 1983, cumulative losses in the 1979–83 period are estimated to be $US 275 million for anhydrous alcohol (in present value terms, $251 million).

Over the 1980–83 period, during which hydrated alcohol production grew exponentially to accommodate the booms in alcohol-powered car sales, net social losses added up to $214 million.[41] These social losses will likely accumulate rapidly, since world oil prices continue to decline in real terms while the alcohol-powered car fleet is already more than 2 million strong.

## Comparing Phases One and Two

*Substitutability in Alcohol Production and Consumption*

No one can say for sure whether Phase One, from the vantage point of 1975, was an economically rational energy adjustment strategy. Trends in world oil prices, interest rates, and commodity prices were subject to fundamental uncertainty at the time. What we do know is that Phase One, though costly, was a measured and flexible response both to the collapse of world sugar prices and to rising world oil prices. Irreversible investments were indeed made in many alcohol distilleries and in some plantations and mills. Yet Brazil did not make an irrevocable commitment to alcohol fuel per se. In the event of higher world sugar or lower world oil prices, the country's plantations and mills could produce more sugar and less alcohol without large adjustment costs. Moreover, the automobile industry and consumers would have been indifferent to the resulting substitution of gasoline for alcohol in the fuel supply since they had yet to invest in alcohol-related capital equipment. The flexibility afforded by these characteristics of the initial alcohol production and consumption systems helped to make Phase One an economically rational response to the extraordinary uncertainties of the time.

[41]In present value terms, $US 155 million. Total production of hydrated alcohol fuel was 0.43 billion liters in 1980, 1.40 billion in 1981, and 1.70 billion in 1982. This estimate of net social losses assumes that 1.70 billion liters were also produced in 1983, although the actual production of this fuel was higher.

## World Sugar Prices

To grasp the importance of the flexibility afforded by Phase One, let us first take notice of the extreme volatility that world sugar prices have exhibited since the early 1970s.[42] These prices are expressed in US cents per pound:

| 1973 | 1974 | 1975 | 1976 | 1977 | 1978 | 1979 | 1980 | 1981 | 1982 | 1983 |
|------|------|------|------|------|------|------|------|------|------|------|
| 9.45 | 29.66 | 20.37 | 11.51 | 8.10 | 7.81 | 9.65 | 28.66 | 16.89 | 8.40 | 8.46 |

One reason why world sugar prices have been so volatile is that the spot market for this commodity is extremely thin. Since bilateral and multilateral agreements regulate the prices and quantities of most of the international trade in sugar, significant production shortfalls can generate extraordinarily high spot prices, as occurred in 1973–74 and 1980–81.[43] Since Brazil was among the top three sugar producers in the world, however, spot prices likely overstate the value of forgone incremental sugar exports during these episodes. The actual opportunity cost of sugar exports for this "large-country" case was presumably bounded on the upside by the spot price and on the downside by the average value Brazil obtained for sugar exports in each year:[44]

| | 1979 | 1980 | 1981 | 1982 | 1983 |
|---|------|------|------|------|------|
| Spot price (1979 cents per pound) | 9.7 | 25.1 | 13.6 | 6.6 | 6.6 |
| Average export price (1979 cents per pound) | 7.4 | 16.0 | 9.9 | 4.7 | 4.8 |

[42]Average nominal U.S. cents per pound, ISA world price. Sources: International Sugar Organization, *Sugar Yearbook, 1980* (London: ISO, 1981), p. 332; and USDA, *Sugar and Sugar Sweetener Outlook* (April 1984):2.

[43]For a useful though dated discussion, see Abdessatar Grissa, *The Structure of the International Sugar Market and Its Impact on the Developing Countries* (Paris: Development Centre of OECD, 1976).

[44]Sources: Central Bank of Brazil, *Annual Report, 1981*; Economist Intelligence Unit, *Quarterly Economic Review of Brazil*, various issues; *International Financial Statistics*; and references listed in note 42. The price deflator is the U.S. wholesale price index.

## Implications for Social Profitability

Consider the social costs of producing sugar during these years. Based on the same data source and method employed above, I estimate total social costs in the Center-South to have risen from about 7 cents per pound in 1979 to about 8 cents per pound in 1980–81 and to have declined to their base period levels in 1982–83.[45] Sugar exports were therefore extremely lucrative in 1980–81 but socially unprofitable in 1982–83. In 1981, for example, sugar exports generated an *average* net return of 2 cents per pound. This return, though small in absolute terms, raised the opportunity cost of sugarcane by more than $US 5.00 per metric ton.[46] The true costs of alcohol production were therefore at least 28 cents per liter, substantially above the value of anhydrous alcohol (20 cents) and far beyond that of hydrated alcohol (17 cents). Clearly, small movements in sugar export prices above Brazil's social cost of production create powerful economic reasons to reduce the output of alcohol relative to sugar.

## The Irony of 1981

These results illustrate the value that should have been attached to the ability to substitute sugar for alcohol in production and gasoline for alcohol in consumption. If Phase One continued, no significant political or technical constraints would have inhibited a substantial increase in sugar exports during 1980–81. But it was during this period that Brazil

[45]These costs are not adjusted for the value of molasses, a by-product of sugar refining, which is a tradable good. Its value could be as much as $0.01 per pound of sugar produced. The reader is also reminded that the data used to estimate the social costs of sugar production are taken from plantations and mills in São Paulo and Paraná and, therefore, probably understate the national average.

[46]Based on industrial yields of 89 kilograms of sugar per metric ton of cane (as reported for 1978–79 by Copersucar). Since 1 kilogram is equivalent to 2.2046 pounds, the conversion factor (from dollars per pound of sugar to dollars per metric ton of cane) is 196. The industrial yield of alcohol is, as above, 70 liters per metric ton.

launched Phase Two and, hence, became committed to alcohol fuel production and consumption. To the extent that sugar exports expanded, they did so at the expense of anhydrous alcohol production rather than that of the less fuel efficient hydrated alcohol. In 1981, the production of anhydrous alcohol declined by 1.1 billion liters (50 percent) while hydrated alcohol production reached 1.4 billion—nearly a threefold increase over the previous year, when alcohol-powered cars were first sold.[47]

## Some Conclusions

With a number of important qualifications, it appears that Phase One of *Proálcool* was a prudent strategy to adjust to adverse conditions in the world sugar and oil markets in the late 1970s and early 1980s. The first qualification is that even after discounting investments in existing plantations and mills as sunk costs, anhydrous alcohol production at annexed distilleries remained socially unprofitable until 1980. There is thus no denying that *Proálcool* was a costly device to protect the sugar industry and the military regime from the embarrassment, once world sugar prices declined, of having invested $US 4.5 billion in the sector during 1973–75. Second, the further, though moderate, expansion of sugarcane production and milling capacity in the late 1970s could not have been justified on efficiency grounds unless the threefold increase in oil prices, the world recession, and the interest rate shock had been foreseen. Third, the rapid expansion of sugarcane cultivation during the early 1980s has created certain socially undesirable effects, including further concentration of landownership and strong tendencies toward monoculture in São Paulo.[48]

Subject to these qualifications, as well as to the caveats underlying the assumptions chosen throughout the analysis,

[47]Conselho Nacional de Petróleo, *Anuário Estatístico, 1982.*

[48]For discussions of these important consequences, see Fernando Homem de Melo, "A agricultura nos anos 80: perspectiva e conflitos entre objetivos

Phase One indeed may have been an economically rational means to generate national income and foreign exchange. Since most observers assumed that world oil prices after the second OPEC shock would keep up with U.S. inflation, the 1980–82 period is an appropriate baseline from which to evaluate Phase One. From this perspective, the production of anhydrous alcohol and its consumption in gasoline engines neatly hedged the country from the effects of cheap sugar and expensive oil. If world sugar prices failed to exceed Brazilian costs of production, the substitution of alcohol for sugar production at annexed distilleries and the substitution of alcohol for gasoline in the fuel supply would generate sufficient returns to cover social costs. At those other times when world sugar prices rose above social costs, the *usineiros* could easily be induced to substitute sugar for alcohol production at the margin. Furthermore, since alcohol-powered cars were not marketed during Phase One, consumers would have been totally indifferent to the quantities of alcohol produced. Brazil's ability to make these adjustments would have been nicely rewarded, as illustrated by the substantial effects of the 2 cents per pound social profit on sugar exports achieved in 1981.

In stark contrast, the autonomous distilleries promoted during Phase Two lacked these substitution opportunities in production. Even if they had produced anhydrous alcohol for cars equipped with gasoline engines, autonomous distilleries would have been able to generate social profits only under a scenario of continuing increases in real world oil prices. This technology also ruled out occasional opportunities for impressive social profits from sugar exports. The second component of Phase Two was equally restrictive. Once consumers made their investments in alcohol-powered cars, a policy to

de política," *Estudos Econômicos* (May/August 1980):57–101; Homem de Melo and Eduardo Gianetti da Fonseca, *Proálcool, Energia, e Transportes* (São Paulo: FIPE, 1981), pp. 51–108; and Quadros da Silva, "O crescimento da lavoura canavieira no Brasil na década de 70."

encourage the substitution of sugar for alcohol in production would be politically risky. To these considerations must be added the fact that in 1982 real world oil prices were about $US 5 per barrel below the level permitting hydrated alcohol production to break even in social prices.

This economic analysis leads us to ask why state authorities began to formulate and implement policies in 1979–80 that strongly encouraged large private investments in autonomous distilleries and alcohol-powered cars. As for the private response to Phase Two, we should ask why producers and consumers were willing to believe that their irreversible investments in distilleries and alcohol-powered cars would become privately profitable—especially given ample evidence that foes of *Proálcool* occupied strategic positions within the Brazilian state. How did a moderate and flexible bailout scheme for the sugar industry become transformed, within four years, into an ambitious program that generated a massive flow of private investment into the production and consumption of alcohol fuel? To these questions about the mutual adjustment of state authorities and private investors we now turn.

# CHAPTER 3

# Market Forces in the Steered Economy

### Strategic and Market Uncertainty

*Private Profitability and Capital Budgeting Methods*

In turning from the efficiency to the control dimension of the resource allocation process, the present chapter leaves the rarefied world of social prices and profits. Instead of focusing on the profitability of an activity for the nation as a whole, let us now examine resource allocation decisions from the viewpoint of key decision makers in market systems: private investors.[1] The capital budgeting (or investment) decisions of

---

[1] In this book, I use the terms *private investors, firms,* and *market agents* interchangeably. The key point is that each of these actors selects capital projects whose value depends on future events. In this sense, an individual purchaser of an automobile is an investor as well as a market agent or consumer.

these economic agents must be explained if we are to account for intersectoral flows of private resources—which, for example, occurred in great volume during Phase Two of Brazil's alcohol program.

Modern finance theory suggests that in all market economies, wealth-seeking investors should value capital projects by forecasting the net cash flows the project will generate and then discounting these estimated net cash flows by the opportunity cost of capital. While this discounted cash flow method is appropriate for valuing risky projects in some market economies, the technique is inadequate for selecting among investment projects in steered economies, where so many activities are closely regulated by the state.[2] Investments in these activities are exposed to *strategic* uncertainty, since sector-specific policies are the product of a mutual adjustment process or game of strategy in which both investors and state officials are influential players. In steered economies, the introduction of strategic uncertainty into the investment selection problem transforms the microeconomic incentives facing wealth-maximizing private investors. In this chapter, I examine these incentives by constructing a simple model of capital budgeting under market and strategic uncertainty. With this analytic device, we may take a first critical step in understanding the interaction between state officials and market agents in steered economies.

## Strategic Uncertainty in Steered Economies

Strategic uncertainty arises when every agent in a system must take everyone else's actions into account in order to know what his or her own actions should be. Mutual adjustment is, therefore, at the heart of strategic uncertainty. Yet these two

---

[2]Of course, there are elements of steered economies in most contemporary market-oriented systems. As discussed in Chapter 1, however, this book is dedicated to the study of those market systems in which pervasive government intervention in capital and goods markets makes the state an especially integral part of the microeconomic process.

concepts are not coextensive. For in the hypothetical case of pure competition, the decisions made by individual producers and consumers are said to have such a small effect on the market that each agent can usefully take the environment as given. In the case of pure competition, then, the agents in the system engage in mutual adjustment but they cannot be said to face strategic uncertainty.[3]

Since few markets mirror the image of perfect competition, strategic relationships among firms are ubiquitous in real-world market economies.[4] For this reason, many economists have devoted vast energy to the study of oligopolistic co-ordination and related forms of mutual adjustment. It would be wise, then, to put these thorny issues aside and focus our attention on what is distinctive about politicized market economies: the strategic interaction between investors and state officials.

Steered economies are not the only market-oriented systems in which public officials must adjust their policies to the actions of private investors in order to achieve their political goals.[5] What is distinctive about the market economy we are studying here, however, is that state guidance of private resource allocation decisions is a critical component of the national political and economic systems. One feature of this type of politico-economic system is that state officials directly control the crucial variables affecting private profits in a substantial number of economic activities—although many other sectors are primarily subject to market forces.

[3]On game theory's modeling concepts and solution techniques, see Martin Shubik, *Game Theory in the Social Sciences* (Cambridge, Mass.: M.I.T. Press, 1982).

[4]For a partisan discussion of the generality of strategic relationships in market systems, see Oskar Morgenstern, "Thirteen Critical Points in Contemporary Economic Theory: An Interpretation," *Journal of Economic Literature* (December 1972):1163–89.

[5]On the "privileged position of business" in market-oriented systems, see Charles E. Lindblom, *Politics and Markets* (New York: Basic Books, 1977), pp. 170–88.

The kind of mutual adjustment process engendered by extensive state microeconomic intervention is significantly different from the kind that arises from macroeconomic intervention. Whereas macroeconomic policy changes tend to affect everyone's fortunes in roughly the same direction, sector-specific policies attract resources into some activities and draw them out of others by lowering or raising expected private profits in specific lines of business. Moreover, when state officials promote a given economic sector, only a limited number of investors usually have the knowledge, capital, and political position to cooperate. These asymmetries among investors as well as the precise focus of sector-specific policy instruments usually transform the state/market interaction over government incentives and private investment choices into a "small numbers" bargaining game. In this context, private investors can often exert substantial indirect control over government policy.[6]

To focus exclusively on what is distinctive about the politicized market economy can lead one to underestimate the variety of mutual adjustment processes *within* these systems. To illustrate the range of variation, we could do worse than cite the alcohol case in Brazil. Potential investors in this activity were as diverse as Volkswagen do Brasil (the largest unit of the giant automaker outside of Germany) and individual buyers of alcohol-powered cars. What is certainly different about these investors, among other respects, is that Volkswagen do Brasil could bargain directly with state officials over alcohol policy, while individual consumers could not. Bargaining between big business and government officials is certainly a familiar form of mutual adjustment. But we must realize that nonbargaining

---

[6]By and large, small numbers of investors are not capable of influencing macroeconomic policy to the same degree. One caveat should be kept in mind, however. Sometimes it is quite difficult to distinguish between a macroeconomic policy action and a sector-specific measure. If the state commercial bank reduces interest rates on loans specifically for new car purchases, for example, this action may be part of a macroeconomic policy designed to stimulate national income.

forms of mutual adjustment between these officials and less organized investors, such as small farmers and consumers, are also important determinants of private resource flows in steered economies.[7]

Suppose that government officials put together a policy package designed to lure private investment into a certain activity.[8] If most of the investors who are in a position to shift their resources into this activity decide that alternative uses of funds would generate greater returns and therefore do not respond, the policy objectives of the relevant state officials will be thwarted. For these goals to be eventually achieved, sector-specific incentives would have to be strengthened. No direct conversation need take place for the policy set to change. Simply by selecting the strategy they think will maximize their wealth, private investors can usually achieve some degree of indirect control over the policy choices of state officials.

In 1980, for example, numerous unorganized, small-scale ranchers in western São Paulo were offered extremely lucrative incentives for new investments in autonomous plantation-mill-distillery complexes. The reasons why state officials wanted to provide these incentives had little to do with the political position of the ranchers per se; these landowners were simply in the best position to cooperate with efforts to expand alcohol production beyond the existing sugarcane plantations. These small players also had the opportunity to invest in alternative activities or remain in ranching. Such substitution possibilities greatly enhanced the ranchers' ability to induce favorable policies toward investments in autonomous distilleries. Without direct bargaining, more attractive policies were eventually

[7]For the distinction between these two forms of mutual adjustment, I am indebted to Charles E. Lindblom. Part II of this study provides ample opportunities to examine the implications of the fact that some investors can engage in bargaining while others are limited to nonbargaining forms of mutual adjustment.

[8]Beginning in the next chapter, we will look closely at the reasons why central decision makers and other state officials engage in mutual adjustment with private investors in specific situations.

formulated and implemented. In fact, the incentives available for investments in autonomous distilleries were probably the most lucrative sector-specific policies followed in Brazil during 1980–81.[9]

## Asymmetries in Mutual Adjustment

Suppose a rancher decided to buy the fixed assets needed for an autonomous distillery complex. In this event, the rancher's resources would become locked into an irreversible investment, since they could not be put to any use except alcohol production. Because a distillery complex is "specific" to one of the most politicized sectors in Brazil, the value of this investment depends primarily on the policies in effect throughout the economic life of the project. Unlike fixed investments, however, sector-specific policies *are* reversible. Although state officials can negotiate with investors over current policies, they can seldom commit the government to a specific set of future policy actions. For example, state officials could not sign an agreement concerning future alcohol prices, production quotas, or the price and availability of working capital credit. Therefore, the rancher who decided to invest in the alcohol sector would become highly exposed to the strategic uncertainty associated with potential policy shifts. This source of uncertainty is unavoidable in a politicized market economy because of its fundamental asymmetry. This asymmetry arises because a large class of future sector-specific policies can be altered by the state at will, whereas the irreversibility of investments in fixed assets binds market agents to their choices well into the future.[10]

[9]The availability of market opportunities is, of course, not the only source of influence available to investors. The subsidies granted during Phase One, for example, cannot be explained by lucrative market substitution possibilities available to the *usineiros*. These policies are best understood by examining the macropolitical context of the policy-making process.

[10]What distinguishes the set of problems analyzed here from the main line of inquiry pursued by contemporary institutional economists is precisely the

## *Limits to a Game-Theoretic Solution*

The theory of games provides the analyst with a useful technique to model systems of interaction in which the players confront strategic uncertainty. In using game theory to analyze the steered economy, however, we immediately bump up against an important problem. The mutual adjustment process we are exploring here does not fit neatly into the categories of cooperative and noncooperative games, since there are elements of both pure types.[11] On the one hand, the extensive communication that occurs between state officials and market agents makes it appropriate to model the steered economy as a cooperative game. On the other hand, noncooperative features are introduced into the game by the fact that the government is not bound to any specific policy set after investors become locked into their strategies. Thus, standard game-theoretic concepts are somewhat inappropriate for predicting the outcome of the strategic interaction between policymakers and investors.

To solve a game, one must first know what payoffs each player will receive under all possible scenarios (that is, the joint outcome of their respective strategies). We can assume that investors maximize their wealth and that the payoffs of a capital project are measured by the present value of the net cash flows these projects generate.[12] But what is it that the

---

inability of investors in "specific" assets to contract with, in this case, the state. On contracts and asset specificity, see Oliver L. Williamson, *Markets and Hierarchies* (New York: Free Press, 1975).

[11]In the words of R. Duncan Luce and Howard Raiffa, *Games and Decisions* (New York: Wiley, 1957), p. 89: "By a *cooperative game* is meant a game in which the players have complete freedom of preplay communication to make joint *binding* agreements. In a *noncooperative game* absolutely no preplay communication is permitted between players." The authors of this classic text also note (p. 105): "We cannot help feeling that the realistic cases actually lie in the hiatus between strict noncooperation and full cooperation.

[12]See any treatment of modern finance theory, such as Eugene F. Fama and Merton H. Miller, *Theory of Finance* (New York: Holt, Rinehart and Winston, 1972).

government should be assumed to maximize? One might simply assume that the state maximizes some arbitrary utility function.[13] To take this tack, however, skirts the fundamental analytic problem. In many steered economies, including the Brazilian one, numerous state agencies are granted some authority over policy-making in the same economic sector. Sector-specific policies are therefore shaped by another complex mutual adjustment process, one that is carried out within the intricate authority network of state politics. Since it is nonsensical to proceed as if "the state" were a unitary actor or, equivalently, a single player, only the investors' payoffs can be defined.

Although a game-theoretic analysis of the state/market interaction over policy and investment cannot generate a neat solution, this approach is still valuable in illuminating the basic structure of the system. Let us build up to a simplified model of the politicized market economy by first suggesting one way investors can be expected to value projects in these systems. This analysis provides what could be termed the microeconomic foundations of the steered economy.

## Capital Budgeting Under Market and Strategic Uncertainty

### *A Simple Portfolio Selection Problem*

Let us begin the modeling effort by examining the simplest hypothetical representation of the capital budgeting problem in a steered economy. Matrix 1 depicts this problem for the case of a single investor. We may assume that this investor is currently endowed with a given amount of liquid wealth and is about to choose an investment strategy. Strategy 1 represents a purchase of real assets that are specific to some sector of the

---

[13]This technique is useful in the formal analysis of certain problems. For an example, see Ralph Bryant, *Money and Monetary Policy in Interdependent Nations* (Washington, D.C.: Brookings Institution, 1980).

|  | $S_1$ | $N_1$ |
|---|---|---|
| Strategy 1: Real Assets | $B$ | $-C$ |
| Strategy 2: Securities | $-B$ | $0$ |

MATRIX 1. *The Capital Budgeting Problem: The Case of One Project*

economy. Strategy 2, the mutually exclusive alternative, is to use the endowment in purchasing government securities. Strategy 2 is said to be "risk-free" since the cash flows yielded by these financial assets are known with complete certainty. In contrast, the cash flows generated by investing in real assets are uncertain at the time the investor chooses between strategies 1 and 2. (The investor is said to make his project selection at $t_0$.)

We may assume that the cash flows yielded by strategy 1 depend to some extent on the sector-specific policy actions taken by state officials throughout the economic life of the project. In the real world, state officials may choose among a wide range of finely differentiated policy sets. For simplicity, let us assume that the policy package in place at $t_0$ is designed to draw resources into the sector associated with strategy 1. But we do not know whether government policy will continue to support this sector at $t_1$, that is, after the investor makes his strategy choice. Let us assume that strategy 1 will yield positive net cash flows if sector-specific policies continue to be favorable for the duration of the project. This eventuality is represented as column $S_1$ in Matrix 1. Alternatively, state officials at $t_1$ might reduce the incentives granted to those who invested in this activity, a possibility that is represented as column $N_1$. Such a policy shift would diminish the cash flows generated by investment strategy 1. For convenience, we may assume that under $N_1$ the net cash flows yielded by strategy 1 will be negative.

Notice that our investor selects his portfolio at $t_0$ while state officials make their move at $t_1$. This representation of the situation stresses the asymmetry created by investment irreversibilities and the investor's inability to contract with the government over future policy. Let me emphasize this asymmetry by referring to $S_1$ and $N_1$ not as government strategies but as "states of the world." The actual state of the world is revealed to the investor at $t_1$, that is, after the investment strategy becomes irreversible.[14]

What would be the payoff of strategy 1 in the event that state of the world $S_1$ occurs? This payoff would be the net present value of the expected stream of cash flows the investment would yield if favorable sector-specific policies continued to be followed. Payoff $B$ in the northwest corner of Matrix 1 summarizes the effects of *known* sector-specific policies, as well as *unknown* marketplace conditions, macroeconomic policy, and nonpolicy shocks.[15] Similarly, payoff $-C$ in the northeast corner of the matrix represents the net present value of strategy 1 in the event that sector-specific policy turns sour.

The payoff of investing in risk-free securities (strategy 2) depends on the value of the alternative strategy of investing in real assets. Let's say our investor chose strategy 2 but $S_1$ occurs. In this event, he would have missed the opportunity to earn $B$,

[14]Of course, current policy is known with certainty at $t_0$. Yet we may assume, for analytic convenience, that the effect of current policy on net cash flows is insignificant in comparison to the effect of future policy. This assumption is most realistic if fixed assets are long-lived.

[15]The state of the world is not known at $t_0$. But for valuing strategy 1 it is useful to estimate the payoffs that would accrue *if* state of the world $S_1$ occurs. Then we can say that uncertainty attaches to the state of the world, rather than to the payoff yielded under a given state of the world. In the language of the state-preference approach to financial theory, payoff $B$ is a *component claim* of the more complex security, strategy 1. The value of strategy 1 depends on both the payoffs and the probability that each state of the world will occur. On this approach to the valuation of investments, see J. Hirschleifer, *Investment, Interest, and Capital* (Englewood Cliffs, N.J.: Prentice-Hall, 1970), pp. 250–62. For an alternative exposition, see Fama and Miller, *Theory of Finance*, pp. 157–59. I am deeply indebted to Carl Alan Batlin for suggesting this modeling approach.

that is, the value of strategy 1 if policy is favorable at $t_1$. So we must penalize our investor for missing this opportunity by subtracting $B$ from what would otherwise be the present value of strategy 2. This penalty is incorporated in payoff $-B$, located in the southwest cell of Matrix 1.[16] If $N_1$ occurs, on the other hand, the payoff of investing in risk-free securities is zero. This is because the investor missed only the opportunity to lose money $(-C)$.

We must remember that the existence of strategic uncertainty is not the only reason why future cash flows are not known with complete certainty at the time the investor makes his portfolio decision. Although future sector-specific policy is often the most important unknown in steered economies, an investor must also consider the effects of variables over which he has no control. A change in demand or supply conditions, for example, might affect the price the investor receives for his products if that price is set in competitive markets rather than in a bureaucracy. Or the introduction of a macroeconomic austerity program could reduce sales drastically. Or an act of nature might impair production levels. These kinds of uncertainty are found in all market economies, and I will use the term *market uncertainty* in referring to them.[17]

While the state-of-the-world approach, employed above, enables us to capture the effects of strategic uncertainty on the value of a project, we must also consider how market uncertainty affects project valuation. Imagine an extreme hypothetical case in which an investment is not exposed to market uncertainty, but only to strategic uncertainty. The output of such an idealized activity can be termed a pure *political product*, since the cash flows generated by these hypothetical invest-

---

[16]Literally $-B$ plus zero, since the investment in securities would earn the risk-free rate of interest and therefore has a zero present value.

[17]In the useful schema of Hirschleifer, my term *market uncertainty* thus includes both "transaction" uncertainty over the outcome of interactions in the marketplace and "productive" uncertainty over the level and quality of production.

ment projects would be completely determined by (politically guided) sector-specific policies.

If strategy 1 is an investment in a pure political product, how does this fact influence the payoff matrix? First, a policy shift at $t_1$ must have severe repercussions on the realized value of strategy 1, since sector-specific policies are the only variables determining the cash flows of pure political products. These repercussions would translate into a wide spread between $B$ and $-C$, reflecting the substantially different cash flows the project could be expected to yield under the two states of the world. Second, the payoffs in Matrix 1 should reflect the hypothetical elimination of market uncertainty from the capital budgeting problem. To know the state of the world, in this example, is to know the net cash flows of the project with certainty. In valuing the project under *either* $S_1$ or $N_1$, the investor should consequently discount the expected cash flows by the risk-free rate of interest.[18]

Now relax the restrictive assumption that strategy 1 represents an investment in a pure political product. For in real-world steered economies, investors bear both market and strategic uncertainty when they commit resources to a specific project. Even in the most extensively regulated sectors, acts of nature or other difficulties may impede production levels or quality.

Yet a distinctive feature of the steered economy is not simply that capital budgeting decisions are made under both market and strategic uncertainty; investors in these systems are normally faced with an opportunity set that includes some projects whose cash flows are highly subject to policy shifts as well as others whose cash flows depend primarily on marketplace outcomes. An investment in sugar production in Brazil, for example, is fairly insulated from the vagaries of the marketplace by the system of state production quotas, price guarantees, credit programs, and the like. But sugar producers

---

[18]When cash flows are known with certainty, no risk premium need be added to the rate that can be earned on risk-free investments.

cannot avoid market uncertainty without cost since they are highly exposed to strategic uncertainty by virtue of the fact that policies such as production prices and quotas can be changed after the sugar-related investments are made. Those who invest in activities where such key variables as production levels or prices are determined in competitive markets, however, are much more exposed to market uncertainty than the sugar producers. And, as a consequence, they are less vulnerable to shifts in sector-specific policies. This trade-off between the relative degrees of exposure to strategic and market uncertainty is characteristic of the capital budgeting problem in steered economies.

Let us see more precisely what this trade-off implies. Suppose we are to compare two nearly identical investment projects. The only difference between them is that the producer price of commodity A is market-determined whereas government agencies set the current and future unit price for commodity B. (I will call the output of the first activity a *market product*.)[19] Investments in commodity A are more *exposed* to market uncertainty than investments in commodity B. In this hypothetical case, the cash flows generated by the market product will exhibit more variability than the cash flows generated by the political product under each state of the world. To reflect the greater variability of commodity A's cash flows under each state of the world, a somewhat higher discount rate should be used in calculating the payoff of this project.

The proposition that an investor should apply a larger discount rate to market than political products may be difficult to operationalize in the real world, where a comparison of the

---

[19]Conceptually, a pure market product is the output of an activity in which sector-specific policies do not affect a project's cash flows. My terms *political product* and *market product* do not refer to these idealized activities; rather, they are used as locational concepts. In a given context, political products are distinguished from market products by the extent to which cash flows are determined by sector-specific policies rather than in the marketplace.

projects in the opportunity set is never as neat as in the example constructed here. Yet, as I show in the analysis of *Proálcool*, these concepts provide some leverage in valuing the alternative projects available to the four sets of players in the game.

## The Form of the Game

I introduced this chapter with a bare-bones description of the interaction between state officials and private investors in steered economies. Then I began to search for the micro-economic foundations of this mutual adjustment process by translating the earlier informal analysis into a formal depic-tion of the investor's choice problem under conditions of market and strategic uncertainty. This methodological ap-proach permits us to derive some useful implications of the assumption that private investors must be induced by the expectation of gain if they are to commit their resources to either political or market products. If, for example, central decision makers are trying to induce private investors to select strategy 1, we should infer that these authorities will be thwarted in their efforts to do so if investors expect strategy 2 to yield greater utility or value.

This stylized analysis of the capital budgeting problem suggests how the mutual adjustment process is structured by the investors' option to make their own resource allocation decisions. If we could complement this microeconomic analy-sis with an equally parsimonious description of the state's decision problem, the cells of Matrix 1 could be filled with ordered pairs, representing the payoffs of each outcome that would accrue to the two players. Then the equilibrium of the game could be predicted by invoking one of the familiar game-theoretic solution concepts.

The politicized market economy cannot be modeled in this way, however, since the payoffs for the state cannot be defined even at the conceptual level. As I have explained, the state is not a unitary player, and only under special conditions can it be said that the entire state apparatus is pursuing a consistent set of operational goals. In fact, sector-specific policy is best understood not as a set of instrument settings, selected to achieve undisputed ends, but as the product of a complex process of partisan mutual adjustment.[20] Therefore, instead of writing down arbitrary payoffs for the state in Matrix 1, I will assume that investors form their own expectations of future policy. These expectations influence the values of $B$ and $C$, for these payoffs reflect the expected net cash flows generated under each state of the world. Investors' expectations of the likelihood that either $S_1$ or $N_1$ will occur can be summarized as a subjective probability distribution across these states of the world.

This simple modeling exercise tells us that the selection of capital projects by private investors depends on three "independent" variables: current policy, investors' expectations of future policy, and market opportunities and risks. But current policy also adapts to private investment decisions, not just the other way around. Moreover, investors' expectations of future policy are shaped by the current policy set. For these reasons, we would misspecify the system by treating current and expected policy as independent or exogenous variables. To specify the system correctly, we must treat private investment decisions, current policy, and expected policy as simultaneously determined, endogenous variables. This system can be said to be in equilibrium only if the values of these three variables are mutually consistent.

My analytic aim, therefore, is to arrive at an implicit solution to this system of relationships. An implicit solution is obtained when the value of each endogenous variable in the system can be said to be constrained by the values of certain other variables. Since we have three endogenous variables, we need three such constraints. In specifying how investors' substitu-

[20]On partisan mutual adjustment, see Charles E. Lindblom, *The Intelligence of Democracy* (New York: Free Press, 1965). This process is discussed in Chapter 4.

tion possibilities structure the game, we are thus identifying one of the equilibrium conditions of the steered economy. A less formal model of the policy-making process, to be introduced in Chapter 4, provides the other two equilibrium conditions.

The one equilibrium condition that can be derived from the model of capital budgeting is a set of investment decision rules. Assume that when investors are faced with a choice between two mutually exclusive projects, they will select the one which yields the greatest expected utility.[21] In the case of Matrix 1, the expected utility of strategy 1 is the sum of two terms: the probability $(p_1)$ that the state continues to support the activity $(S_1)$ times the utility of the investment if it does so *and* the probability $(p_2)$ that policy sours $(N_1)$ times the utility of the investment under that eventuality. Now assume, purely for expositional convenience, that investors are risk-neutral with respect to strategic uncertainty. In this case, the utility of strategy 1 is the probability weighted average of the investment's net present value under $S_1$ and $N_1$. In symbols:

$$U \text{ (strategy 1)} = E_1 = p_1 \cdot B - p_2 \cdot C$$

Similarly, for the alternative strategy of investing in risk-free securities,

$$U \text{ (strategy 2)} = E_2 = -p_1 \cdot B$$

By algebra, it can be shown that $E_1 \gtreqless E_2$ as[22]

[21]On the expected utility approach, see Fama and Miller, *Theory of Finance*, p. 190, and Hirschleifer, *Investment, Interest, and Capital*, p. 215. An alternative decision rule for selecting projects is the maximin criterion. This solution to the capital budgeting problem would be appropriate for investors who desire security against the worst possible state of the world. It is also a solution concept frequently applied to noncooperative games of strategy. See Luce and Raiffa, *Games and Decisions*, pp. 278–80.

[22]In words: The expected value of strategy 1 is greater than (equal to/less than) the expected value of strategy 2 as $p_1$ is greater than (equal to/less than) $C/2B + C$, respectively. Note that in this case $p_2 = (1 - p_1)$.

$$p_1 \gtrless \frac{C}{2B + C}$$

In the special case where $B = C$, the expected value of an investment in real assets would be greater than that in securities if $p_1 = 0.33$. On the other hand, if the downside risks are twice as large in absolute value as the upside gains ($C = 2B$), strategy 1 would still dominate so long as $p_1 > 0.5$. These somewhat surprising results reflect the opportunity cost of investing in securities if $S_1$ obtains. If $p_1$ rises, strategy 1 improves not only because $E_1$ increases but also because $E_2$ must decrease. Of course, the incentives to invest in these real assets would be weakened somewhat by the more realistic assumption that investors are risk-averse with respect to strategic uncertainty.

## The Case of Two Projects

The simple case of two investment strategies discussed above served to clarify the main outlines of the analysis. In the present section, a more complex situation is explored, one in which the entrepreneur is faced with two mutually exclusive projects as well as the option of investing in risk-free securities.

Four states of the world may obtain in this case. First, both sectors are supported ($S_1S_2$) at $t_1$. Second, sector 1 is supported and sector 2 is neglected ($S_1N_2$). In the third case, the reverse situation occurs ($N_1S_2$). In the fourth case, neither sector is supported by state policy at $t_1$ ($N_1N_2$). This game takes the form shown in Matrix 2.

The rationale for these payoffs is identical to that of Matrix 1. This case, however, introduces an additional set of opportunity costs under some states of the world. For example, an investor in sector 1 will lose the opportunity to earn $B_2$ if $N_1S_2$ obtains, in addition to suffering the decline in the value of investments in the unfavored sector (represented by $-C_1$).

|  | STATES OF THE WORLD | | | |
|---|---|---|---|---|
|  | $S_1S_2$ | $S_1N_2$ | $N_1S_2$ | $N_1N_2$ |
| Strategy 1: Sector 1 | $B_1\dagger$ $2B_1 - B_2\ddagger$ | $B_1$ | $-C_1 - B_2$ | $-C_1$ |
| Strategy 2: Sector 2 | $B_2\dagger$ $2B_2 - B_1\ddagger$ | $-C_2 - B_1$ | $B_2$ | $-C_2$ |
| Strategy 3: Securities | $-B_1\dagger$ $-B_2\ddagger$ | $-B_1$ | $-B_2$ | $0$ |

$\dagger$if $B_1 > B_2$

$\ddagger$if $B_2 > B_1$

MATRIX 2. *The Capital Budgeting Problem: The Case of Two Projects*

The notion of opportunity cost is somewhat more subtle if both projects are supported by the government at $t_1$. If strategy 1 is chosen and $S_1S_2$ obtains, the investor receives a payoff of $B_1$. However, the larger payoff of $B_2$ is forgone if $B_2 > B_1$. Since the two investments are mutually exclusive, the opportunity cost is the difference $(B_2 - B_1)$, which must be subtracted from payoff $B_1$. The value of an investment in sector 1 under $S_1S_2$ is therefore $2B_1 - B_2$ if $B_2 > B_1$ and simply $B_1$ if this opportunity cost does not exist $(B_1 > B_2)$.[23]

When the future state of the world is known with certainty, the optimal strategy choice is unambiguous.[24] Under the opposite case of complete ignorance or maximal strategic uncertainty, it is also possible to derive clear decision rules. Such a state of affairs occurs when investors believe that all defined states of the world are equally likely. By simple

[23]The same argument applies to strategy 2 under $S_1S_2$, where the payoff is $B_2$ if $B_2 > B_1$ and $2B_2 - B_1$ if $B_1 > B_2$. The payoff under strategy 3, investing in risk-free securities, is simply the negative of the best payoff under each state of the world.

[24]Strategy 1 is optimal under $S_1N_2$ and, if $B_1 > B_2$, under $S_1S_2$. Strategy 2 is preferred under $N_1S_2$ and, if $B_2 > B_1$, under $S_1S_2$ as well. Strategy 3 yields the highest payoff under $N_1N_2$ only.

algebra, it can be shown that the expected values of the three strategies are related by the following expressions:[25]

$$E_1 \gtreqless E_2 \quad \text{as} \quad B_1 - B_2 \gtreqless \tfrac{1}{2}(C_1 - C_2) \qquad (1)$$
$$E_1 \gtreqless E_3 \quad \text{as} \quad B_1 \gtreqless \tfrac{1}{2}C_1 \qquad (2)$$
$$E_2 \gtreqless E_3 \quad \text{as} \quad B_2 \gtreqless \tfrac{1}{2}C_2 \qquad (3)$$

These three relationships determine when each strategy is preferred under complete strategic uncertainty. The strategy of investing in risk-free assets dominates all others only when the downside risks of both projects are more than twice as large as their respective upside gains ($C_1 > 2B_1$ and $C_2 > 2B_2$). If either condition fails to obtain, decision makers will invest in one of the two sectors.

By definition, market players will be indifferent between strategies 1 and 2 if these are perfect substitutes ($B_1 = B_2$ and $C_1 = C_2$). Equation (1) shows that as these two equalities are relaxed individually, the optimal strategy choice becomes evident.[26] When both equalities are relaxed simultaneously, it is clear that sector 1 is preferred if its payoffs are greater under all states of the world (that is, when $B_1 > B_2$ and $C_1 < C_2$).

In a politicized market economy, however, these inequalities often have the same direction. If $B_1 > B_2$ because sector 1 produces a more political product than sector 2, it is likely that $C_1 > C_2$: Since cash flows in sector 1 are enhanced by its political status under $S_1$, unfavorable policy ($N_1$) will have greater negative consequences for the value of assets in this sector than for assets in sector 2 ($N_2$). Which strategy is preferred under these conditions depends on the spreads between the respective $B$'s and $C$'s. Specifically, Equation (1) shows that the market sector will dominate only if the difference between $C_1$ and $C_2$ is twice as large as that between $B_1$ and $B_2$. This asymmetric result is driven by the opportunity

---

[25]These conditions hold whether $B_1 > B_2$ or $B_2 > B_1$.

[26]For instance, if $C_1 = C_2$ and $B_1 > B_2$, strategy 1 is preferred. If $B_1 = B_2$ and $C_1 > C_2$, strategy 2 is preferred.

costs of failing to choose the more political sector if it is
favored.[27] Thus, in this example, the incentive to invest in
political products is magnified by the opportunity costs of not
doing so, even under maximal strategic uncertainty.

Complete ignorance is, of course, a special case of decision
making under strategic uncertainty. The decision maker
generally has some information about the future. This information, which can be described by a subjective probability
distribution, is used to calculate the expected value of alternative investments. The decision rules of this care are analo-
gous to those of Equations (1) to (3):[28]

$$E_1 \gtrless E_2 \quad \text{as} \quad p_1(2B_1 - 2B_2) + p_2(2B_1 + C_2) - p_3(C_1 + 2B_2)$$
$$- p_4(C_1 - C_2) \gtrless 0 \tag{4}$$

$$E_1 \gtrless E_3 \quad \text{as} \quad p_1(2B_1) + p_2(2B_1) - p_3(C_1) - p_4(C_1) \lessgtr 0 \tag{5}$$

$$E_2 \gtrless E_3 \quad \text{as} \quad p_1(2B_2) - p_2(C_2) + p_3(2B_2) - p_4(C_2) \gtrless 0 \tag{6}$$

By casual observation it is apparent that few interesting
general statements can be made about these equations. The
optimal strategy depends on the probability distribution
across states of the world and on all the payoffs. It is therefore
appropriate to turn to the specific case of the alcohol program,
not only to illustrate the results of the model but to identify the
differential incentives facing market players in the game.

## Investment Incentives of Alcohol Producers

### The Technological-Institutional Context

The opportunity set facing the *usineiros* in the early years of
*Proálcool* was vastly different from that available to potential
alcohol producers not initially linked to the sugar industry.
Before the onset of the alcohol program, many sugar pro-

[27] If these costs are excluded from the payoffs of strategies 1 and 2, it can be
shown that $E_1 \gtrless E_2$ as $(B_1 - B_2) \gtrless (C_1 - C_2)$.

[28] If $B_2 > B_1$, then $p_1$ in Equation (4) is weighted by $(B_1 - B_2)$ instead of
$(2B_1 - 2B_2)$.

ducers already had small distilleries annexed to their milling and refining complexes. In most instances, these distilleries were designed to convert the residual material from sugar refining—molasses—into alcohol. By and large, sugarcane juice was not converted *directly* into alcohol. This clearly subsidiary position of alcohol within the sugar production process changed markedly after the inauguration of the National Alcohol Program.

*Annexed and autonomous distilleries.* In order to enter the alcohol sector, potential producers initially *outside* the sugar industry would have to invest in agricultural equipment and sugarcane mills, in addition to the distilleries. These potential investors primarily considered the option of constructing autonomous plantation-mill-distillery complexes that would be incapable of producing sugar as an alternative end use. The capital outlays needed to purchase mills and equipment for autonomous distilleries would be enormous relative to those for most alternative activities in the agricultural sector.[29] Furthermore, the lead time needed to achieve full production from autonomous distillery complexes would be approximately four years; an annexed distillery could be operational in less than a harvest season. The effects of the differential capital requirements and lead times of annexed distilleries and autonomous distillery complexes are formally reflected in their net present values under each state of the world.

*Uncertainty on the output side.* These payoffs also reflect the fact that alcohol is a quintessential political product. Consider, for example, the two key uncertainties that attach to the marketing of any good: the quantity demanded and price received. Alcohol producers are insulated from these uncertainties by the authority granted to the Institute for Sugar and

[29]Of course, interested producers outside of agriculture would need to purchase the necessary land as well, unless they had idle landholdings as a hedge against inflation.

Alcohol (IAA), which sets output prices and regulates supply through quotas. Although the IAA can insulate alcohol producers from direct confrontation with these market uncertainties, the quota and price policies carried out by the agency are necessarily constrained by the final demand for alcohol fuel. Over this variable the IAA maintains no direct control. But final demand is not wholly determined in the marketplace, either. Liquid fuels policy is ostensibly the preserve of the National Petroleum Council (CNP). In the case of gasohol, the quantities of alcohol permitted in the fuel supply (hence final demand) were determined by central decision makers, the CNP, and an interministerial commission. Since only gasohol was sold during Phase One, consumers did not have any direct control over the relative consumption of gasoline and anhydrous alcohol at that time. In contrast, under Phase Two consumers could influence the relative demand for gasohol and pure alcohol through their automobile purchase decisions. As we will see, the choice between engine types was affected in large measure by the comparative inefficiency of alcohol-powered cars and by the relative retail prices between the two available fuels. Since these prices were set by the National Petroleum Council, the demand for hydrated alcohol was strongly influenced by expected outcomes of the policy-making process.

*Uncertainty on the input side.* Now consider uncertainties that attach to the production process, aside from variable weather and technical difficulties. Some key input prices, such as wages and land rental rates, are market-determined, but in all probability these variables affect all agro-industrial sectors in a similar way. Turning to the other essential input, we find that *commercial* credit tends to be of little interest to the agro-industrialist. Loans provided by commercial institutions normally bear interest rates substantially above the rate of inflation (except under certain monetary policy regimes). Instead, agricultural producers have borrowed principally from the government, usually at highly negative interest rates, in order to finance working capital and fixed investments. The real value of the debt service was well below the value of the initial loan because these liabilities were not indexed to inflation and carried relatively low nominal interest rates.[30] Given the obvious importance of access to state-subsidized credit, the interest rates that affect private profitability can be said to rest exclusively in the hands of state officials.

During the late 1970s and early 1980s, the government offered the same terms for working capital loans to producers of all agricultural commodities. However, there was no guarantee that this principle of equality would be retained over the life of the private investment. One reason why the relaxation of this principle might have been feared, especially when a period of austerity was on the horizon, was that credit terms for *fixed* investments varied greatly from activity to activity. If the policy of granting equal terms for working capital loans were relaxed, producers of the "neglected" commodities would bear an additional opportunity cost. The same fear did not apply to loans on fixed investments, since investors could lock in credit terms by signing contracts with the Banco do Brasil or other financial agents of the state.

*Comparisons.* Relative to sugar and alcohol, most crops in Brazilian agriculture are market products.[31] Since price floors are rarely binding, producer prices and output levels are essentially determined in the marketplace.[32] Final demand for

[30]For a terse discussion of the relationship between this policy and the overall politico-economic strategy of Planning Minister Delfim Netto, see Edmar L. Bacha, "Vicissitudes of Recent Stabilization Attempts in Brazil and the IMF Alternative," in *IMF Conditionality*, ed. J. Williamson (Cambridge, Mass.: M.I.T. Press for the Institute for International Economics, 1983), pp. 323–34.

[31]Coffee is an exception, since this sector has been regulated by the state since the turn of the century. The Brazilian Institute of Coffee (IBC) was created at about the same time as the IAA and was given the same kind of regulatory mission.

[32]It is commonly observed that minimum prices are raised above market-clearing levels only during the year following unacceptably low levels of output for politically sensitive crops such as basic foodstuffs.

these market products is primarily dependent on the domestic and world markets rather than on government policy, and the marketing channel for alternative agro-industrial activities is in private hands.[33] On the input side, as we have seen, uncertainty attached mostly to the possibility that working capital credit terms would eventually vary by commodity.

### Annexed Distilleries

In Part II, we will see that *Proálcool* had few committed allies within the state during the 1970s, but that some of these allies were in high places. President Ernesto Geisel, for example, had put a great deal of his personal prestige and influence behind the idea of alcohol energy. Geisel was also largely responsible for those few absolutely critical policies that permitted alcohol to become more than a subsidiary commodity in the sugar production process. These policies, as well as President Geisel's personal intervention, generated extremely positive signals about the future of alcohol production in Brazil. On the other hand, the words and deeds of state officials in the financial bureaucracy and Petrobrás signaled that any attempt to expand *Proálcool* beyond a minimal sugar industry protection scheme would almost certainly fail. Given these contradictory signals, it might be said that investments in annexed distilleries were made under maximal strategic uncertainty: Favorable and unfavorable policies, $S_1$ and $N_1$, respectively, were equally likely.

To make an irreversible investment in a highly politicized activity under conditions of maximal strategic uncertainty

[33]Although its role is often underemphasized, the marketing system is obviously crucial to price formation; for a discussion, see C. Peter Timmer, Walter P. Falcon, and Scott R. Pearson, *Food Policy Analysis* (Baltimore: Johns Hopkins University Press, 1983), chap. 4. Producers are especially sensitive to the difference between a government-controlled distribution chain and one dominated by private middlemen who are known to benefit from monopoly power.

would seem completely irrational, since the value of such a project is almost wholly dependent on future sector-specific policies about which the investor knows little. But do we wish to claim that the rapid growth of distillery capacity and alcohol production during the 1977–79 period was due to irrational behavior on the part of the *usineiros?* How else can we explain why these "economic agents" invested in distilleries in spite of lengthy delays in the approval of investment credits by the state financial bureaucracy and the general uncertainty surrounding future policy?

The explanation for this puzzling behavior lies in the fact that investments in annexed distilleries at existing plantations and mills would be privately profitable even under maximal strategic uncertainty. Although the *usineiros* did not know which state of the world was more likely, they were not totally ignorant, either. The *usineiros* must have understood, for example, that the political basis of the alcohol program rested firmly but uniquely on the perceived legitimacy of protecting their industry from the effects of low world sugar prices.[34] This kernel of political analysis made it clear that favorable policies toward alcohol production would be sustained $(S_1)$ only if world sugar prices failed to recover or that, equivalently, *Proálcool* would turn sour $(N_1)$ if normal conditions returned to the sugar market. Since state officials, in essence, were providing the *usineiros* with a hedge against uncertainty in the world sugar market, it is intuitively clear why these producers would be fairly well off under either state of the world.

Formal analysis of the private profitability of investments in annexed distilleries parallels the analysis of Phase One in the previous chapter. To the extent that the decline in exports would have idled existing sugarcane production and milling capacity, the marginal private cash flows generated by a new distillery would have been substantial under $S_1$. Conversely, without producing alcohol, the value of existing investments in

[34]See Chapters 5 and 6.

plantations and sugar mills could be extremely low. Since the construction of an annexed distillery did not represent a major capital outlay, *net* cash flows also would be great under this scenario.[35] The *usineiros* would then discount these net cash flows by approximately the risk-free rate, reflecting the fact that alcohol is nearly a pure political product. Payoff $B_1$ therefore would be large indeed. Alternative investments in market products could not yield such net cash flows (under $S_2$), and the higher risk premiums used to discount the cash flows of the market products would further reduce the value of these alternative investments relative to those in annexed distilleries. Therefore, $B_1 > B_2$.

State $N_1$ would obtain if world sugar prices recovered at $t_1$, since in that case the political support underlying favorable alcohol policies would most likely vanish. When the *usineiros* switched back to sugar production, the value of the new annexed alcohol distilleries would be greatly diminished (since they would be underutilized). However, the relatively small initial outlay would prevent $C_1$ (the downside risks) from taking on high values and, under this state of the world, sugar production would provide an alternative source of cash flows. Under these conditions, in which $B_1 > B_2$ and $C_1 < C_2$, investments in alcohol distilleries would be rational even under maximal strategic uncertainty. The *usineiros* were therefore fortunate to be in a political position in which market uncertainty would be borne largely by the government.[36]

*Autonomous Distilleries*

The private profitability analysis of Phase Two also parallels the social profitability analysis of the previous chapter. Compared to the installation of an annexed distillery, net cash flows

[35]Moreover, government credit terms were lucrative and "down payments" small.

[36]Indirectly, these costs were borne by the public, which paid for the credit subsidies in large part via the inflation tax. See Part II of this study.

from investments in autonomous distilleries would be extremely weak. These complexes would require investments in agricultural equipment, a sugar mill, and a distillery. It would have been impossible for most agricultural producers to finance such huge investment projects out of their own resources. Some investors, however, including cooperatives owned by ranchers in western São Paulo, could receive financing for as much as 90 percent of the capital outlays. Aside from the subsidies attached to these loans, the *Proálcool* credit scheme would enable these investors to leverage their equity greatly. This leveraging effect would increase $B_1$ relative to $B_2$, since alternative sectors did not present such extraordinary financing opportunities.[37]

The difference between $B_1$ and $B_2$ was further increased by alcohol's status as a political product. First, an equivalently favorable policy set for alcohol, in comparison with the alternative of producing a market product, would have a greater positive effect on the cash inflows of the investment in alcohol production. Second, the higher cash flows generated by the autonomous distillery complex would be discounted at a reduced rate because of the smaller exposure of this project to market uncertainty.

There is, however, a darker side to investments in autonomous distilleries. If policy at $t_1$ turned unfavorable, the greater initial outlay for capital-intensive sugarcane and alcohol production *plus* the enhanced sensitivity of cash flows to policy shifts could raise $C_1$ well above $C_2$. Even small unfavorable turns in policy could be disastrous if, for example, these policy shifts created bottlenecks in the chain from production to consumption.[38] Hence $B_1 > B_2$ and $C_1 > C_2$.

---

[37]Long lead times for autonomous distilleries would make a difference in the timing of these cash flows by lowering to some extent the value of autonomous distillery projects relative to investments in market products.

[38]In particular, there might be little demand for the output of autonomous distilleries if a substantial fleet of alcohol-powered cars failed to materialize.

In this situation, whether the expected payoff of an investment in an autonomous distillery $(E_1)$ would exceed that of alternative opportunities $(E_2)$ depends on the relative magnitudes of these payoffs. Consider the following numerical example in which $B_1 = 10$, $B_2 = 8$, $C_1 = 15$, and $C_2 = 10$.[39] From Equations (1) and (3), it is clear that if each state of the world is equally likely, value-maximizing investors would choose sector 2. In the less restrictive case where agents have some information to form expectations, the alcohol sector would be preferred if[40]

$$p_1(4) + p_2(20) - p_3(31) - p_4(5) > 0 \qquad (4')$$

Given these payoffs, it is possible to identify the probability of $S_1$ that is sufficient for $E_1 > E_2$. Consider the case in which investors attach a probability of 0.7 to $S_2$. By definition, the joint probability distribution over the four states of the world then depends on the investors' estimate of $p(S_1)$. It can be shown that $p(S_1)$ must exceed 0.663 for strategy 1 to be selected under these circumstances.[41] Not surprisingly, as $p(S_2)$ is assumed to decline, the probability of $S_1$ required for $E_1 > E_2$ falls as well.[42] More specifically, the break-even $p(S_1)^*$ declines at a constant rate as $p(S_2)$ is diminished. Finally, it is clear from Equation (4) that $p(S_1)^*$ is more sensitive to changes in $B_1$ and $B_2$ than to changes in $C_1$ and $C_2$.[43]

---

[39]These numbers are selected to indicate that the difference between the two values of the downside risks is likely to be greater than the difference between the respective upside gains.

[40]Equation (6) implies the additional stipulation that $p_1(20) + p_2(20) - p_3(15) - p_4(15) > 0$. But in the example discussed here, this constraint is not binding.

[41]This result is derived as follows. First recall that $E_1 > E_2$ as the left-hand side (LHS) of Equation (4) exceeds zero. The value of LHS is a linear function of $p(S_1)$ for given payoffs and a given value of $p(S_2)$. In this example, LHS $= -23.2 + 35[p(S_1)]$. By simple algebra, LHS $> 0$ as $p(S_1) > 0.663$.

[42]And vice versa. This observation follows from the linear expression $p(S_1)^* = 0.143 + 0.745[p(S_1)]$, where $p(S_1)^*$ represents the probability of $S_1$ necessary for $E_1 > E_2$.

[43]This result derives from the opportunity cost structure of the politicized market economy, discussed earlier in other examples.

A few simple conclusions follow from the analysis of the decision problem for potential entrants in the alcohol sector. First, the substitution possibilities for this group were considerably closer than for the *usineiros* because of the lower discounted cash flows per unit of investment under $S_1$ and the considerably greater risks under $N_1$. Second, state officials would not be able to induce private resources to move into the autonomous distillery sector unless the investors' subjective estimate of $p(S_1)$ reached relatively high levels.[44] Third, increases in the level of market uncertainty due to macroeconomic policy or nonpolicy shocks would raise $E_1$, the value of the political product, relative to $E_2$, the value of the market product.

## Investment Incentives in Alcohol Consumption

### *The Automobile Industry*

So far, the automobile industry in Brazil has remained in the shadows of my discussion of the alcohol program. During Phase One, Volkswagen, General Motors, and Ford were quietly supportive of the alcohol program. These companies could afford to remain on the sidelines because they had no reason to expect that the production of alcohol-powered cars would ever become a real possibility. Nonetheless, investments were made in the technological development of alcohol-powered engines. By the time that alcohol was touted as a top priority of President Geisel's newly appointed successor in 1979, the automobile industry was technologically, as well as politically, prepared for Phase Two. As we will see in Part II, the multinational automobile industry became the key social force behind this risky extension of Brazil's commitment to alcohol fuel.

Why were normally cautious corporate executives willing to take the risk that alcohol policy would become favorable and remain so in Phase Two? Aside from the knowledge that their

[44]Assuming that investors would expect the next best alternative activity to be supported as well.

industry's own involvement in *Proálcool* would greatly enhance the probability of favorable future policies, there were several other interrelated reasons why investments in the production and marketing of alcohol-powered cars looked attractive in 1979–80.

In the midst of the second oil shock, automobile executives realized that the continuing escalation of world oil prices might permit initially favorable policies toward the alcohol sector to be sustained $(S_1)$. Moreover, under $S_1$ rising consumer fuel prices (reflecting the cost of imported crude oil) would depress the sales of gasoline-powered cars. In this scenario, the funds invested in retooling plants to produce alcohol engines could generate huge marginal cash flows; the value of the industry's tremendous investment in Brazil might thereby be preserved.

But what if the world oil market improved and policy became less favorable $(N_1)$? In that event, sales of gasoline-powered cars could return to their former levels. Given the modest incremental investments needed to produce and market alcohol-powered cars, it would be easy for $(B_1 - B_2)$ to exceed $\frac{1}{2}(C_1 - C_2)$, where strategy 2 represents the next best alternative use of funds. Consequently, the industry had an incentive to join the effort to launch Phase Two even if $S_1$ and $N_1$ were equally likely. The choice problem facing the automobile industry was thus similar to that of the *usineiros*, who had to decide whether to make incremental investments in alcohol distilleries. What the *usineiros* and the auto companies had in common was that the state provided each of them with a way to hedge market uncertainty (that is, the effects of changes in world sugar and oil prices, respectively). Investments in both annexed distilleries and factory retooling could rationally be made even under maximal strategic uncertainty.

### Consumers

In ordinary language, the terms *consumer* and *investor* are not interchangeable. But those consumers who were in the market to purchase an automobile during Phase Two were faced with a decision similar to that of the *usineiros*, the ranchers, and the automobile industry. In all these cases, the decision makers were considering irreversible investments. What differentiated the consumer's capital budgeting decision was that the value of an investment in an automobile would not depend on the cash flows generated by this productive asset; rather, its value would depend on the relative cost of producing "transportation services" from either alcohol-powered or gasoline-powered cars. These costs, in turn, depended on the degree to which alcohol engines were less fuel efficient than gasoline engines, on the relative consumer price between alcohol and gasohol, and on the price and financing terms of the initial purchase. These last two sets of variables were objects of state policy.

Subsidies and taxes on the purchase of automobiles were among the instruments available to state officials to drive a wedge between the private costs of alcohol and gasoline cars. In 1981, for example, the government permitted consumers to amortize their state-provided automobile loans over thirty-six months if they purchased an alcohol-powered car, whereas loans on gasoline-powered cars would have to be paid back within twelve months. In an environment where inflation was more likely to rise than fall, this extension of the amortization period for alcohol-powered cars could be extremely valuable.

By lowering the user cost of capital under all states of the world, this policy enhanced payoff $B_1$ (the value of an alcohol car under $S_1$) relative to $B_2$ (the value of a gasoline car under $S_2$) and decreased $C_1$ relative to $C_2$. The policy of imposing lower excise taxes (the *Taxa Rodoviária Única*) on alcohol-powered cars also increased the value of this investment under all states of the world.

In an effort to strengthen incentives further, the National Petroleum Council initially set the pump price of alcohol fuel at a level that more than compensated for the relative fuel inefficiency of alcohol-powered engines. This policy drove an additional wedge between $B_1$ and $B_2$. But unlike the cost differential introduced by the lenient credit terms, consumers had no guarantee that the fuel costs of alcohol-powered cars would remain lower than those of gasoline-powered cars. A policy that raised alcohol fuel prices at $t_1$ relative to gasoline prices would increase operating costs and thereby impose a capital loss on purchasers of alcohol-powered cars. Since gasoline and alcohol cars were otherwise *close substitutes*, the choice between them was extremely sensitive to the probabilities consumers attached to changes in relative fuel prices and availabilities. In fact, the alcohol boom was largely touched off by changes in these expectations under the extraordinary political conditions of 1980–81, when support for Phase Two of *Proálcool* had apparently coalesced.

# The
# Politicized Market
# Economy

## Information, Expectations, and Outcomes

Analytically, we have seen, the mutual adjustment process between state officials and private investors cannot be squeezed into either the categories of cooperative or noncooperative games. This process always falls short of a cooperative game since state officials, in their attempts to lure private resources across sectors at $t_0$, cannot usually bind the government to a specific set of incentives at $t_1$. Because of this constraint, the precision of government control over resource flows in steered economies depends heavily on whether investors fear that current policy and stated intentions are poor predictors of future policy.

Although mutual adjustment in these systems is not fully cooperative, investors typically know far more about their decision-making environment than they would if the game were purely noncooperative. So important are sector-specific policies to the Brazilian politico-economic system, for example, that the press devotes considerable attention to policy developments.[1] Relying solely on public sources of information, it is usually possible to identify the pattern of policy-making authority over a given political product. Furthermore, using these and other information sources, experienced investors are normally capable of sizing up the longevity of favorable policies toward the political products in their opportunity set.[2]

### Mutual Adjustment Between Central Decision Makers and Privileged Investors

We have already seen that the cooperative features of the mutual adjustment process can greatly outweigh its noncooperative aspects. Take, for example, the relationship between the *usineiros* and central decision makers during Phase One. To be sure, the *usineiros* were extremely exposed to strategic uncertainty; virtually every critical variable determining net cash flows in the sugar and alcohol sector was in the hands of state officials. But central decision makers perhaps needed the cooperation of the *usineiros* almost as much as these producers needed the cooperation of top authorities. As we will see in greater depth in Chapter 5, the São Paulo *usineiros* embodied many of the developmental goals of the Brazilian military regime, especially those relating to the promotion of a privately owned, modern, export-oriented productive structure. The promise of these developmental goals, in turn, was a central component of the "legitimacy formula" used by the military regime to achieve popular support for its now displaced system of rule.[3]

---

[1]Coverage of the alcohol program, for example, was extensive and detailed, as will be seen in Part II of this study.

[2]Among the other sources of information are, of course, personal contacts with state officials.

[3]The leading works on the military regime include Alfred Stepan, *The*

Because of their important position in this scheme, the *usineiros* could successfully demand a set of socially costly policies, namely the alcohol program in its early years, to hedge themselves against uncertainty in the world sugar market. With these policies initially in place, the *usineiros* knew that some features of the alcohol program would be implemented while sugar export prices remained weak. For this inference to be drawn from historic and ongoing events did not require brilliant political analysis. The single unambiguous feature of Phase One was that neither the policy permitting the direct conversion of sugarcane into alcohol nor that allowing the addition of increasing quantities of anhydrous alcohol into the fuel supply could be effectively opposed by any state official so long as the industry was being "threatened" by external events. The certainty of this linkage between low sugar prices and support for *Proálcool* allowed the interaction of the *usineiros* and state officials, analytically, to approximate that of a cooperative game during Phase One.[4]

The same kind of cooperative interaction, this time between central decision makers and the foreign-owned automobile industry, helped make Phase Two a reality. For Volkswagen, Ford, General Motors, Fiat, and Mercedes-Benz, the Brazilian market was an extremely important source of growth. As an indication, the production of transport equipment grew by annual rates above 20 percent throughout the Brazilian economic miracle (1968–74).[5] Although aggregate growth

*Military in Politics: Changing Patterns in Brazil* (Princeton: Princeton University Press, 1971); Alfred Stepan, ed., *Authoritarian Brazil* (New Haven: Yale University Press, 1973); Guillermo A. O'Donnell, *Modernization and Bureaucratic-Authoritarianism* (Berkeley: Institute of International Studies, 1973); and David Collier, ed., *The New Authoritarianism in Latin America* (Princeton: Princeton University Press, 1979).

[4]The regulatory/advocacy role played by the Institute for Sugar and Alcohol (IAA), as well as the mutual dependence of the *usineiros* and central decision makers, enhanced the cooperative features of the game. See Chapters 5 and 6.

[5]Werner Baer, *The Brazilian Economy: Its Growth and Development* (Columbus, Ohio: Grid Publishing, 1979), p. 96.

rates subsequently diminished, automobile production increased in every subsequent year until 1977.[6]

Executives at the headquarters of these enterprises were not only counting on Brazil; central decision makers in Brasília counted on the further growth of the automobile industry, too. During the "miracle" years, this sector contributed significantly to the expansion of consumer durable production and privately owned manufacturing activity, as well as to the generation of national income and employment.[7] Helped along by generous amounts of consumer credit, provided by the government, the automobile generally became *the* symbol of the style of production and consumption that the military regime tried earnestly to foster in this period. For individuals, moreover, the automobile emerged as the clearest symbol of social success and, hence, a primary focus of material aspiration. For this reason, among others, the presence of the automobile industry perhaps came to mean more to middle and upper-class Brazilians—key supporters of authoritarian rule at least during its first decade—than did the accomplishment of many earlier developmental feats, such as the implantation of a domestic steel industry in the 1940s or that of Petrobrás in the 1950s.[8] The pivotal role of the automobile in the industrial sector as well as in the structure of everyday life helps to explain why central decision makers in 1979–80 were willing to make the tough decisions needed to provide these companies with an opportunity to hedge uncertainty in world oil markets.

[6]*Conjuntura Econômica* (January 1984):20.

[7]For analysis of the miracle period, see Albert Fishlow, "Some Reflections on Post-1964 Brazilian Economic Policy," *Authoritarian Brazil*, ed. A. Stepan (New Haven: Yale University Press, 1973), pp. 69–118; Baer, *The Brazilian Economy*, pp. 89–113; Pedro S. Malan and Regis Bonelli, "The Brazilian Economy in the Seventies: Old and New Developments," *World Development* (January/February 1977):19–46; and Edmar L. Bacha, "Issues and Evidence on Recent Brazilian Economic Growth," *World Development* (January/February 1977):47–67.

[8]On the origins of the national steel and petroleum industries, see John D. Wirth, *The Politics of Brazilian Development, 1930–1954* (Stanford: Stanford University Press, 1970).

These two examples illustrate one of the crucial factors that mitigate the risks of investments in highly political products. Speaking in a general way, investors can comfortably bear wide exposures to strategic uncertainty if they embody central decision makers' vision of the desired politico-economic order.[9] Since the political support for top authorities in steered economies usually rests in good measure on their ability to realize this kind of vision, central authorities become dependent to some degree on the economic strength of such privileged investors. What breathes life into this interdependent relationship are past commitments of public resources to specific production, consumption, and ownership patterns. For example, the rapid growth of the modern São Paulo sugar complex and the expanding demand for passenger cars were both financed in large part by the government. These past commitments were not to be abandoned when conditions changed in the world sugar and oil markets; on the contrary, central decision makers were led to consider and eventually favor successive new commitments to alcohol production and consumption. Consistent with this circular pattern, the *usineiros* and the auto executives must have understood that their respective decisions to undertake alcohol-specific investments would create strong incentives for central decision makers to promote the alcohol sector for years to come. More formally, the private investment decisions made by these privileged producers at $t_0$ were likely to constrain the sector-specific policy objectives that central decision makers would pursue at $t_1$.

Other significant variables that reduce the risk of investing in political products are opportunities for collective action among the investors themselves. For example, the concentration of the São Paulo sugar industry plus the strength of their association and joint venture, Copersucar, helped to make the interaction between the *usineiros* and state officials more

[9]In the special case in which a single agency has autonomous policy-making authority over a sector, a cooperative relationship may easily arise between investors and that agency. In this event, whether investors enjoy a privileged relationship vis-à-vis central decision makers may be irrelevant.

surefooted. The same can be said for ANFAVEA, the political organization of the five-member automobile industry. Aside from enhancing syndical power, it is well known that collective action improves the quality of information transmitted between state officials and market agents. These organizational considerations are perhaps especially important after investments become irreversible, since it is useful to be able to make one's voice heard as soon as sector-specific policies begin to turn sour.[10]

Now let us tie these two factors together. Highly concentrated or tightly organized sectors that embody the developmental vision of central decision makers face lower levels of strategic uncertainty, all other things being equal, than their less concentrated, organized, or politically privileged counterparts. An important inference might be drawn from this theoretical observation: Investors with the political and organizational capabilities of the *usineiros* and the automobile industry in Brazil are best able to use the government to hedge themselves against market uncertainty.

### Mutual Adjustment Between Central Decision Makers and Ordinary Investors

The deeper commitment to alcohol production and consumption during Phase Two made the mutual adjustment process much less cooperative after 1979 than it was in the preceding four years. To increase alcohol output to the targeted 10.7 billion liters within five years, the government had to gain the cooperation of hundreds of potential investors, many of whom, like the ranchers, were traditionally involved in less politicized activities than sugar or alcohol production. Since they were not so central to the military regime's development model as the *usineiros*, these smaller-scale and less modern

[10]See Albert O. Hirschman, *Exit, Voice, and Loyalty: Responses to Decline in Firms, Organizations, and States* (Cambridge, Mass.: Harvard University Press, 1970), pp. 30–43.

producers could not be assured of unflinching support for their large irreversible investments down the road. Moreover, because of their large numbers and small scale, collective action among these businessmen would be extremely difficult to achieve. These political and organizational factors pushed the interaction between state officials and potential investors in alcohol production complexes in the noncooperative direction.

By the time these businessmen seriously considered entering the alcohol sector, the automobile industry had announced its intention to produce alcohol-powered cars. Since these vehicles were not yet on the market, however, consumer interest in alcohol-powered cars was unknown. Consumer acceptance of this slightly differentiated product would ultimately determine whether the demand for alcohol fuel would fall short, or perhaps exceed, the targeted supply at any given time.

In a sense, consumers were ordinary investors *par excellence*. Although middle-class support was considered essential to the authoritarian system of rule, the importance of any single consumer was infinitesimal. Moreover, since society specializes in production rather than in consumption, opportunities for collective action were limited indeed. These political and organizational factors made it much less rational for an individual consumer to participate in the alcohol program than it was for any of the other players in the game. Nonetheless, consumers presumably realized that as the privately owned fleet of alcohol-powered cars expanded, central decision makers would bear higher political costs in the event they neglected the alcohol program. The individual incentives to purchase an alcohol-powered car therefore became stronger as other consumers made their own commitments to alcohol-specific technology. Among these atomistic market agents "collective" action thus could only arise spontaneously through a sequence of individual buying decisions.

Once potential investors in new alcohol production complexes were confident that state officials would consistently support Phase Two, the pace of the alcohol expansion was determined, in large measure, by consumers' response to the marketing of alcohol-powered cars. The chain from production through consumption, however, was only as strong as its weakest link. Since the form of mutual adjustment between state officials and consumers was certainly of the noncooperative variety, consumers were least likely, other things being equal, to ignite the alcohol boom. Under a certain constellation of current and expected future policies, of course, consumer cooperation could be induced. But the participation of consumers in Phase Two added a crucial element of instability. Not only were the expectations held by these unorganized market agents likely to be extremely elastic with respect to changes in such key signals as the relative price between alcohol fuel and gasohol; the close substitutability of alcohol and gasoline cars made consumer purchase decisions highly sensitive to changing expectations. Individuals who cannot engage in deliberate collective action and who have close substitution opportunities, Albert Hirschman has written, are more likely to respond to a deterioration in circumstances by choosing "exit" rather than "voice."[11] If this is true, Phase Two of the alcohol program was inherently unstable. That this instability was exacerbated by certain factors specific to the Brazilian politico-economic system is a possibility I consider in this study.

### The Role of Political Signals

Before investigating the reasons why consumers and ranchers eventually formed favorable expectations of future policy toward the alcohol sector, let us examine more carefully the kinds of information available to both ordinary and privileged investors.

Since state officials know that investors are trying to estimate the degree and longevity of support for political products,

[11]Ibid.

these authorities engage in a variety of actions expressly designed to alter investors' expectations of future policy. Proponents of the alcohol program, for example, frequently claimed that *Proálcool* was a top national priority. To illuminate this claim, they set ambitious production targets and suggested periodically that further incentives were under consideration. Although such general declarations provide some indication of support for a political product, specific evidence of policy implementation is of greater value. Observers probably estimated the strength of support for the alcohol program by keeping close tabs on the number of projects approved, the amount of subsidized credit disbursed by the state's financial agencies, the limits on converting sugarcane into alcohol or on mixing alcohol into the fuel supply, the production quotas and producer prices of sugar and alcohol, and the relative price of gasohol and alcohol charged to consumers, as well as on a variety of less important indicators of policy implementation. Such actions speak louder than general pronouncements about the priority some state officials attach to a political product. Concrete policy measures are therefore often undertaken *primarily* to influence expectations of future policy.

To characterize this sort of interaction, in which information is provided in order to sway expectations, economists have developed the concept of signaling. Since the signals referred to here are designed to influence investors' perception of the support for political products, I will use the term *political signals* to describe any information that affects these perceptions. As we probe the role of political signals, it is important to remember why the signaling process figures so prominently in the mutual adjustment of state officials and private investors. This reliance on signaling is due to the fact that at $t_0$, investors in political products become locked into a two-period strategy while the government is free to change most incentives at $t_1$. Taking advantage of this asymmetry, state officials could conceivably misrepresent the actual degree of support for a political product in order to induce resources to shift between sectors at $t_0$. The potential for such opportunism is inherent in the structure of the mutual adjustment process studied here.[12]

Recent advances in the study of economic institutions have illuminated the issues of opportunism and signaling.[13] By and large, however, the institutional contexts in which these problems have been studied are relatively simple in comparison with that of the steered economy. The interactions modeled by economists most often involve buyers and sellers of goods or assets, each of whom is assumed to be a unitary agent with well-defined objectives.

One classic example comes from the literature on corporate finance.[14] Top corporate managers ordinarily have a great deal more information about the underlying strength of their franchises than they can make available to participants in financial markets. If these managers can benefit from higher stock prices in the short run, they might signal to investors, say by raising dividends, that the future looks bright even if it does not. Given management's incentives and the inherent information asymmetry, investors do not necessarily believe these signals.[15]

What initially deserves emphasis, however, is that management can be expected to know whether the signals they provide are true. Herein lies the difference between the nature of the signaling problem in the corporate finance and politicized market economy contexts. Since policy-making authority for the same political product is typically delegated to more than

---

[12]On opportunism, or self-interest with guile, see Oliver L. Williamson, *Markets and Hierarchies: Analysis and Antitrust Implications* (New York: Free Press, 1975).

[13]Perhaps the most widely known contribution to this literature is George A. Akerlof, "The Market for Lemons," *Quarterly Journal of Economics* (August 1970):488–500.

[14]See Stephen A. Ross, "The Determination of Financial Structure: The Incentive-Signalling Approach," *Bell Journal of Economics* (Spring 1977):23–40.

[15]When signals are not believed, inefficient signaling results. Later in the chapter I discuss the possibility of inefficient *political* signaling.

one agency, an individual state official usually does not know whether future policy—the analytic equivalent of future corporate earnings—is likely to be at variance with the political signals he provides. If an individual agency is not the autonomous policymaker for a political product, investors must use great sophistication in interpreting the signals this agency emits. Investors must ask themselves, for example, what these signals reveal about the likely outcome of the mutual adjustment process among all the agencies granted authority over the political product in question.

## *Evaluating Political Signals*

In this complex environment, the rational investor must first try to understand the objectives each of the relevant policymakers wishes to achieve. This task does not necessarily require highly cultivated political instincts. The personal goals of state officials are often generally congruent with the objectives of the agencies they lead.[16] Each agency, in turn, may pursue an unambiguous mission. The mission of the IAA, for example, has been to promote the Brazilian sugar and alcohol industry. Similarly, the primary mission of the Central Bank and the Ministry of Finance is to set and achieve macroeconomic goals, including the reduction of inflation and excessive balance of payments deficits. Apart from pursuing their substantive missions, most agencies also attempt to expand the autonomy and breadth of their respective jurisdictions.

If every relevant agency, under whatever conditions, doggedly pursued its substantive mission, the task of forecasting future policy would only require knowing the pattern of authority and the missions of the relevant agencies. But self-interest in state politics sometimes leads an agency to defer to

---

[16]There are, of course, many exceptions to this analytically useful generalization. In the United States, for example, it has recently become common for central decision makers to assign their appointees the task of reducing the role or effectiveness of the agencies they lead.

attempts by central decision makers or other agencies to control its policy actions. These attempts at mutual control, which are made through a variety of devices including authority, persuasion, and negotiation, are fundamental processes at work in shaping policy.[17] For this reason, the rational investor must understand, at least in rough outline, how control devices are used in policy-making. In particular, investors must strive to learn why attempts at mutual control are sometimes highly effective and why, at other times, agencies steadfastly pursue their substantive missions.

The variability of central decision makers' control over the policy-making process was particularly evident during the evolution of *Proálcool*. In Phase One, for example, the Brazilian Central Bank and the state-owned Banco do Brasil both openly defied President Geisel's explicit demands to speed up disbursements of subsidized credit for annexed distilleries. Moreover, Petrobrás did its best to protect the sanctity of its legal monopoly over the production of liquid fuels, which would be jeopardized by an expanding alcohol sector. This pattern of behavior contrasted starkly with that of the 1980–81 period, during which the alcohol program's earlier opponents acted as if they were its best friends. Petrobrás, for example, contributed to the appearance of support by restraining its previously intense criticism of the program and by importing heavier crude oil to accommodate the rise in alcohol consumption.[18] Furthermore, the Central Bank and the Banco do Brasil, after spending years holding off the approval of credits for annexed distilleries, suddenly began to disburse nearly all the funds requested by interested investors in both autonomous and annexed distilleries. Finally, the National Petroleum Council stepped in to assure that the alcohol marketing chain would link production to consumption. Since the substantive missions of these agencies did not change over so short a

---

[17]Charles E. Lindblom, *The Policy-Making Process*, 2d ed. (Englewood Cliffs, N.J.: Prentice-Hall, 1980), pp. 43–55.

[18]See Chapter 2.

period, we may presume that central decision makers, during 1980, became much more effective in their attempts to control the policy actions of *Proálcool*'s opponents.

What the variability of central control over policy-making indicates, more generally, is that expectations of future policy do not depend solely on the degree to which investors and central decision makers are mutually dependent, the principal factor highlighted above. For example, investors who attempt to assess the likelihood of a policy reversal must determine whether the attractiveness of current policy is due to effective central control of the state apparatus. If some of the agencies granted authority over the political product have indeed deferred to central decision makers, rational investors must attempt to identify the conditions under which these agencies are likely to wrestle free of central control.[19] The task of forecasting future policy therefore requires investors to pay attention not only to political signals; they must also develop a clear conception of the various linkages in the system of mutual controls, including those guiding the mutual adjustment process among state officials. The information value of political signals, in effect, is greatly enhanced when investors interpret them in light of such a conception of the policy-making process.

As outside observers of episodes such as the alcohol booms, we must first identify the specific political signals that were generally available at the time. We can then infer the expectations investors held by filtering these signals through what we suspect was the model of the policy-making process investors used. The first of these steps is empirically easier to take than the second. To take the second step, I draw on an idea that has recently achieved widespread respect in theoretical econom-

---

[19]Or in the case where central decision makers are opposed to favorable policies toward a sector in which a cooperative relationship between producers and their regulatory agency has been established, we can ask under what conditions this agency will have to defer to top authorities. The two cases are analytically identical.

ics.[20] It is now common for an economist to assume that when market agents forecast such variables as inflation, they do so in a manner consistent with the structure of the economy as modeled by the economic theorist. Given an assumed series of values for monetary and fiscal policy, for instance, public expectations of inflation are inferred by solving the model of the economy for the future price level. These inferred expectations are then used to analyze the theoretical response of the economy (income, employment, price level, and the like) to macroeconomic policy actions.[21]

In a similar though less formal way, I will set out a simple model of the policy-making process in the next section. To infer investors' expectations, I will assume that these agents filter political signals through a model of this form. I invoke this extremely weak version of the rational expectations hypothesis in analyzing the politicized market economy not only because this assumption firmly grounds the model in current theories of microeconomic optimization. More important, interviews with a wide range of private investors in Brazil convinced me that these economic agents have become keen analysts of the policy-making process.[22]

For certain purposes, the purely theoretical aspects of this approach are useful in themselves. As an example, I will use this model and the assumption about how expectations are formed in order to identify some important factors that can reduce central control over sector-specific polices and private investment flows. But this approach especially comes to life in

[20]The seminal article is J. Muth, "Rational Expectations and the Theory of Price Movements," *Econometrica* (July 1961):315–35.

[21]For a classic article in this tradition, see Robert E. Lucas, "Econometric Policy Evaluation: A Critique," in Lucas, *Studies in Business-Cycle Theory* (Cambridge, Mass.: M.I.T. Press, 1981), pp. 104–30.

[22]The model of the policy-making process used by a given investor could be more or less sophisticated than the one I will present. Whether ordinary consumers have developed such an understanding is more debatable than, say, is the case of Volkswagen do Brasil. Nonetheless, we should not underestimate consumers' motivation or understanding of the main outlines of their politico-economic system, at least in the Brazilian context.

Part II, where I provide a close empirical analysis of the development of *Proálcool*. Basing my study almost entirely on published material, such as newspaper reports, I will suggest how commonly available political signals changed during the 1975–84 period of the alcohol program. In this way, I attempt to explain why, for example, in 1980–81 many investors expected the government to continue to provide favorable incentives for alcohol production and consumption, triggering the first alcohol boom.

## Mutual Adjustment Among State Officials

### Preliminary Remarks

In analyzing the policy-making process, it is important to probe the basic structure of the political system within which proximate decision makers adjust to each other. In *The Policy-Making Process*, for example, Charles Lindblom discusses how the multifaceted "privileged position of business" constrains what government officials can seek and achieve.[23] As another important example, Peter Katzenstein compares advanced industrial systems by identifying the dominant political coalition in each country as well as the degree of centralization of power within the state and within society.[24] In some contexts and for some analytic purposes, these and other political factors can be usefully abstracted from a variety of less important ones. In analyzing the basic political structure of the Brazilian steered economy during the 1975–84 period, I instead focus on the intense contradictions between the military regime's objectives and on the segmentation of the state apparatus. Before I examine the logical implications of these parameters, let us develop a better understanding of why they were chosen.

[23]Lindblom, *The Policy-Making Process*, pp. 71–82.
[24]Peter J. Katzenstein, ed., *Between Power and Plenty: Foreign Economic Policies of Advanced Industrial States* (Madison: University of Wisconsin Press, 1978).

*Contradictions of Rule.* After taking power in 1964, Brazil's central decision makers championed a certain vision of the politico-economic order to build support for military rule. Aside from an order free of "politics," the military promised the restoration of economic growth, partly through the promotion of an economy capable of producing in large scale its own capital and durable goods. What has greatly impressed many observers about the implementation of this macropolitical strategy is the extent to which the government itself was the engine of growth.[25] In addition to steering the private economy to a greater extent through both macroeconomic and sector-specific policy intervention, the state greatly increased its role as entrepreneur. In some sectors, such as electricity generation and petroleum refining, state enterprises grew and operated independently of private capital. In a wide array of other sectors, usually the most technologically modern and complex, state enterprises often formed joint ventures with multinational corporations and, sometimes, with elite segments of the locally owned private sector. For the most part, the only sectors that state enterprises could not penetrate, for political reasons, were traditional strongholds such as textiles.

In his highly regarded and impressive book, *Dependent Development: The Alliance of Multinational, State, and Local Capital in Brazil*, Peter Evans argues that, over the years, the exclusion of all but the elite segments of the national bourgeoisie from the most modern and potentially high-profit zones of the economy tended to undermine the "Triple Alliance."[26] By undermine, Evans appears to mean that these tendencies weakened the relative economic position of local private capital at the same time that the political support of this group

[25]See, for example, Baer, *The Brazilian Economy*, pp. 135–60; Peter Evans, *Dependent Development: The Alliance of Multinational, State, and Local Capital in Brazil* (Princeton: Princeton University Press, 1979); and Evans, "Reinventing the Bourgeoisie: State Entrepreneurship and Class Formation in Dependent Capitalist Development," in *Marxist Inquiries*, ed. M. Burawoy and T. Skocpol (Chicago: University of Chicago Press, 1982).

[26]Evans, *Dependent Development*, pp. 274–97; and Evans, "State Entrepreneurship."

remained essential for the authority of military rule. The first visible evidence of this contradiction in the Brazilian model was the so-called antistatization movement launched in the mid-1970s by a loosely organized group of local capitalists against, in essence, public enterprise property rights. Importantly, as we will see, the alcohol program became a test case of the statization issue, especially in 1975 and 1979.

The identification of this contradiction between the social bases of authoritarian rule and the political consequences of heavy reliance on state and multinational firms in the Brazilian industrialization process provides us with a key thread to interpret the policy and investment outcomes of the alcohol case. At least two other contradictions of the Brazilian model also became more intense over the period studied here, and their identification similarly enables us to make sense of the alcohol experience.

For instance, the extent to which credit subsidies were used to bolster segments of local private capital grew precipitously over this period. This development encouraged the World Bank, in a confidential report, to characterize the Brazilian system as a "transfer economy" in which the bulk of the transfers from the public to the private sectors are received by businesses rather than by individuals. In a similar vein, Albert O. Hirschman refers to the extraordinary use of subsidized credit as a mechanism to transfer income between sectors and groups and, hence, as the functional equivalent of the infamous arrangement of trade and exchange rate policies that helped finance Brazil's earlier industrialization.[27]

After the mid-1970s, these subsidized loans and certain other incentives were increasingly financed by monetary creation rather than by taxes. The progressive escalation of inflation in the late 1970s and early 1980s was caused, in part, by this policy. Having been identified as the culprit for the infla-

---

[27]Albert O. Hirschman, "The Social and Political Matrix of Inflation: Elaborations on the Latin American Experience," in Hirschman, *Essays in Trespassing: Economics to Politics and Beyond* (Cambridge: Cambridge University Press, 1981), pp. 188–92.

tionary spiral, the use of this mechanism for subsidizing segments of the private sector has been greatly restricted (more recently at the behest of the International Monetary Fund). To the extent that this device had been important to the maintenance of bourgeois support for the military regime and to the extent that the provision of subsidized credit fueled inflation, the Brazilian "model" during this period tended to undermine itself seriously in this respect as well.

A third basic contradiction was perhaps more long-standing. Since the Great Depression, political authorities and intellectuals have elaborated an ideology of economic policy-making sometimes termed *developmental nationalism*.[28] This ideological development gradually became institutionalized in the 1940s and 1950s, during which time economic growth was primarily driven by import-substituting industrialization.[29] With the coup d'état of 1964, developmental nationalism received a new impetus. As part of the justification for extended military rule, Brazilian ideologists such as General Golbery explicitly linked developmental nationalism with the military's own national security doctrine.[30] While continuing to employ the rhetoric of developmental nationalism, however, economic policy under the military regime encouraged the further integration of Brazil into international goods and financial markets.[31] This strategy contributed importantly to

[28]See Wirth, *Brazilian Development*; Peter Flynn, *Brazil: A Political Analysis* (Boulder, Colo.: Westview Press, 1978), pp. 94–189; and Albert O. Hirschman, "Ideologies of Economic Development in Latin America," in Hirschman, *A Bias for Hope: Essays on Development and Latin America* (New Haven: Yale University Press, 1971), pp. 270–311.

[29]On import substitution, see Albert Fishlow, "Origins and Consequences of Import Substitution in Brazil," *International Economics and Development: Essays in Honor of Raul Prebisch*, ed. L. E. DiMarco (New York: Academic Press, 1972), pp. 316–419.

[30]Alfred Stepan, "The New Professionalism of Internal Warfare and Military Role Expansion," in *Authoritarian Brazil*, ed. A. Stepan (New Haven: Yale University Press, 1973), pp. 47–65.

[31]Fishlow, "Post-1964 Brazilian Economic Policy," pp. 94–113; Baer, *The Brazilian Economy*, pp. 117–32.

rapid economic growth during the miracle period and cushioned the effects of the two oil shocks.

Yet this departure from developmental nationalism was never provided with an explicit ideological justification. When Brazil was under great pressure to adjust to higher world interest rates and oil prices in the early 1980s, it was therefore particularly awkward for policymakers to respond to this "external threat" by encouraging, as they did, further integration into the world economy. Few measures could be taken for nationalistic reasons that would also, for example, facilitate Brazil's continued access to world credit markets. One such measure, to anticipate Part II, was the National Alcohol Program.

*Segmentation.* By segmentation, I refer to a systematic tendency to diffuse policy-making authority over the same political product to numerous collegial state agencies. My focus on this parameter was triggered by two important theoretical trends, one in the United States and the other in Brazil. Peter Katzenstein's *Between Power and Plenty* is a classic example of the first trend. The principal task of this volume is to explain why foreign economic policies are so different in "statist" countries, such as France and Japan, than in the United States and Britain. Among the variables Katzenstein uses to describe the variation in political structures among these countries is the centralization of power within the state. One major theme of this work is that the centralization of policy-making authority in such agencies as Japan's MITI or France's Commissariat du Plan greatly enhances the coherence of sector-specific policies in those countries.[32]

Responding to a different *problématique*, political scientists in Brazil, during the late 1970s, began to expose some of the myths about state-led industrialization under authoritarian rule. Sergio Abranches, for example, argues that political conflict did not disappear in 1964—contrary to the military's

---

[32]Katzenstein, *Between Power and Plenty*, pp. 295–336.

promise to eliminate politics from government—but was instead refracted into the sphere of sector-specific policy-making.[33] Under close examination, this policy-making process barely resembled the technocratic image of efficiency cultivated by the military regime. Based on a threefold case study of industrial policy-making during the authoritarian period, Abranches concluded:

> Obstacles to the formulation of coherent, comprehensive and articulated policies come out of both the fragmentation of interests and the segmentation of the state apparatus. Comprehensive plans have almost no other function than providing the ideological grounds for negotiation and for the legitimation of governmental actions. Most policies are effectively made by sectoral agencies, state banks and [state] enterprises.[34]

The tendency to diffuse policy-making authority in Brazil was similarly evident in the alcohol case. Faced with competing claims for control over the program, central decision makers granted some regulatory authority to almost every agency with an interest in the production, marketing, or consumption of alcohol fuel. For example, a National Alcohol Council was established to determine project selection criteria and to approve individual plans to construct distilleries. This council could count among its members seven independent agencies, including the Ministries of Industry and Commerce, Finance, Energy, Agriculture, and Planning. The recently established ministerial-level Council for Economic Development reserved the right to set production targets and producer prices for alcohol. As for the policies affecting consumer prices and changes in gasoline production, these were left in the hands of the National Petroleum Council and Petrobrás. How much credit would be made available to the alcohol program, and

[33]Sergio H. Hudson de Abranches, *The Divided Leviathan: State and Economic Policy Formation in Authoritarian Brazil* (Ann Arbor: University Microfilms, 1978).

[34]Ibid., p. 440.

on what terms, was officially decided by the National Monetary Council, comprising representatives of the monetary and fiscal authorities.

The authority to implement the program was also widely dispersed. An interested investor in a distillery, for instance, would have to submit a detailed technical proposal which would be evaluated by the IAA. If the proposal was approved, any member of the National Alcohol Council could effectively veto it later. Once these hurdles were jumped, a financial proposal had to be submitted to the Banco do Brasil in order to receive cheap investment credits. But even if this state commercial bank approved a credit line, the Central Bank could reject a proposed financial contract. This kind of extensive segmentation, I submit, intensified conflict over the alcohol program and greatly magnified uncertainty over future policy.

### The Analytic Framework

Since all the proximate decision makers for the alcohol program were nominally members of the executive branch, we can rely extensively on organization theory to clarify the key variables that drive the mutual adjustment process between these officials. This analysis, however, need not involve an inquiry into "bureaucratic politics."[35] As I indicated above, the sector-specific policy-making process is one of the key terrains on which macropolitical strategies are played out in Brazil. Since the role of political structures, such as contradictions between regime objectives, is not emphasized in most treatments of bureaucratic politics, I would prefer to characterize the following as a model of state politics and policy-making.

*Organization Theory and Extensions.* The set of concepts I draw most heavily upon are associated with the names of Herbert

[35]In fact, my model abstracts from bureaucratic politics, as it is specifically defined in Graham Allison, "Conceptual Models and the Cuban Missile Crisis," *American Political Science Review* (September 1969):689–718.

Simon, James March, and Richard Cyert.[36] This approach, which has been dubbed the "neo-Weberian synthesis,"[37] is especially useful here because it addresses the way in which complexity and ambiguity can create opportunities for lower-echelon officials to dominate certain outcomes within a formally hierarchical context. Conversely, these concepts help explain why under certain conditions the "staff" decides to follow the "ruler" or "entrepreneur."

I extend this neo-Weberian synthesis into the realm of state politics by, for example, emphasizing how intense contradictions between the nonoperational objectives of top authorities can impair, for better or for worse, effective central control of policy-making. Another proposed extension is to identify the specific factors that enhance conflict or contribute to its resolution. I also make this approach somewhat more dynamic by emphasizing the strains that new commodities place on the inherited pattern of authority. Intense competition over the authority to regulate and produce new political products can not only impede decision making but may lead top authorities to diffuse policy-making authority to many collegial agencies. As a consequence, conflict over actual policy-making may be exacerbated down the road.[38] With the introduction of these simple extensions of the neo-Weberian synthesis, we can analyze the logical interconnections between policy outcomes and a few key macropolitical and commodity-specific parameters.

[36]Herbert A. Simon, *Administrative Behavior*, 3d ed. (New York: Free Press, 1976), especially chaps. 1 and 4; Simon, "The Architecture of Complexity," in Simon, *Sciences of the Artificial*, 2d ed. (Cambridge, Mass.: M.I.T. Press, 1981), pp. 193–229; and Richard M. Cyert and James G. March, *A Behavioral Theory of the Firm* (Englewood Cliffs, N.J.: Prentice-Hall, 1963).

[37]Charles Perrow, *Complex Organizations: A Critical Essay*, 2d ed. (Glenview, Ill.: Scott, Foresman, 1979), pp. 139–73.

[38]Throughout this chapter, I follow Weber in limiting the use of the term *conflict* to situations in which agencies disagree on the formulation and implementation of policies. I restrict the term *competition* to situations in which agencies attempt to enlarge their jurisdictions. See Max Weber, *Economy and Society*, ed. G. Roth and C. Wittich (Berkeley: University of California Press, 1978), p. 38.

*The Dependent Variable.* The outcome of the policy-making process is the equilibrium policy set. By policy set, I mean the set of policy actions selected by central decision makers, state bureaucracies, or state-owned corporations. By equilibrium, I mean that these policy actions are adjusted to each other in such a way that there is no tendency *internal* to the relationship between policymakers that would lead to the selection of different policies. This equilibrium could be disturbed, however, by a shift in the value of any variable exogenous to the system.[39]

Policy actions are decisions made by state officials that directly or indirectly affect the value of an investment in a political product. For example, the implementation of a new subsidy or tax on a specific commodity is a policy action. Or an increase in the interest rate charged on loans for working capital. Or the public announcement and justification of a production target by top authorities. Another example of a policy action is the elaboration of a plan to coordinate the actions of a group of independent agencies, each charged with the authority to regulate one or another aspect of the production, marketing, or consumption of the same political product.

### Central Decision Makers and the Task Environment

As we have already seen, the policy-making process is guided, in part, by central decision makers' sector-specific policy objectives. These specific objectives often derive from top authorities' macropolitical goals, such as maintaining authority or the achievement of a certain politico-economic order. President Geisel's interest in the alcohol program, for example, was whetted by the opportunity to safeguard the position

---

[39]For a useful discussion of what the equilibrium method of analysis does and does not mean, see Fritz Machlup, "Equilibrium and Disequilibrium: Misplaced Concreteness and Disguised Politics," in Machlup, *International Payments, Debts, and Gold* (New York: Scribner's, 1964).

of the São Paulo *usineiros*, who represented this order in the agricultural sector.

Whether favorable policy toward a sector enhances central decision makers' macropolitical goals depends on a variety of factors, including what Herbert Simon would term their "task environment."[40] Among the variables that affect these goals are, for example, international economic trends, investor confidence, geopolitical events, public opinion, and specific demands made by key supporters of top authorities.

The precise ways in which central decision makers adapt to their task environment depend on the macropolitical goals they pursue. These goals are said to rest at the apex of the state's hierarchy of goals. By *hierarchy of goals* is meant the system of ends-means linkages among goals or policies in which "each level is to be considered as an end relative to the levels below it and as a means relative to the levels above it."[41]

If the highest-order goal of a regime is to maintain its authority, objectives such as promoting national security or fostering local capital accumulation are second-order regime goals. These second-order goals are among the most general *means* by which top authorities often attempt to enhance their rule. Third-order objectives, then, are the most general means to achieve the second-order goals of the regime; they might include, for example, maintaining a standing army and promoting exports. These high-order goals can be said to "map" the task environment into the specific policy objectives of central decision makers.

Since it is difficult to measure the attainment of such goals or, similarly, the effects of concrete actions upon them, macropolitical objectives are not operational.[42] Thus, none of these general goals implies any set of specific policy actions

---

[40]Simon, *Sciences of the Artificial*, pp. 6, 98.
[41]Simon, *Administrative Behavior*, p. 63.
[42]Ibid., p. xxxiv.

without making additional judgments about how they will contribute to one or another of the macropolitical goals.

Macropolitical objectives are also alike in that they are slow to change. Central decision makers, for example, rarely abandon the goals of strengthening national security or promoting growth. Since a regime's goals change only slowly in stable political systems, they may be treated as *parameters* of a short-run model of the policy-making process.

### Central Decision Makers and the State Apparatus

If central decision makers formulated the details and actually implemented sector-specific policies, predicting the policy set would be nearly as simple as examining how these authorities adapt to their task environment. But in all states, weak or strong, central decision makers delegate most of the authority for choosing actions to various state agencies. Granted such authority, we have seen, bureaucracies and state corporations sometimes defy the wishes of their superiors. Let us now begin to account for this pattern of behavior.

Although central decision makers, in theory, can easily revoke a grant of policy-making authority, this form of punishment is rarely practiced. After an agency has used its authority to take a set of policy actions over a period of time, this routinized pattern of behavior develops its own legitimacy.[43] The value attached to the existing network of authority relations is further enhanced by the fact that grants of policy-making authority, when initially made, derive their legitimacy from the specific macropolitical objectives that the agency is assigned to promote. Consequently, challenges to the long-exercised, specific authority of a bureaucracy or state corporation would rub against not only the value of stability in

---

[43]A well-known proposition in organization theory is that "a relatively stable structure of assignments and authority comes to be valued within a bureaucracy." See Charles E. Lindblom, *Politics and Markets: The World's Political-Economic Systems* (New York: Basic Books, 1977), p. 28.

assignments but, in some measure, the authority of the state as well.

Once authority is granted to an agency, central decision makers usually must rely heavily on persuasion or various forms of tacit negotiation in order to control sector-specific policy.[44] But when authority has been clearly defined and exercised for decades, why might persuasion be effective? One reason is that the facts and analysis mobilized by top authorities might convince an agency that certain policy actions would enhance the regime's macropolitical objectives and the agency, therefore, should act accordingly. If these efforts fail on a crucial issue, central decision makers could conceivably threaten to withdraw an established grant of authority.[45] Overt threats to withdraw authority, however, are usually not necessary to mold the volitions of ministers and executives of state corporations. These political officials are notably careful to adjust their actions to the possibility that their agencies' existing prerogatives might be challenged. Moreover, since today's pattern of authority may not correspond to the problems faced by the state tomorrow, an agency always has an incentive to act in a way that promises to extend its authority to new policy actions.

With this institutional analysis in mind, let us begin to develop a number of hypotheses designed to explain the variability of central control over the policy-making process:

1. State agencies will bend their policy actions in response to attempts by central decision makers to control them if

[44]On persuasion as a mechanism of social control, see Lindblom, *Politics and Markets*, pp. 52–62.

[45]In some countries, the legislature can also withdraw the authority previously granted to a government agency. In July 1982, for example, legislation was introduced into the U.S. Congress that, if passed and signed into law, would have restricted the Federal Reserve Board's authority to conduct monetary policy. Soon thereafter, the Fed expanded bank credit substantially and short-term interest rates fell by more than seven percentage points.

their long-run objectives will be compromised by failing to defer to top authorities.

2. Since these long-run objectives include attaining or at least maintaining the widest possible autonomous jurisdictions, agencies will most likely defer to central decision makers when their authority is threatened or when the ability to extend their authority to new policy actions will be reduced by failing to do so.

3. An agency's authority is most likely to be challenged or ultimately attenuated if it takes policy actions that are perceived to be illegitimate in the context of state politics.

4. Policy actions are illegitimate in the context of state politics when they are highly inconsistent with the macropolitical goals of the regime.[46]

Since the connection between a specific policy action and the nonoperational goals of the regime is fraught with ambiguities, the legitimacy of a policy action is always subject to dispute. Consequently:

5. State agencies are more likely to bend their policy actions in response to attempts by central decision makers to control them *to the degree* that the perceived ambiguity between specific policy actions and the goal of maintaining the regime's authority is reduced.

Hypothesis 5 is in many respects simply a restatement of the familiar hypothesis that "goal ambiguity" reduces central control over an organization. In analyzing state politics, however, more can be said. Let us consider several implications of the observation that in some states there are clear and persistent contradictions among macropolitical objectives:

---

[46]This hypothesis is related to the proposition that officials will not oppose a specific policy action if it clearly favors the achievement of the general, nonoperational goals of the organization to which they belong. See Weber, *Economy and Society*, pp. 48–56.

6. A policy action is legitimate so long as a persuasive argument can be made that the action is a means to achieve *at least one* of the macropolitical objectives of the regime.

7. If there are intense contradictions among the regime's goals, any given set of policy actions favored by central decision makers is unlikely to be consistent with *all* the goals of the regime.

8. State agencies can often justify their own preferred policy actions by appealing to one or more goals of the regime that would be hindered if they deferred to central decision makers' *specific* policy objectives. It follows that central control over policy-making tends to be impaired when top authorities pursue intensely contradictory macro-political objectives.

This line of reasoning does not imply that central decision makers in a country with intensely contradictory regime goals are always less able to bend the policy actions of state agencies than are their counterparts in a country where those contradictions are less intense. Many situational factors could militate against this tendency. For example, the task environment could be so threatening that the intensity of contradictions among the regime's goals is greatly softened, as in wartime. Or in safer times, an activity might be so located in the political economy that its promotion is consistent with several generally contradictory goals of the regime. As we will see, alcohol fuel was so located in the Brazilian political economy in 1980–81 and 1983–84.

*Competition: The Struggle over Authority*

Let us now investigate further difficulties that central decision makers face in a dynamic steered economy. As society's assortment of commodities evolves, as it does with techno-logical innovations, current patterns of policy-making author-ity may fail to correspond precisely to the new structure of economic activity. Seizing the opportunity to extend or defend its range of control, a state agency will often argue that the principle upon which its authority rests implies that the agency should be granted control over the new activity as well. Since most new commodities share attributes of more than one old commodity, however, the legitimacy of such a claim is rarely self-evident. Competing jurisdictional principles, consequently, are often at issue. This is one reason why central decision makers are faced with a serious dilemma when state agencies compete for exclusive authority over new commodities.[47]

To describe more carefully the objects of this struggle, we should distinguish between what I call *productive* and *regulatory* control. Productive control refers to entitlements conferred upon either public or private enterprise, or both, to produce a certain kind of commodity. Regulatory control refers to the authority to regulate a specific political product. This distinction is often blurred in practice, for when a state enterprise is granted *exclusive* productive control over a commodity, a good deal of regulatory control is often implied. Nonetheless the distinction must be maintained: The struggle over productive control may reflect a deeper conflict between public and private enterprise property rights, whereas the struggle over regulatory control is less likely to be linked with a contest over fundamental institutions.

The competition over productive control is particularly difficult to resolve because, on the one hand, central decision makers usually value state enterprises, especially when these institutions develop impressive financial and technical capabilities. On the other hand, there are usually political limits to

---

[47]In dynamic economies, new commodities arise all the time. For a classic discussion, see Joseph A. Schumpeter, *Capitalism, Socialism, and Democracy* (New York: Harper & Row, 1950), pp. 59–86. Any systematic treatment of the evolution of private law is chock-full of evidence for the proposition that new commodities, because they grow out of existing patterns of economic activity, create conflicts between regulatory principles or entitlements. For a fascinating example, see Morton J. Horwitz, *The Transformation of American Law, 1780–1860* (Cambridge, Mass.: Harvard University Press, 1977).

the range of important sectors in which state enterprises can be allowed to compete with local capitalists. If these limits are persistently ignored, top authorities could find that the only social base for their rule is the state bourgeoisie.[48]

Since both private and state enterprises can bring substantial resources to the struggle for productive control, this competition can become extremely intense. Occasionally a struggle, such as that over the alcohol sector in Brazil, may take on symbolic importance. Underlying the symbolic issues are, nonetheless, real concerns. Each time competition over productive control is resolved, new precedents are created. These precedents are vital political resources for the next struggle.

While the struggle over *regulatory* control is usually less dramatic, this kind of competition is also shaped by the ability of some agencies, such as ministries of industry or agriculture, to rally the support of societal allies. Other bureaucracies, such as the state-owned banks, can draw upon acknowledged administrative capabilities in attempting to expand their regulatory jurisdictions.

When several agencies bring principled arguments to bear in the competition for authority, the strategy of granting each of them some jurisdiction over the same new commodity is normally the path of least resistance. By enabling central decision makers to avoid choosing between legitimate but contradictory claims, this approach deflects the difficulties underlying the struggle for authority away from the center of political power. However, these difficulties usually resurface as conflicts over substantive policy.

*Segmentation.* By coping with fundamental conflicts in this way, central decision makers unavoidably contribute to the diffusion of state authority. But the diffusion of authority over a commodity or "issue area" is also enhanced by other

[48]Evans, *Dependent Development*, pp. 274–97; and Evans, "State Entrepreneurship."

factors.[49] The extreme diffusion of authority over *Proálcool*, for example, was exacerbated by the sheer variety of tasks to be performed, most notably in Phase Two. Thus, the complexity of an issue area should be held constant in defining the concept of segmentation. We arrive, therefore, at the following definition: An issue area rises in *complexity* as the number of interrelated policy actions grows.

Both technological and market linkages raise the complexity of an issue area. Technological linkages may be thought of in terms of input-output relationships. Policy actions regulating alcohol production and consumption, for example, were linked to those affecting all other liquid fuels because of the joint production of petroleum derivatives. Market linkages, in contrast, arise from the behavioral dimension of economic choice. The ability of consumers to choose between alcohol and gasoline engines during Phase Two, for instance, con-strained the prices of gasohol and gasoline the National Petroleum Council could set.

With this issue-area characteristic in mind, let us define segmentation:[50] When the number of independent agencies granted some authority over equally complex issue areas is systematically larger in one state than in another, the former is said to be more *segmented*.[51]

It seems likely that segmentation does not significantly enhance the dispersion of authority if the issue area is simple. Even in Brazil, authority over simple issue areas is often conferred upon a single agency. In the early 1930s, for

[49]An *issue area* is a set of interrelated policy actions. Two policy actions are interrelated if both affect the cash flows generated by investments in the production, marketing, or consumption of the same commodity.

[50]*Complexity* is one of three issue-area characteristics I identify here. *Age* is another characteristic, since this dimension influences the level of competi-tion over policy-making authority. The third characteristic, *size*, is discussed in the next section.

[51]One agency is independent of another if the relationship between them is collegial (Weber, *Economy and Society*, pp. 271–82). Collegiality may be difficult to determine empirically in some cases.

example, central decision makers created two separate agencies to focus policy-making authority for the coffee and sugar sectors, respectively. Moreover, the particular institutional form chosen—the autarky—provided these agencies with the autonomous resource bases they needed to steer clear of the constraints that fiscal authorities otherwise could have imposed.

If this line of argument is correct, it is useful to conceive of the relationship between segmentation and complexity as multiplicative:

$$\text{Dispersion of authority over old issue areas} = \text{Segmentation} \times \text{Complexity}$$

Since the struggle for new authority is rooted in the current pattern of authority and economic activity, we can predict the number of agencies that are able to compete over a new issue area in a similar fashion:

$$\text{Number of agencies in competition} = \text{Segmentation} \times \text{Complexity}$$

*Some consequences.* One reason why competition is problematic is that in every organization, uncertainty over the future pattern of authority impedes substantive policy-making. Moreover, when the struggle over authority is resolved by dispersing authority, the policy-making process is more likely to be beset by intense conflict over substantive policy.

To anticipate a later discussion, we might also consider how competition adds to uncertainty over future policy. When competition is intense, investors have to anticipate the eventual pattern of authority, in addition to the policy actions each agency is likely to take once granted clear authority. This possibility might be of minor importance if the struggle over authority quickly dissipates. There are, however, many obstacles to the quick resolution of competition. For example, the strategy of dispersing authority may disappoint all of the competing agencies, together with their societal allies. The fact that any kind of decisive allocation of authority is somewhat costly may lead central decision makers to delay the resolution of competition as long as possible. Since the existing pattern of authority in some cases can temporarily accommodate policy-making for new commodities, competition might be allowed to persist for extended periods. We will see, for example, that the competition for both regulatory and productive control of the alcohol sector was not fundamentally resolved until nearly four years after the inception of the program—that is, six months before the alcohol boom.

### *Conflict: The Struggle over Policy*

Although the struggle over authority is ubiquitous in the policy-making process,[52] for analytic purposes we can now abstract from competition and focus on the formulation and implementation of substantive policies. In this section, I will further abstract from the specific process in which central decision makers and state agencies draw upon devices, such as persuasion and tacit negotiation, to control each other's policy actions. Instead, I will identify a few key variables whose values raise or lower the probability that the equilibrium policy set will be "consistently favorable" for a given political product.[53]

My argument begins with a tautology: A political product that generates high levels of conflict among state officials will not benefit from a consistently favorable policy set unless the conflict is substantially resolved. With this tautology in mind, we can separate the struggle over policy into the twin processes of conflict generation and conflict resolution.[54] This step is

[52]For a lucid conceptual discussion of the struggle for authority, see Lindblom, *Politics and Markets*, pp. 17–32, 119–30.

[53]A consistently favorable policy set obtains when *all* agencies granted authority over a political product take policy actions designed to draw resources into that activity.

[54]In *A Behavioral Theory of the Firm*, Cyert and March identify a process they label "the quasi-resolution of conflict." However, they do not explicitly direct the reader's attention to sources of variability in the level of conflict.

absolutely critical in the present context because potential investors in a political product can be more confident about the future if the attractiveness of current policies does not rest on potentially precarious central control.

To make use of the separation of the conflict-generation and conflict-resolution processes, we should carefully define some terms. A *conflict* is said to arise when the unconstrained volitions (or interests) of two or more state agencies, each with some authority over the issue area, are mutually incompatible with respect to a given policy action. An agency's volitions are said to be *unconstrained* when they depend solely on its substantive bureaucratic, political, or entrepreneurial mission. By definition, *unconstrained volitions* are formed independently of central decision makers' specific policy objectives. A conflict is said to be *resolved* when volitions are so constrained that they are no longer mutually inconsistent.

*The Effects of Diffuse Authority.* We may expect that conflict, so defined, increases as more agencies are granted some policy-making authority over the same political product. For the simple reason that no two agencies are likely to have identical missions, some incompatibility between the institutional interests of each agency is likely to arise. The Brazilian Ministry of Industry and Commerce, for example, had a strong political interest in speeding up the alcohol program, whereas the Banco do Brasil had many bureaucratic and financial incentives to slow down the disbursement of subsidized credit for the program until 1980. Many other examples from the first four years of the alcohol program would further illustrate the direct relationship between interagency conflict and the diffusion of policy-making authority.

This somewhat mechanical proposition also conforms to political intuition. An agency presumably would be created only if existing agencies at the time could not serve the distinct purpose that central decision makers then believed should be served. Moreover, these separate identities tend to be maintained, since each agency, once created, becomes an institutionalized vision of at least one role the state should play in society. To oversimplify, the Ministry of Industry and Commerce, for example, has come to promote the interests and ideology of private capitalism. Petrobrás similarly represents the interests and ideology of state capitalism. Or, for another example, the Ministry of Planning personifies, so to speak, the state's responsibility to plan Brazil's economic affairs synoptically. Because these institutions represent different normative visions of the state, we should expect conflict to arise between agencies which are jointly assigned authority over the same political product.

A related, though slightly different, reason why the diffusion of responsibility breeds conflict follows from the peculiar nature of the authority relation—specifically that the repeated exercise of authority often helps to maintain it.[55] Deliberate efforts by an agency to maintain its authority can create conflict even when no substantive reason is presented. The IAA, for example, frequently rejected proposals to install annexed distilleries, despite its mission to promote the sugar and alcohol industry, precisely to indicate the importance of its authority to make technical evaluations of such projects![56]

*Segmentation and Complexity.* As we have seen, the diffusion of policy-making authority is greatly enhanced when the issue area is complex and when central decision makers resolve the struggle for authority by creating overlapping jurisdictions. Hence, we may expect conflict to be greatest over complex issue areas in highly segmented states and expect conflict to be lowest for simple issue areas in less segmented states.

Aside from the sheer number of interrelated policy actions to be taken in complex issue areas, we should also pay attention to how tightly these decisions are coupled. To illustrate the concept, during Phase One the set of policies affecting the

---

[55]Lindblom, *Politics and Markets*, p. 19.

[56]This point was made to me by a number of observers of the alcohol program.

supply of alcohol could be chosen relatively independently of the refining policies of Petrobrás.[57] But once Phase Two was under way, these and other policy actions became tightly coupled. For example, the policies designed to attract investments in new alcohol production complexes were sensitive to investor interest. Potential investors in alcohol production, in turn, monitored consumer demand for alcohol-powered cars. Consumers paid attention to the relative price of alcohol and gasohol. The National Petroleum Council (CNP) set this relative price to balance the supply and demand for alcohol and gasoline. But in 1981 an excess supply of gasoline appeared, in part, because of Petrobrás's refining structures and practices. This accumulation of gasoline stocks led the CNP to change the relative price of gasohol and gasoline, which significantly (though temporarily) reduced consumer interest in alcohol-powered cars. Investor interest in alcohol production subsequently subsided as well. Conflict was thus extremely high during Phase Two not only because there were more links between, for example, alcohol supply policies and Petrobrás's refining policies; conflict was also enhanced because the tight coupling of policy actions made each agency deeply concerned about even small changes in each other's policy decisions.

*Size.* Complexity is an issue-area characteristic that reflects the direct links between policy actions, whether created by technological or behavioral relationships. Let us now turn to the indirect connections *between* issue areas.[58] All issue areas are related in an aggregate way, since the state's ability to finance or subsidize private investments is inherently limited. Whether this aggregate relationship matters depends on the size of the

[57]Because of the initial flexibility in Petrobrás's refineries and the overwhelming incentives for the *usineiros* to invest in annexed distilleries. See Chapters 2 and 3.

[58]See the theory of nearly decomposable systems in Simon, "The Architecture of Complexity."

issue area: An issue area becomes *larger* as the level of public resources it absorbs (or would absorb if policy became more favorable) rises relative to the availability of those resources.

The role of size, so defined, in generating conflict is well known not only in social science but in the real world. Cyert and March, for example, call attention to what amounts to the inverse of size when they discuss "organization slack."[59] According to their model, in which organizations attack problems sequentially, slack reduces conflict by making it more difficult to see precisely how much one goal can be achieved only at the expense of another. Albert O. Hirschman, another long-time student of slack, has specifically called attention to this phenomenon in describing typical reactions of state agencies when major projects are sponsored by other agencies:

> A government that decides to undertake a major effort in one particular sector or region will frequently find that, as a result of these highly visible favors, demands from other sectors or regions have become activated and have to be granted at least in part for the purpose of putting together the political coalition that will permit the original plan to go forward.[60]

The potential for this effect increases, of course, as the issue area in question becomes larger. To state this relationship in negative terms, when an issue area becomes large, so that the demand for resources becomes significant relative to their availability, even those agencies not granted authority over the issue area might be effective in opposing its further expansion. Hence, conflict is greatest for large and complex issue areas in segmented states.

Alcohol was a small issue area during Phase One, in good measure because (for reasons discussed in Chapters 2 and 3) the amount of credit needed to augment annexed distilleries

[59]Cyert and March, *A Behavioral Theory of the Firm*, pp. 36–38.
[60]Hirschman, "Social and Political Matrix of Inflation," p. 196.

and thereby reach the relatively modest production goal was limited. This example suggests that the most important and highly varied factors influencing the demand for resources, aside from access to the policy machinery, include the ambitiousness of the production and investment targets, the degree of capital intensity, net social profitability, investors' expectations of future policy and market opportunities, and capacity conditions.

Turning to the denominator of size, the amount of resources available to promote specific sectors at any given time depends on a complex set of structural and policy constraints on tax collection, internal and external debt finance, and monetary creation. These relationships are both theoretically complex and empirically ambiguous and thus cannot be discussed here. Before passing over this critical factor, however, we should remember that perception is often more important than reality.[61] For example, the perception that credit subsidies were creating an inflationary spiral in 1980–81 was more relevant than any empirical measure of the precise connection between the two. As we will see, the growth of this perception during the period accentuated conflict over every political product whose promotion absorbed public resources, paradoxically helping to trigger as well as defuse the alcohol boom.

*Conflict Resolution.* In making the distinction between the generation and resolution of conflict, in effect we ask how consistent or favorable the policy set would be *if* the policy-making process attained equilibrium before any conflicts were resolved. Let us now examine the incentives for state officals to resolve conflict through mutual adjustment.

One key incentive was identified in the earlier section on central decision makers and the state apparatus. There I

---

[61]For one of his most elaborated discussions of this point, see Albert O. Hirschman, "The Turn to Authoritarianism in Latin America and the Search for Its Economic Determinants," in *The New Authoritarianism in Latin America*, ed. D. Collier (Princeton: Princeton University Press, 1979), pp. 61–98; reprinted in Hirschman, *Essays in Trespassing*, pp. 98–135.

mentioned the commonplace notion that central decision makers are better positioned than other officials in attempting to bend the policy actions of state agencies. This position is due not only to the ability of central decision makers to grant and withdraw policy-making authority. These officials can also use their special command over symbolic resources to manipulate the perceived connections between specific policy actions and the regime's nonoperational objectives. This basic principle of political systems suggests the following hypothesis:

9. In extraordinary times, when conditions in the task environment pose a clear and present danger to the country or to the authority of the regime, central decision makers can more effectively manipulate political support among state officials for their specific policy objectives. The ability of top authorities to bend the policy actions of the staff is enhanced during extraordinary times because a threatening task environment tends to reduce the ambiguity between some specific policy actions and the regime's nonoperational goals. In this sense, a threatening task environment tends to suppress contradictions between macropolitical goals, even in countries where these contradictions are particularly intense.[62]

In normal times, the argument of Hypotheses 1 to 8 is more likely to hold. To summarize:

10. When the contradictions between macropolitical objectives are intense, a state agency opposed to central decision makers' favored activities can perhaps justify its uncooperative actions by arguing, in effect, that the specific regime goals pursued by the agency would be

[62]In these situations, many intrastate conflicts are displaced by conflicts between the state and its task environment. "Every major conflict overwhelms, subordinates, and blots out a multitude of lesser ones." See E. E. Schattschneider, *The Semisovereign People* (Hinsdale, Ill.: Dryden Press, 1975), p. 65.

compromised if it deferred to central decision makers. As a consequence, in states with contradictory regime goals, the policy set is likely to attain equilibrium before many conflicts are resolved. The principle exceptions to this proposition during normal times are those sectors so located in the political economy that their promotion appears to be consistent with each of the otherwise contradictory regime goals.

11. Obstacles to consistently favorable equilibrium policy sets are those that generate conflict and impair conflict resolution. This analysis implies that mixed or unfavorable policy sets are associated with complex and large issue areas, segmented states, intensely contradictory regime goals, and normal times.

*Three Digressions.* I have not made much explicit use of the familiar distinction between policy formulation and policy implementation (partly because this dichotomy rubs against the notion of a hierarchy of ends-means connections). For at least two interrelated reasons, central control is weaker over the implementation process. One is that the ends-means connection between policy-formulation actions and central decision makers' specific goals is always less ambiguous than is the connection between these goals and policy-implementation actions. Another reason is that concrete measures are almost invariably guided by technical considerations. Since implementing agencies are often granted such authority because of their specialized technical competence, many state agencies are quite safe when conforming to their standard operating procedures. Consequently, even agencies opposed to the development of a given sector are often willing to bow to central decision makers' policy-formulation objectives simply because these agencies will likely have the last say in policy implementation. We may therefore suppose that the equilibrium policy set might be mixed—that is, contain both favorable and unfavorable policy actions—precisely because state agencies are much more likely to defer in the policy-formulation process.

It should also be mentioned that central decision makers can constrain some agencies more easily than others. For example, agencies whose assets include both specialized technical competence and an autonomous resource base tend to be more fully insulated from central control than agencies that are devoid of these political assets. State enterprises are therefore prime candidates for defiant behavior. Similarly, the state financial apparatus is more capable of withstanding pressure from above than are purely bureaucratic agencies. Of these bureaucracies, agencies closely allied with important groups in society are better able to oppose central decision makers on specific issues than are those which do not have such ties.

To complicate matters further, suppose that in state politics there is safety in numbers. That is, it may be much less costly for an agency to be one among many defying the wishes of central decision makers than for an agency to be the sole holdout in the struggle to gain control over policy. If this is true, one would expect that most agencies will quickly "tip in" to the trend toward favorable policy actions as soon as the resistance to central decision makers' specific objectives begins to crumble.[63]

These are just three of the useful extensions that could be made to the simple model of mutual adjustment among state officials developed here. In the interest of simplicity, I defer further speculation to the historical analysis of the alcohol program.

## Inefficient Political Signals and Policy Ineffectiveness

Let us quickly retrace some steps before pushing on to analyze the conditions under which central decision makers are likely to be thwarted in their attempts to induce private resources to shift between sectors of the economy. We began with the simple

[63] On "tipping" effects, see Thomas C. Schelling, *Micromotives and Macrobehavior* (New York: Norton, 1978), pp. 99–102.

point that political signals play an important role in helping investors forecast future policy. This role becomes even more important if investors use a model of the policy-making process to interpret political signals. By employing such a model, I argued, investors could more accurately estimate the probability that future policy would be less favorable than current policy. This kind of subjective probability information could then be used to value alternative projects, and to select among them, in the manner suggested in Chapter 3.

### Conflict Generation, Conflict Resolution, and Political Signaling

When favorable signals fail to generate optimistic expectations, economists say that the signals are "inefficient." Similarly, when favorable political signals, such as a consistently favorable current policy set, do not engender optimistic expectations of future policy, we can say that political signals are inefficient. In a steered economy, inefficient political signaling obviously impairs central decision makers' control of private investment flows.

Suppose central decision makers favor promoting an activity, as they did in the case of alcohol, and that whatever conflict is generated by this activity is resolved; hence, current policy is consistently favorable. We should expect that, all else being equal, investors are more likely to fear a policy reversal in a high-conflict situation than in a low-conflict setting. Although conflict in both cases is currently resolved, high levels of conflict make policy reversals more likely in the future. Therefore, signaling inefficiency declines as conflict increases. From the previous section, it follows that the efficiency of political signals is at least somewhat impaired for large and complex issue areas in segmented states.

We might also conjecture that, all else being equal, the equilibrium attained when conflict resolution is strong is more precarious if the regime's goals are intensely contradictory. This conjecture is based on the supposition that a given shock

TABLE 3. *Conflict Generation, Conflict Resolution, and the Policy Set*

|  | LOW RESOLUTION | HIGH RESOLUTION |
|---|---|---|
| Low Conflict | Moderately inconsistent current policy set at $t_0$ | Highly consistent current policy set at $t_0$ |
|  | Minimal risk of policy reversal at $t_1$ | Moderate risk of policy reversal at $t_1$ |
|  | (*Proálcool*, Phase One) |  |
| High Conflict | Highly inconsistent current policy set at $t_0$ | Consistent current policy set at $t_0$ |
|  | Moderate risk of policy reversal at $t_1$ | High risk of policy reversal at $t_1$ |
|  | (*Proálcool*, 1979) | (*Proálcool*, 1980) |

to the task environment—such as falling real oil prices—will have a more substantial effect on an agency's incentives to defer to central decision makers when the latter pursue intensely contradictory macropolitical goals. If this is so, these contradictions are another source of impairment in signaling efficiency. To take one further step, we could surmise that signaling efficiency is also impaired when the task environment is especially unstable, as indeed has been the case for Brazil over the last decade.

For illustrative purposes, Table 3 presents some likely relationships between high and low conflict generation and resolution, the consistency of policy at $t_0$, and the risk of a policy reversal at $t_1$.

## The Implicit Solution

In formal terms, we have found that the inefficiency of political signals, while a significant source of impairment of central control over investment flows, is not a "free" parameter of my model of the steered economy. This parameter depends specifically on macropolitical structures, such as the regime's

goals and state segmentation, as well as on issue-area characteristics, such as size and complexity.

*Competition.* As we have seen, competition is especially
intense for new and complex issue areas in segmented states.
Since competition raises uncertainty about the future pattern
of authority over a political product, segmentation as well as
an issue area's age and complexity tend to impair the efficiency
of political signals.

*Privileged vs. Ordinary Investors.* The mutual adjustment of
privileged investors and central decision makers, we have seen,
is a more cooperative process than that between top authorities
and ordinary investors. This cooperative relationship entails
greater access to state officials and, presumably, better information about the support for a political product than is
available to ordinary investors. Moreover, I have argued that
the structural position privileged investors occupy in the
politico-economic system enables them to be more assured of
stable policy than ordinary investors can be. The political,
economic, and organizational factors contributing to this
structural position improve, in effect, the efficiency of political
signals for privileged, relative to ordinary, investors. Thus,
signaling efficiency is greatest when the following circumstances obtain: privileged investors; old, simple, and small
issue areas; minimally segmented states with relatively compatible regime goals; and stable task environments.

*Central Control.* Two more pieces of the puzzle need to be put
into place to address one of the questions at hand: Why are
central decision makers in steered economies, though they
have formal authority over a wide array of sector-specific
policy instruments, under certain conditions generally ineffec-
tive in inducing resources to shift between sectors of the
economy?

In discussing the sources of signaling inefficiency, I supposed that central decision makers achieved control over the

policy-making process but that, nonetheless, they were unable to assure investors that consistently favorable policies would be around in the future. Now if we relax the assumption that such control is initially achieved, two more familiar channels of policy ineffectiveness are immediately apparent. If central decision makers cannot control current policy, they will not be able to use this powerful signaling device to sway investors' expectations of the future. Moreover, the direct effect of favorable current policies on the value of investments in political products is substantially weakened as well.

To close the system, we must note that central control over private investment flows depends also on investors' opportunities to invest in market products. To the extent that investments in market products appear attractive, central decision makers will have a more difficult time inducing resources to shift into political sectors. We can expect, in sum, central control to be most impaired when the following circumstances obtain: ordinary investors; new, complex, and large issue areas; segmented states where top authorities pursue intensely contradictory regime goals; normal times; and attractive market opportunities.

*Interdependent investors.* Finally, we should remember that the private value of any single investment can depend on whether other investors similarly commit their resources to a political product. As we have seen, for example, both consumers and investors in new alcohol-production complexes were dependent upon each other's reactions to political signals; a coordination failure could leave alcohol producers without a demand for their product or consumers without fuel for their cars. Consumers, in particular, also had individual incentives to let other consumers buy their alcohol-powered cars first. These complex linkages meant that the stability of Phase Two rested on how consumers—extremely atomistic participants with close substitution possibilities—reacted to political signals over the course of time. Given the multiple sources of signaling inefficiency in Brazil for these critical investors, in this immensely complex issue area, the first alcohol boom perhaps could only have been an unstable equilibrium.

## From Statics to Dynamics

To explain the alcohol case, I will often use the term *equilibrium* in describing a situation. As in any system, all the agents in the politicized market economy must take mutually consistent actions for a stable equilibrium to be reached: "An *equilibrium* is a situation in which several things that have been interacting, adjusting to each other and to each other's adjustment, are at last adjusted, in balance, at rest."[64]

For a steered economy to be conceptually at rest, two conditions must be met. First, the actions of state officials must be so adjusted to each other that policy cannot become either more or less favorable to the specific sector in question *without* the occurrence of some exogenous shock. Second, the decisions of private investors must be so adjusted to the policy actions of state officials that neither investment trends nor the policy set has any tendency to change in the absence of some external disturbance.

I will argue in Part II, for example, that the relationship between policy and private investment in 1976–78 roughly met these conditions for a stable equilibrium. During this period, the support for an alcohol program rested on an extremely thin political consensus within the state. Essentially, state agencies could not effectively oppose *Proálcool* so long as the practical objective of the program was to provide the *usineiros* with an outlet for their excess sugar production capacity. Central decision makers' attempts to relax the legal restrictions on the conversion of sugarcane into alcohol were therefore unopposed. On the other hand, President Geisel consistently failed to persuade Central Bank and Banco do Brasil officials to speed up the approval of credits for annexed distilleries. Alcohol production, nonetheless, grew rapidly during this

[64]Ibid., p. 25.

period (though admittedly from a minimal base). Once it was realized that the *usineiros* could expand alcohol production without a deeper commitment of state credit resources, the Central Bank's position seemed to harden even further. This position encouraged the sugar producers to invest in annexed distilleries in advance of receiving subsidized credits. Alcohol production statistics could therefore continue their upward trend despite the Central Bank's policy. In this sense, state policy actions and investors' behavior reinforced one another between 1976 and 1979.

This stable equilibrium was disturbed by the feedback effects generated by the expansion of alcohol production at existing plantations and mills. These effects tended to eliminate the very flexibility in the system that had allowed the alcohol program to glide along on top of an extremely thin political consensus. For instance, the expansion of alcohol production reduced the initial oversupply of sugarcane cultivation and milling capacity. Similarly, the opportunities for installing new annexed distilleries diminished as these same investments were made. Alcohol production therefore could continue to grow at a rapid pace much beyond 1979 only if huge new investments in agricultural machinery and sugarcane mills were made. This dynamic process of absorbing excess capacity, which was a direct consequence of the initial short-run equilibrium, helped to transform alcohol into a large issue area by 1979.

During this same period, two other feedback mechanisms gradually increased the complexity of the alcohol issue area. First, the flexibility afforded by the existing consumption system was slowly eliminated as alcohol began to approach 20 percent of the gasohol fuel supply. If these capacity constraints were reached before alcohol-powered cars were developed and sold on the market, *Proálcool* would become dead in the water. This eventuality was averted, however, by the automobile industry's decision to produce alcohol-powered cars. As a consequence, the tasks of pricing alcohol and gasoline and of ensuring the wide availability of alcohol fuel became extremely complex in 1980. Second, the flexibility of the existing

Petrobrás refineries slowly became exhausted as gasoline consumption declined relative to the demand for diesel fuel. The onset of this technical constraint eventually made alcohol policy and outcomes tightly coupled with decisions and trends in the entire liquid fuels sector. This rise in the complexity of the issue area did not simply make Phase Two more difficult to coordinate in a technical economic sense; for as a consequence, the immediate future of the alcohol program was placed in the hands of an unsympathetic Petrobrás.

The growing size and complexity of the issue area, plus the possibility that a long-term commitment to alcohol fuel would be made, initially punctured the thin political consensus in 1979. Yet the high levels of conflict and competition over expanding the program were eventually overcome. By tracking the process by which public and private expectations converged upon a stable, long-term commitment to alcohol energy in Brazil, we can develop a clear characterization of the way in which political signals are generated, interpreted, and acted upon in a steered economy.

We will see, for instance, how the alcohol production statistics of 1976–78 signaled that a significant alcohol program might not just remain the dream of economic nationalists. Or how the sequence of agreements between the automobile industry and the state pushed the program into its second phase. Or how external shocks, such as OPEC-2 and the Iranian Revolution, made it more costly for state agencies to oppose central decision makers' growing support for an alcohol program. Or how the elimination of credit restrictions and incremental changes in the implementation of *Proálcool* signaled that political support for an expanded alcohol policy had solidified. Or how the support for the alcohol program by international bankers signaled that favorable policies did not rest simply on the dynamics of Brazilian state politics. Or, finally, how these signals, combined with the shock of the 1979 maxidevaluation and the 1980 Iran–Iraq War, enabled central decision makers to portray the alcohol sector as the arsenal of Brazil's new "war economy."

The analysis of the resulting alcohol boom will show us that under extremely rare political conditions even a state such as Brazil's—characterized by intensely contradictory regime goals and segmented policy-making authority—can temporarily induce huge flows of private resources into a new, complex, and large sector or issue area. What the sudden *collapse* of the first alcohol boom demonstrates, however, is that even under these political conditions central decision makers' control of private investment is extremely fragile and can vanish with small negative perturbations in political signals.

One reason why the first boom was so fragile is that alcohol's preeminence among political products in 1980 was due primarily to the program's ability to remain intact while Brazil's continued economic growth appeared to be nearing the end of its tether. At this time, the country's already high inflation rates also started to climb steeply. Key economic policymakers then began to place heavy blame for this turn of events on the state's subsidized credit policies. We can readily understand, therefore, why the removal of credit restrictions for alcohol-related investments in August 1980 had sent the strongest possible political signal to potential entrants in this sector. However, the phenomenal ability of the program to attract distillery proposals subsequently created enormous demands for the very resource that was becoming increasingly scarce: subsidized credit.

The stability of the alcohol boom was also undermined by signals that the production and consumption of alcohol was economically inefficient. By 1981, the flexibility of Petrobrás's existing refining system had reached its outer limits, and the firm's executives had until then refused to invest in the expensive equipment that could further change refinery cracking ratios (that is, reduce refineries' gasoline output per barrel of crude input). At the margin, therefore, alcohol consumption merely created an excess supply of gasoline. Although investors did not know whether alcohol production was economically inefficient, they were attuned to the fact that alcohol had to appear to be the Brazilian "exit" from the energy crisis in order for its political support to be sustained. When news of accumulating gasoline stocks made the alcohol program seemingly create more problems than it solved, investors' expectations of the future became extremely sensitive to other adverse political signals. These came in June 1981, when new credits for alcohol distilleries were "temporarily" suspended. During the next few months, alcohol-powered car sales plummeted and new proposals for distilleries failed to arrive on the government's docket. In late 1981, the alcohol program thus moved swiftly away from its zenith. Then, over a year later, *Proálcool* resurged as the country wrestled with an external payments crisis, an IMF stabilization plan, and an excess supply of alcohol fuel. Not least among middle-class Brazilians' fears at the time were rumors of the impending rationing of gasoline.

# The National
# Alcohol Program in Brazil:
# History and Analysis

CHAPTER 5

## From Sugar
## Industry Bailout to
## Energy Strategy

### The Sugar and Alcohol Tradition

Sugarcane dominates the history of alcohol in Brazil, as it does much of the early history of the country itself. During the sixteenth century, the Portuguese introduced sugarcane into the Brazilian northeast in order to generate the income they needed to defend the territory from external aggression. Today, four hundred years later, sugar exports no longer represent the principal economic activity of a much-transformed Brazil. Yet sugar remains the mainstay of the Northeast economy, especially in the states of Pernambuco and Alagoas, and this traditional crop continues to be extremely prominent on the now diverse Brazilian agricultural landscape.

*Northeast Dominance and the Great Depression*

Direct state involvement has been central to the development of the sugar industry for nearly forty years. In 1933, President

129

Getulio Vargas created the Institute of Sugar and Alcohol (IAA) to ameliorate the disastrous condition of the sugar industry, which was plagued by the 1929 collapse of world commodity prices. The demands of the dominant Northeastern producers for government control and protection of the sugar market meshed well with the Vargas regime's propensity to intervene in the ailing agricultural economy.

The immediate problem faced by the IAA was excess production. Since world sugar prices were extremely low, a profitable export strategy was clearly not a short-term possibility. In protecting the industry from the contraction in the world sugar market, emergency actions taken by the Vargas government were designed to stabilize prices by decreasing production and by developing an alternative nonfood use for the remaining surplus. The IAA therefore created a system of production quotas and other rules. A second policy of the 1930s promoted the production of alcohol as a motor fuel. Expanding on this base, alcohol came to provide nearly 50 percent of the fuel supply in some regions during the petroleum-scarce years of World War II.

This early experience with alcohol is sometimes celebrated as an ingenious response to the temporary scarcity of petroleum. But IAA-sponsored central distilleries were operated principally to maintain an equilibrium between production and consumption of sugar at supported price levels.[1] Alcohol continued to serve primarily as a device to regulate the sugar market until 1980.

### The New Internal Market Orientation: 1933–65

According to Barbara Nunberg, government policies toward the sugar industry typified the strengthening nationalist ideological currents of the depression period:

---

[1]Barbara Nunberg, "State Intervention in the Sugar Sector in Brazil: A Study of the Institute of Sugar and Alcohol" (Ph.D. diss., Stanford University, 1978), chap. 4, p. 7.

The dominant strategy of the planners in the Institute of Sugar and Alcohol was to export sugar only when internal demand had been supplied and there was an excess which could be exported at a reasonable, compensatory price. This strategy was followed not only because of the very real needs of internal consumption and the expanding domestic market, but also in an effort to protect the sugar sector from the shocks which nearly destroyed it during the Depression.[2]

This autonomous development strategy was strongly reinforced by the country's overvalued exchange rate policy. Although overvaluation contributed to the import substitution process, it also greatly discriminated against sugar and other exports. Between the late 1940s and the early 1960s, export earnings increased by only 13 percent while the gross national product expanded by 140 percent.[3]

*The Rise of the São Paulo Sugar Industry: 1930–75*

Without much active encouragement from the IAA, sugar production has expanded over the course of the last few decades principally on the former São Paulo coffee plantations. Rapid production increases on these lands are often attributed to the efforts of hardworking Italian immigrants and their descendants who have purchased huge tracts of land since the 1930s. These efforts were nicely rewarded, in part, because of the São Paulo *usineiros'* close proximity to the country's rapidly expanding urban markets. The state's rich and relatively flat lands, moreover, were conducive to mechanization and permitted high yields.[4]

These factors ultimately allowed the Center-South to dwarf the production of the Northeast. In 1933, when the IAA was created, the Northeast produced 80 percent of Brazil's sugar.

[2]Ibid., chap. 1, p. 20.

[3]Ibid.

[4]For technical, economic, and institutional background on the sugar sector, see Tamás Szmrecsányi, *O Planejamento da Agroindústria Canavieira do Brasil, 1930–1975* (São Paulo: Editora HUCITEC, 1979).

(The remainder was produced in the Center-South.) Although national production has since increased ten times, the Northeast's output has increased by only a factor of three. In 1977, the Center-South produced 75 percent of the nation's sugar, while the Northeast produced only the remaining 25 percent.[5]

Despite the efforts of the IAA to cushion the impact of this trend, it was clear by the mid-1960s that the São Paulo producers were becoming the most powerful force in the Brazilian sugar industry.[6] Sugarcane, in turn, had become dominant in São Paulo agriculture. By 1976, cane occupied 17 percent of Paulista agricultural lands and even surpassed the gross income generated by coffee production in that year.[7]

Several important trends accompanied this growth. First, the cultivation of food crops decreased due to the expansion of sugarcane plantations. Second, landownership became increasingly concentrated as many small-scale suppliers of cane sold their properties.[8] Sugar production in São Paulo was soon dominated by a few families, such as the Omettos, whose *usinas*[9] produced more than 12 percent of the nation's sugar in 1975—apparently more than any individual *state* except for São Paulo and Pernambuco.[10] Third, the use of temporary

[5]Nunberg, "State Intervention," chap. 7, pp. 1–3, cites data from the statistical service of the IAA.

[6]Nunberg, "State Intervention," chap. 7, p. 3.

[7]Ibid., pp. 3–4.

[8]In 1964, some 60 percent of all cane was furnished by these suppliers, whereas in the late 1970s they supplied less than 40 percent of the Center-South's sugar production. The concentration process was largely carried out legally, aided by occasional suspensions of the quota system when the sugar export market was strong. See Nunberg, "State Intervention," chap. 7, pp. 7–8.

[9]The term *usina* refers to sugar mills and the sugarcane plantations. Owners of *usinas*, such as the Omettos, are called *usineiros*.

[10]Regina Machado Curi, "Os Barões de Açúcar," *Veja* (21 June 1976):23–29, cited in Nunberg, "State Intervention," chap. 7, p. 5. Within São Paulo, the Omettos are responsible for 27 percent of production, followed by the Zillo group (10 percent) and the Atalla group (5 percent). Interview with Mauro G. Paschkes, FINASA-ACLI (commodity brokers), São Paulo, July 1979.

labor increased, since sugarcane requires substantial attention only during the harvest season, which lasts merely half the year. Consequently, urban migration accelerated among those laborers who had once cultivated the now displaced subsistence crops.[11] These trends eventually became important social issues in the debate over the alcohol program.

### The Late 1960s and the World Sugar Market

The growth of the São Paulo sugar industry during the 1960s and 1970s was influenced not only by the expanding urban areas of São Paulo and Rio de Janeiro but by a renewed Brazilian interest in the international sugar market. This interest commenced with the United States decision to embargo purchases of Cuban sugar in "retaliation" for the 1959 revolution and its aftermath. As a result:

> Brazil, as a potentially large producer and exporter, was awarded a lion's share of this quota, which became increasingly large as the Brazilian sugar industry proved itself capable of reliably delivering greater quantities of sugar each year. Thus, by the 1970s, the IAA's traditional emphasis on maintaining a balance between internal consumption and production began to yield somewhat to the growing desire to export sugar to the North American and world markets.[12]

During the 1960s and early 1970s, the trend toward increased exports, while evident, was not dramatic. In 1965, Brazil exported 15 percent of its sugar production, equivalent to 3.5 percent of the sugar traded on the world market. By 1971, the population exported had grown to 19 percent, increasing the country's share in the international trade of

[11]Nunberg, "State Intervention," chap. 7, p. 7. See also Maria Conceição D'Inção e Mello, *O Bóia Fria: Acumulação e Miséria* (Petrópolis: Editora Vozes, 1975).

[12]Nunberg, "State Intervention," chap. 6, pp. 2–3.

sugar by two percentage points.[13] The extraordinary export increases came only during subsequent years.

### The IAA Modernization Program: 1971–75

The sugar industry's rapid export growth during the first half of the 1970s was caused by a seemingly propitious conjuncture: Highly unusual conditions in the international sugar market appeared in the midst of the military regime's sugar modernization program. Largely in anticipation of higher world sugar prices, the IAA's modernization program was designed to improve the agro-industry's extremely low productivity.[14] In the first phase of the program, these goals were to be achieved by eliminating, merging, or relocating numerous small, uneconomical mills which were prominent in the Northeast. The execution of this phase of the program between 1971 and 1973 "made clear the IAA's intention to encourage the development of large-scale capital-intensive sugar production and the further concentration of landowner-ship."[15] For the first time, the IAA no longer attempted to protect less efficient Northeastern producers from Center-South competition.

The government's scheme envisaged a second phase in which the industry's technology would be modernized. The IAA therefore established a subsidized financing system for the expansion and modernization of plantations and mills. The financial resources needed to carry out the modernization project were to be supplied by the IAA's Special Export Fund with revenue generated from the difference between the established price paid to *usineiros* and the international market price received by the IAA. Higher world sugar prices would therefore automatically provide more resources for the in-dustry's expansion and modernization. The interest rates and terms of the IAA's loans would be extremely favorable relative

[13]Ibid., chap. 5, p. 4.
[14]Ibid., chap. 10, p. 12.
[15]Ibid., p. 6.

to the commercial capital market.[16] Since interest rates were, in effect, negative due to inflation, the IAA funding offer created a strong incentive for *usineiros* to undertake modernization projects.

### Unguarded Optimism: 1973–75

Briskly expanding exports and the completion of the first phase of the modernization scheme set the stage for the extraordinary events of 1973–75. Due to sugar crop failures in major producing countries, the world price of sugar began to skyrocket in the second half of 1973. At its peak during the latter part of 1974, the world sugar price reached $US 1400 per ton (70 cents per pound), representing a *tenfold* increase over the preboom levels. Revenue from sugar exports surpassed $US 1.26 billion in 1974, a 125 percent jump over the previous year.[17] In 1974, Brazil's share of the world sugar market almost reached 12 percent (it was 3.5 percent in 1965).[18] The value of sugar exports in 1974 even overtook that of coffee for the first time.

According to Nunberg, the IAA became euphoric over this extraordinary situation, typified by the agency's prediction that prices would remain high on the international market:

> Brazil can take advantage of the permanence of the current situation to renovate the structure of its sugar economy with a certain tranquility. Along these lines, Brazil could even become the principal exporter by the end of the decade.[19]

Although there was much skepticism about the IAA's assumptions, the institute launched its New Sugar Policy (*Nova Política*

---

[16]Interest rates on IAA loans ranged between 10 and 12 percent per annum with at least twelve years to repay and three years before the first payment became due. See Nunberg, "State Intervention," chap. 10, p. 11.

[17]Ibid., chap. 5, p. 5.

[18]Ibid., chap. 6, p. 4.

[19]Álvaro Tavares do Carmo, president of the IAA, quoted in Nunberg, "State Intervention," chap. 6, p. 7.

*Açúcareira*) in 1974 to further expand production, productivity, and exports. This ambitious program was financed by the enormous resources which were accumulating in the Special Export Fund. The subsequent harvest (1975–76) surpassed the previous production records as capacity and productivity grew.

Just as the New Sugar Policy was well under way, however, the volatile sugar market deteriorated rapidly. In mid-1975, as supplies continued to increase while demand contracted, world sugar prices plummeted. In that year, Brazil's sugar export earnings decreased 23 percent to $US 1.1 billion. But 1975 was only the beginning. The world price in 1976 fell to $US 150 per ton, disastrously low compared to its 1974 peak of $US 1400 per ton. Export earnings from sugar shrank to only $US 202 million in 1976—a drop of 77 percent from its peak value.[20] At that time, moreover, no international sugar agreement had been reached, the United States preferential price system for sugar had expired, and Washington had raised its sugar import tariffs by 300 percent.[21] The IAA thus decided to suspend all spot sales of raw sugar abroad and honor only its long-term contracts.

### Overcapacity in the Sugar Industry and the State's Response

*The Options in 1975*

Once Brazil had withdrawn from the spot market, a serious problem of overcapacity in the sugar industry quickly emerged and was likely to worsen as long-term contracts expired. Brazil's response to this situation paralleled that of the 1930s: The government protected the sugar industry from cheaper imports and helped it turn toward the domestic market.

As part of a renewed internal orientation, domestic sugar

[20]Ibid., pp. 5–13.
[21]Ibid., p. 13.

consumption could be encouraged. Between 1967 and 1975, per capita consumption of sugar in Brazil increased by 10 percent to a level half that of the United States.[22] Since this trend was caused by overall economic growth, however, no immediate policy options were available to raise the demand for sugarcane in this way. But there was another traditional fallback position: alcohol. With government action, some of the excess production capacity could be used to generate motor fuel in larger quantities than had been produced in the recent past.

### The Influence of the São Paulo Sugar Elites

The sugar industry has been influential in the Brazilian political economy, in part, because it is concentrated in a small number of producers in the Center-South who benefited greatly from the government's modernization program. The industry's key political force is Copersucar, the São Paulo producers' cooperative. This organization was founded in 1959 to defend the interests of the area's sugar producers. At the time, the São Paulo *usineiros* felt neglected by the IAA, whose institutional mission was more closely linked to the Northeastern sugar industry. In order to receive protection from the 1967 crisis of sugar overproduction in Brazil and elsewhere, many Paulista *usineiros* relied on Copersucar's political efforts. Eventually, Copersucar became a prominent economic and political force in Brazil:

> Within the state of São Paulo, it accounts for 90 and 91 percent respectively of sugar and alcohol production. Clearly, it not only constitutes one of the most powerful forces within the Brazilian sugar industry, but is also one of the most important private firms in Brazil as a whole.[23]

Since the modernized, large-scale, and capital-intensive sugar sector in the Center-South embodied the development

[22]Ibid., p. 20.
[23]Nunberg, "State Intervention," chap. 8, p. 2.

values of the military regime, the São Paulo *usineiros* received special access to highly placed state officials. Nunberg reports that Copersucar unofficially became the representative of all private sugar interests in the Center-South and was able to deal directly with the president of the republic rather than working through the IAA.[24] The clearest evidence of Copersucar's extensive influence is that it existed at all. Under Brazilian law, such cooperatives were illegal until recently, yet the group's operations were unobstructed by this technicality. More spectacular evidence of Copersucar's ability to influence government policy was provided by the cooperative's multinational ventures. The drive to expand Copersucar's interests beyond the Brazilian sugar industry was led by the cooperative's well-known and extremely wealthy president, Jorge Wolney Atalla. Assuming the presidency in 1968, following a successful campaign to increase alcohol production during the 1966–67 overproduction crisis, Atalla turned Copersucar into one of the largest corporations in Latin America.[25]

Examples abound of Atalla's ability to receive highly unusual support from the Banco do Brasil, even when the debt of Copersucar and Atalla himself had grown enormously. Atalla's influence was buoyed by his staunch support of the military regime. According to Nunberg, writing in the mid-1970s: "Atalla is considered to be a close friend of [former] President Geisel, and he is one of the few private businessmen who can get an audience with the President."[26]

Atalla fell from the presidency of Copersucar in July 1979, due to extreme personal financial difficulties and his loss of support from important groups within the cooperative. But in 1975, when world sugar prices were plummeting and the industry appeared to be entering a period of deep trouble, the influence of Atalla and Copersucar were still strong.

[24]Ibid., p. 8.
[25]Ibid., p. 19.
[26]Ibid., p. 22.

## A Second Crisis by 1975

At the same time, another key international event was putting pressure on Brazil's balance of payments. The 1973–74 quadrupling of crude petroleum prices by the OPEC countries appeared to wreak havoc on Brazil's economic miracle. The country's extreme sensitivity to OPEC's action was sharply reflected in the trade account. In 1973, Brazil's expenditures on petroleum imports equaled 16 percent of its export earnings. Only a year later, 40 percent of the country's exports were required to pay for imported petroleum. As Brazil imported 80 percent of its oil, the OPEC shock made future economic prospects highly uncertain.

When the 1973–74 oil shock hit Brazil, President Geisel was already acutely aware of energy issues. He had earlier served as president of Petrobrás, the state-owned petroleum monopoly. In mid-1975, Geisel visited Brazil's Center for Aeronautical Technology (CTA):

> In the course of a visit to Brazil's space agency in São José dos Campos, he stopped at a newly founded laboratory investigating alcohol as a motor fuel and was fascinated by the experimental results. He is said to have prolonged what was to have been a brief, ceremonial visit into a lengthy session, and to have quickly grasped the possibilities.[27]

## The Official Rationale for the Alcohol Program: 1975

On 14 November 1975, President Geisel officially promulgated the National Alcohol Program.[28] The principal stated objective of the program was to save foreign exchange by using alcohol as a supplement to the nation's gasoline supply and as a petrochemical feedstock. The 1975 decree also stated that a variety of national goals, in addition to saving foreign exchange, could be furthered by an ambitious alcohol pro-

[27]Allen L. Hammond, "Alcohol: A Brazilian Answer to the Energy Crisis," *Science* (11 February 1977):564.
[28]Decree No. 76,593.

gram. First, alcohol production (it was claimed) would reduce income inequality among regions in Brazil by permitting the production of alcohol from manioc in poor sections of the country. Second, alcohol would reduce inequality in the size distribution of income by creating rural employment in the Center-South and Northeast regions. Third, the plan claimed that *Proálcool* would generate national income by putting untapped land and idle labor to work. Finally, technological and other economic benefits would flow from the expanded production of capital goods (mills and distilleries) by local manufacturers.

These stated objectives reflected a political arrangement worked out by state officials and important interest groups. The selection of the foreign exchange savings and income distribution objectives in the November decree indicates that sufficient questions had been raised to encourage policymakers to position the program in a politically more popular way than as a bailout scheme for the sugar industry. Intense negotiation transformed the alcohol program into an explicit energy strategy. This transformation coincided with the mobilization of state agencies and producer interest groups which, like President Geisel, "quickly grasped the possibilities" of the alcohol option.

### State Politics Before the November Decree

The initial justification for the alcohol scheme appeared in a June 1975 proposal written by Minister of Mines and Energy Shigeaki Ueki and Minister of Industry and Commerce Severo Gomes.[29] The primary motivation cited in that proposal was to reduce the serious effects of low world prices on the sugar industry. The ministers emphasized the need to maintain rural employment and to make use of the extensive investments which had recently been committed to the sector. OPEC oil

[29]"Produtividade, meta fundamental," *O Estado de São Paulo*, 12 July 1975.

price increases were mentioned in justification, but only as a secondary consideration. Alcohol should be produced, they argued, only if world sugar prices remained low. For this reason, ministers Ueki and Gomes recommended the promotion of annexed distilleries rather than autonomous ones. With annexed facilities, the production of sugar for export could be quickly increased merely by reducing the production of alcohol. According to the proposal, autonomous distilleries would be built or expanded only under special circumstances determined by the Ministries of Mines and Energy, Industry and Commerce, and Agriculture. Moreover, the ministers did not propose to offer lenient financing terms. Ueki and Gomes were obviously proposing an alcohol program of limited scope and priority.

Within two months, the character of the alcohol option had changed considerably. In mid-September 1975, the Council for Economic Development (CDE) established a working group to study and present conclusions about the "utilization of alcohol to reduce petroleum imports."[30] The CDE told the group to report back within thirty days with an alcohol policy. By September 1975, the substitution of petroleum had evidently become an urgent political goal.

During the following month, forces inside and outside the state mobilized themselves in an attempt to maximize the gains and minimize the losses that could accrue from what was perceived to be a potentially enormous alcohol program. Promoting itself and the sugar industry, the IAA authorized the establishment of six autonomous distilleries in October 1975, just a few weeks after the announcement of the CDE mandate.[31] The IAA must have taken this action in order to stimulate public interest in the alcohol program, since the institute generally preferred the expansion of annexed distil-

[30]"CDE adianta os estudos para adicionar o álcool à gasolina," *O Estado de São Paulo*, 12 October 1975.

[31]Herval C. A. Faria, "Definida a fonte de recursos, surgem os projetos do álcool," *O Estado de São Paulo*, 12 October 1975.

leries.[32] An ambitious program that permitted sugar exports to increase easily with the return of higher world prices would be less risky to the IAA's institutional interests. For the most part, the interests of the *usineiros* were in harmony with those of the IAA. Only the question of control over alcohol distribution led Copersucar and the IAA to disagree.

### Debate over Raw Materials, Control, and Incentives

Once the alcohol option came to be seen principally as an oil import substitution scheme rather than a response to the sugar crisis, the desirability of sugarcane as the exclusive raw material for alcohol production began to be questioned. Technocrats in the Ministry of Agriculture and the Ministry of Industry and Commerce tended to support the inclusion of manioc (cassava) in the alcohol program. Manioc is cultivated principally by small-scale farmers as a food crop in all parts of the country. In fact, Brazil is the world's largest producer of manioc. Its use as an alcohol feedstock, proponents argued, could have significant positive effects on income distribution. Instead of further concentrating income in the hands of the São Paulo *usineiros*, they contended, manioc producers (most of whom were poor) could benefit from participation in the alcohol program. Proponents of this idea failed to point out, however, that poor *consumers* of manioc would face rising food prices unless productivity improved or consumption was subsidized.

Faced with the possibility that another crop would be favored, the IAA, the sugar industry, and the São Paulo Secretariat of Agriculture lobbied for the nearly exclusive use of sugarcane in alcohol production. They argued that cane was a "natural" choice, since the country could draw on its long experience in sugar cultivation. Moreover, since national industries produced mills and distilleries, neither technology nor capital goods would need to be imported. Finally, the industrial processing phase could be self-sufficient in energy

[32]Ibid.

since the pulp residue from the cane (bagasse) could supply the power to mills and distilleries.[33]

While bureaucratic and producer interests competed for support of their respective positions, the manioc option acquired a surprising but extremely powerful proponent: Petrobrás. Since its creation as Brazil's state-owned petroleum company during the 1950s, Petrobrás had maintained a legal monopoly over the production of liquid fuels. With a potentially large alcohol program in the offing, the giant state enterprise had no intention of losing its tight control over the liquid fuels sector.

Petrobrás announced that it would establish a manioc plantation and distillery complex in Minas Gerais. In a related maneuver, Petrobrás rumored that it might be willing to promote the utilization of manioc by offering agricultural and industrial financing and by establishing a minimum price for alcohol produced from manioc.[34] If the company established control over a significant manioc sector, Petrobrás could conceivably preempt the sugar industry and the IAA and thereby preserve its monopoly over liquid fuels.

Before reporting back to the Council for Economic Development, the working group made public its proposal to give the IAA a monopoly over the commercialization of all the alcohol and molasses produced in Brazil.[35] This trial balloon started a sharp debate over what had become a central unresolved question of the program: Who would control the alcohol sector? Petrobrás demanded that in keeping with its liquid fuels monopoly, it be designated the sole purchaser of alcohol, rather than the IAA.[36] Of course, the IAA was delighted with the working group's proposal.

[33]"Álcool carburante, um tema de opção nacional," *Visão* (27 October 1975):17–20.

[34]"Indefinição sobre o monopólio retarda a política do álcool," *O Estado de São Paulo*, 1 November 1975.

[35]"Projeto do álcool gera protestos no setor privado," *Jornal do Brasil*, 11 November 1975.

[36]"Indefinição sobre o monopólio retarda a política do álcool."

In a departure from their otherwise consistent support of the IAA, the *usineiros* vigorously opposed both the working group's suggestion and the counterproposal made by Petrobrás. Sugar producers were fearful that the state would first try to maximize its control over alcohol distribution and then eventually take over production itself. This perspective should not be attributed to mere paranoia, since the Petrobrás monopoly over liquid fuels had attained a high degree of legitimacy. The enterprise was first created, in part, to ensure that the liquid fuels sector would be controlled by the state for the "public interest." Petrobrás, furthermore, appeared committed to protecting its privileged position.

Led by its president, Copersucar launched an attack on the working group's plan.[37] To mobilize support for his position, Atalla capitalized on the emerging debate over state ownership in the economy.[38] By winning on this issue, the sugar industry's efforts to control the alcohol sector would be enhanced. On another issue, Copersucar demanded subsidized credit to expand sugarcane production and install distilleries.[39]

These deep conflicts—over raw materials, control, and incentives—remained after the CDE's eight hours of discussion in mid-November 1975. Nonetheless, enough deals were made to establish an official alcohol program.

### Concrete Decisions of the CDE: November 1975

Several important decisions were made by the Council for Economic Development. First, the CDE placed control over alcohol marketing in the hands of the state. The National Petroleum Council (CNP), which formally controlled Petrobrás, was to guarantee a market and price for alcohol for both

[37]See advertisement, "Perigo da estatização da comercialização do álcool," *O Estado de São Paulo*, 6 November 1975.

[38]Atalla received the support of the *Estado:* "O processo de estatização," *O Estado de São Paulo*, 8 November 1975.

[39]"Gasolina: petróleo + álcool (cana ou mandioca?). O governo não vai aceitar pressões para decidir," *Jornal da Tarde*, 7 November 1975.

fuel and petrochemical end uses. But the CNP was not to be given a *monopoly* over alcohol marketing, since producers could sell their product directly to gasoline distributors or to the petrochemical industry. This decision was evidently a victory for the sugar industry.[40]

The more critical conflicts over control and raw materials were by no means resolved by the CDE in the decree of 15 November 1975. Productive control would depend, in part, on whether sugarcane or manioc became the dominant raw material. Since the decree permitted alcohol production from sources other than sugarcane, the announcement could be couched in the jargon of improved income distribution and agricultural development.[41]

Regulatory control was ostensibly delegated to a new National Alcohol Council (CNAl) to be composed of representatives from the IAA and the Ministries of Industry and Commerce, Mines and Energy, Agriculture, Finance, Interior, and Planning. The CNAl was given responsibility for establishing project selection criteria and targeting alcohol production levels. The creation of this body signified that policy decisions for the alcohol program would be made at a broader level than that of the IAA. Since the conflicting views and interests of such diverse commission members would be difficult to reconcile, it is evident that the Council for Economic Development was unable to specify the direction the National Alcohol Program would take.

Certain issues, however, were settled by the presidential decree. First, a goal of 3 billion liters of alcohol fuel was set for 1980 in order to supplement the projected gasoline supply by

[40]"CNP garantirá compra e preço do álcool anidro," *O Estado de São Paulo*, 9 November 1975. The previous day the *Estado* reported that the IAA would remain responsible for marketing alcohol for the chemical industry while Petrobrás would buy the alcohol destined for mixture with gasoline. President Geisel's involvement may have affected the outcome. See "Geisel convoca ministros para a decisão do álcool," *O Estado de São Paulo*, 8 November 1975.

[41]"Feliz início do Programa do Álcool," *O Estado de São Paulo*, 18 November 1975.

20 percent. This limit was based on technical research which confirmed that alcohol could safely constitute 20 percent of the gasoline supply without modifying ordinary automobile engines. Second, the decree raised the producer price for alcohol relative to that of sugar. Third, the November 1975 decree authorized a subsidized financing scheme to encourage the expansion of alcohol production.[42] To construct a distillery or cultivate new lands, the entrepreneur would be required to submit a proposal to the IAA. After the institute evaluated the project from a technical standpoint, the proposal would be sent to CNAl for approval. If approval was granted, a separate proposal for subsidized credit would be sent to the Banco do Brasil, which would evaluate the project's financial viability.

### Explaining the November 1975 Decree

To explain the creation of the National Alcohol Program in 1975 is hardly an insurmountable task in light of the evidence presented above. We are, in fact, confronted with an embarrassment of explanatory riches: the long-standing tradition of state intervention in the sugar sector, the deeply rooted ties between economic nationalism and sugar policy, the multiple precedents of transforming excess sugarcane into alcohol (in the mid-1930s, early 1940s, and late 1960s), the military's consolidation and modernization scheme for the sugar industry (early 1970s), the New Sugar Policy (1974), the emergence of Copersucar and the pattern of its special access to top authorities, the country's growing dependence on imported oil, the convergence of the sugar and oil shocks, the potential uniqueness of this Brazilian energy strategy, as well as President Geisel's special expertise in energy matters and style of personal intervention in the economic policy-making process.

---

[42]Annual interest rates on distilleries would be 17 percent over a twelve-year period, with three years before the first payment was due. For new lands brought under cultivation, interest rates would be 7 percent per year over five years, with two years before the first payment. See "Está pronta o Plano Nacional do Álcool," *Folha de São Paulo*, 31 October 1975.

To say that the formulation of the National Alcohol Program was a high-probability event perhaps understates the case.

While the OPEC shock surely added to the probability of the 1975 decree, this second threat to the Brazilian model of politico-economic development may not have been necessary for the launching of the National Alcohol Program. The rapidly declining value of Brazilian sugar exports was itself a pressing problem for central decision makers—and not only because sugar had become a major credit item in the balance of trade. For behind these numbers lay a key component of the development model that the military regime had tried earnestly to promote through greater microeconomic intervention. By virtue of a series of authoritative measures and financial inducements, the *usineiros* came to represent one aspect of the military's preferred style of production, consumption, and ownership in Brazil. More specifically, by 1975 the sugar industry symbolized how sector-specific policies could be used to fashion a large-scale, concentrated, capital-intensive, export-oriented, and privately owned activity within the often neglected agricultural sector. In the language of Chapter 4, the *usineiros* were therefore privileged investors *par excellence*.

To this privileged position within the post-1964 system must be added the sugar industry's central location in the longer-standing ideological framework of developmental nationalism. As we have seen, the IAA was one of the first institutional manifestations of the ideology of state-guided, inward-looking development. Moreover, the idea of producing alcohol in times of weak external demand for sugar was as familiar to Brazilian policymakers as it was innovative to admirers abroad. These ideological considerations smoothed the way toward the institutionalization of a sugar industry bailout scheme under *Proálcool*.

The privileged position of the *usineiros* and the ideological embellishment provided by economic nationalism were probably sufficient for policymakers to take the relatively innocuous step of announcing some measures to increase the production of alcohol and its consumption as gasohol in the existing automotive fleet. To this explanation could be added a variety of related but distinct macropolitical considerations, associated with President Geisel's precarious position within the military regime. The president had taken office in 1974, following six years of stiff repression. As a result of his effort to relax the most authoritarian aspects of military rule, Geisel had generated stiff opposition from hard-line officers and from "powerful industrial and financial interests, both national and international, afraid of a threat to the profitable workings of the system built up since 1964."[43] During 1975, when Geisel's position was apparently weakest, the president therefore had strong incentives to bolster important allies and salient representatives of the Brazilian model such as the *usineiros*.[44]

The argument that the sugar shock was sufficient for *Proálcool* does not imply that the role of the OPEC shock was purely epiphenomenal. For example, President Geisel's enthusiasm for the idea was certainly related to the military's long-standing concern with petroleum supply and, in particular, to the president's own energy expertise. Geisel began his association with Petrobrás in 1955 as a refinery superintendent and, following a lengthy interlude in other military-related positions, served as director of the state petroleum monopoly in the late 1960s and early 1970s. Moreover, Geisel's ascension to the presidency of the republic in the midst of the first OPEC shock was partly triggered by his long experience as an oil man: "a man at the helm familiar with problems of oil and energy at just the time when soaring oil prices represented the most serious external threat to the balance of payments and the

[43]Peter Flynn, *Brazil: A Political Analysis* (Boulder, Colo.: Westview Press, 1978), p. 488.

[44]For a wide range of insights about dynamics within the regime as well as the effects of election outcomes during this period, see Flynn, *Brazil*, pp. 472–512.

continued success of the Brazilian 'model'."[45] Thus, the OPEC shock made the military strongly interested in General Geisel as a presidential aspirant and, in turn, contributed to President Geisel's extremely active role in *Proálcool*.

Whatever the motives for linking alcohol with the energy crisis, this ordinarily sensible maneuver almost backfired. To see why the suggestion that alcohol was more than a sugar industry bailout scheme became a liability, we must recognize that by 1975 state officials and the informed public understood that the military's macropolitical strategy had fallen well short of its mark. By then there were already sure signs that the regime was starting to lose the support of certain segments of local private capital. These signs were most apparent in the growing attention the press gave to complaints that state and multinational enterprises had encroached too far into the terrain of the national bourgeoisie. Although this source of discontent did not yet translate into the movement for democratization, central decision makers had cause for alarm.[46]

Several of the contradictions in the political model thus became apparent in 1975 at the same time that the energy crisis

---

[45]Flynn, *Brazil*, p. 473. Flynn also argues (p. 478) that Geisel broke with the recent past by becoming more personally involved in policy-making than his predecessors and by offering several new initiatives: "It was precisely this search for a new line, a different 'project' for Brazil, which most fueled speculation about the Geisel government from the start, with expectations of a different approach both to the economy and to politics."

[46]Peter Evans, *Dependent Development: The Alliance of Multinational, State, and Local Capital in Brazil* (Princeton: Princeton University Press, 1979). In his careful investigation of several industrial sectors, Evans discovered that only a small number of firms managed to find an economic niche in high-profit sectors of the economy, such as pharmaceuticals and petrochemicals. Moreover, these "groups" were able to enter such coveted sectors only if they participated in joint ventures with multinationals and state enterprises. Conversely, most segments of local capital eventually discovered that they were protected from the competition of the multinationals and state enterprises, either naturally or politically, only in less profitable or traditional sectors, such as textiles. Evans provides a crisp summary of his findings in *Dependent Development*, pp. 274–90.

continued to strike the economic model in a most vulnerable place. Brazil was dependent on petroleum imports for 80 percent of its oil supply; the transportation sector was based almost completely on cars and trucks; and the recent slowing of economic growth was associated with the energy crisis, at least in the public mind.[47] Under these circumstances, many observers must have guessed that central decision makers might seize upon the alcohol program in an attempt to reverse the growing contradictions of their political and economic model of development. More specifically, it could be imagined that a large-scale alcohol program would not only enhance political support for the regime by expanding the economic domain of local private capital; at the same time, this political strategy would give central decision makers the opportunity to show the public that they were trying hard to achieve energy adjustment.

One problem with this strategy was that it stepped on the toes of Petrobrás, the biggest and most powerful state enterprise in Brazil. Once alcohol was positioned as a gasoline substitute, Petrobrás could make a reasonable case that the production of alcohol by private capital violated its legal monopoly over liquid fuels.[48] This huge organization also had the capability to make its voice heard. To a similar extent, the *usineiros* could use the organizational resources of Copersucar

[47] Several papers were subsequently published which showed that the oil crisis cannot be cited as the sole explanation of tougher economic times. See, for example, Edmar L. Bacha, "Issues and Evidence on Recent Brazilian Economic Growth," *World Development* (January/February 1977):47–67. Moreover, one economist has shown that the direct effects of the oil shock on inflation were less significant than the indirect effects of higher import prices for goods (with embodied energy). See Marcelo Lara Resende, "Energy Prices and the Post Oil/Energy Crisis Brazilian Inflation: An Input-Output Study" (Ph.D. diss., Yale University, 1982).

[48] It should also be emphasized that Petrobrás's cherished monopoly over petroleum exploration was being challenged at precisely the same time. As the result of Petrobrás's failure to find as much oil in Brazil as was expected at the time of its creation (as well as subsequently), central decision makers reluctantly decided to offer multinational oil companies contracts for oil exploration in October 1975.

to assert their compcting claim. Given the impressive ability of these two organizations to defend their perceived interests, we should not be surprised if a potentially serious national commitment to alcohol energy gave rise to a struggle for productive control.

What *is* surprising, however, is the timing and intensity of this struggle. In 1975, one would have needed a fertile imagination to foresee an irreversible, large-scale, national commitment to alcohol fuel per se. For starters, the technology to produce alcohol-powered cars did not yet exist. Alcohol constituted less than 1 percent of the gasoline supply in 1975, well below the 20 percent limit imposed by the existing engine technology. Moreover, investments in autonomous distilleries were out of the question, since the real problem, after all, was what to do with the country's excess capacity to produce sugarcane. These factors together meant that the *Proálcool* of November 1975 would not yet break the traditional political bonds between sugar and alcohol.

Although a struggle for productive control tends to arise whenever a new commodity comes onto the scene, the intensity of the competition over the alcohol program in 1975 (when a significant commitment to alcohol energy was only a distant possibility) shows us how farsighted the carriers of public and private enterprise property rights can be in a system like the Brazilian one.

In its attempt to defuse the threat of an expanding alcohol sector, Petrobrás tried to gain the authority to regulate the alcohol marketing chain. For if Petrobrás became the sole legal purchaser of alcohol fuel, its ability to control the program would be formidable. To make its claim persuasive, Petrobrás attempted to capitalize on the legitimacy that its monopoly over the production and refining of liquid fuels had attained. This claim was directly opposed by the IAA, of course, which vaunted its historic authority to control the marketing of sugar and the previously subsidiary commodity, alcohol. Central decision makers were therefore faced with mutually exclusive jurisdictional claims. Both these claims were legitimate, in the sense that both Petrobrás and the IAA could reasonably argue that the autonomous control of the alcohol marketing chain was closely allied to its existing authority.

Once the idea of using manioc to produce alcohol was in the air, Petrobrás grasped the opportunity to promote this alternative source of alcohol. By doing so, Petrobrás asserted that the sugar producers did not have an exclusive right to control alcohol *production*. If this principle were established, Petrobrás would be in a stronger position to control alcohol policy in the future. This strategy would complement the state oil monopoly's efforts to obtain exclusive control over the alcohol marketing chain. The purpose of these two efforts was to reduce the likelihood that alcohol one day would become a major threat to Petrobrás's secure market for liquid fuels.

Faced with these competing claims, central decision makers followed the path of least resistance. President Geisel apparently used his personal influence, for example, to strike a balance between the claims made by the IAA and Petrobrás. Although they were unsuccessful in their bids to control the alcohol marketing chain, both contestants as well as the *usineiros* probably found the outcome satisfactory. None of these groups could feel that their fundamental interests would be in jeopardy, since the National Petroleum Council was granted limited authority. Moreover, the CNP was composed of high-ranking military officials who were known to have close ties with both central decision makers and Petrobrás. As for the role of Petrobrás in manioc production, this possibility was not excluded by the November 1975 decree.

The natural tendency for central decision makers to follow the path of least resistance in the face of competing claims for regulatory control was illustrated in the creation of the seven-member National Alcohol Council, which was given the authority to establish project selection criteria and set alcohol production targets. Authority over the financial component of the program was ostensibly granted to the Banco do Brasil.

The pattern of authority over other policy actions would unfold over the ensuing months and years. The liabilities of resolving the competition for regulatory and productive control in this way began to appear as early as 1976.

CHAPTER

**6**

# Phase One
# (1976–78): Alcohol
# Without *Proálcool*

Within four years of the presidential decree which created the
National Alcohol Program, alcohol production surpassed its
targeted goal for 1979 of 3 billion liters. In applauding this
outcome, some of the program's international observers
claimed that *Proálcool* was one of the military government's
greatest accomplishments since it assumed power more than
fifteen years earlier.[1] A closer examination of the events of
1975–79 indicates, however, that the rapid increase in alcohol

---

[1]"Easing Up in Brazil," *Christian Science Monitor*, 18 January 1980, taken
from *London Times*. Another article sounded the same general theme: "Fuel
grown on farmlands? That is not so fanciful as it sounds, as fuel-short Brazil
has been demonstrating for the past decade. . . . With the United States just
now beginning its own serious study of gasohol as a commercial supplement
to short fuel supplies, it could well look to Brazil for inspiration." See James
Nelson Goodsell, "Brazil Turns Sugar Cane into Sweet Oil Savings,"
*Christian Science Monitor*, 10 January 1980.

production had little to do with the government's program. Even in mid-1979, most people close to the issue claimed that "although there is alcohol in Brazil, *Proálcool* does not yet exist."[2]

## The Easy Phase of *Proálcool*

Once it had achieved some initial momentum, the alcohol program benefited from many technical, economic, and political characteristics that allowed Phase One to be the "easy" phase of this import substitution scheme. So long as alcohol production did not surpass 20 percent of the gasoline supply, automobile engines would not have to be modified, new alcohol pumps would not have to be installed at filling stations, and the existing storage and distribution infrastructure might be reasonably adequate. Moreover, since *Proálcool* was portrayed as a nationalistic response to OPEC price rises, it was imprudent for state officials to oppose the program publicly—at least while world sugar prices remained low. The opposition to *Proálcool*, therefore, particularly questioned the wisdom of expanding alcohol production to a level beyond the equivalent of 20 percent of the motor fuel supply. Moving beyond this level would require expensive modifications of the energy production, distribution, and consumption systems.[3]

While the question of the ultimate scale of *Proálcool* one day would have to be addressed, the automobile industry and certain government technocrats could maintain a wait-and-see attitude for some time to come. After driving a prototype alcohol-powered car as part of a publicity stunt in mid-1976, for example, Minister of Industry and Commerce Severo Gomes refused to promise that the government would try to move beyond the 20 percent limit.[4] Although Gomes was head of the ministry most ardently in favor of expanding production, it was clear that much progress had to be made before the

[2]Interview with Márcio Gotlib, Copersucar, São Paulo, July 1979.
[3]See Chapter 2.
[4]Aluísio Raimundo, "Custa da troca de gasolina por álcool," *O Estado de São Paulo*, 20 June 1976.

prospect of modifying automobile engines would become a serious issue.[5]

Meanwhile, the automobile industry was quietly supportive of the alcohol program. Although the industry did not want to invest large sums of capital to retool their factories without an assurance of supply, automakers began to conduct technical research on alcohol engines.[6] As early as August 1976, General Motors, Ford, and Volkswagen announced that there were no major technological barriers to the production of these special engines.[7] Privately, however, automobile producers remained extremely skeptical of the alcohol program.[8] At that time, alcohol constituted less than 1.2 percent of the gasoline supply, while in 1959 it had surpassed 8 percent even without an alcohol program.[9] In mid-1977, the president of ANFAVEA, the automobile producers' association, asked the government to continue the alcohol program at least until a constant proportion could be added to the gasoline supply across the whole nation.[10]

## Coalition Building in State Politics: 1976–78

### *Otimistas* and *Negativistas*

Actors in the policy formulation debate and program implementation process can be separated, in a general way, into two

[5]"Volks mostra autos com motor a álcool," *O Estado de São Paulo*, 22 September 1976.

[6]"Como tornar viável o Proálcool?" *Jornal da Tarde*, 1 June 1977.

[7]"Álcool: defendida a adição padronizada," *O Estado de São Paulo*, 5 August 1976. See also "Volks mostra autos com motor a álcool."

[8]Interview with Georg Pischinger, Volkswagen do Brasil, S.A., São Paulo, August 1979.

[9]"Morosidade no Programa do Álcool," *O Estado de São Paulo*, 26 April 1977.

[10]"Álcool: ANFAVEA pede continuidade do Plano," *O Estado de São Paulo*, 27 May 1977. ANFAVEA is the acronym for the Associação Nacional dos Fabricantes de Veículos Automotores. This group is a private association rather than a federation or syndicate sanctioned by the state as part of its corporatist organization. Such private organizations have gained prominence in the representation of interests in the Brazilian political system.

groups: the *otimistas* and the *negativistas*. The former included President Geisel, the Ministry of Industry and Commerce (MIC), the sugar interests, and the few entrepreneurs who quickly received permission to construct new autonomous distilleries.[11] The *negativistas* included principally the minister of mines and energy, Shigeaki Ueki, Petrobrás, and financial bureaucracies such as the Ministry of Finance, the Central Bank, and the Banco do Brasil. This second coalition did not hold sway in the interministerial Council for Economic Development (CDE), which continued to set certain goals for *Proálcool*. Nevertheless, in pursuing their institutional missions during the policy implementation phase, the *negativistas* slowed down *Proálcool* considerably.

It would be misleading to suggest that the policy positions of the *otimistas* and *negativistas* were determined exclusively by institutional interests. Indeed, much uncertainty about the economic attractiveness of the alcohol option pervaded the public and private debates. While benefit-cost analyses such as that presented in Chapter 2 were apparently not widely conducted,[12] some government technocrats doubted that alcohol production would be economically efficient in the long run. One well-placed observer suggested to me strongly in 1979 that alcohol, from an economic point of view, had always been an unsettled question. Both the *otimistas* and *negativistas* could therefore bring powerful opposing arguments to policy-making discussions.[13]

[11]The key figure among these entrepreneurs was Lamartine Navarro, Jr., a construction consultant, who received early permission from the National Alcohol Council (CNAl) to build an autonomous distillery complex in western São Paulo state. Lamartine Navarro later emerged as an important private spokesperson for the *otimistas*.

[12]A Brazilian representative at the annual Alcohol Fuels Technology International Symposium in 1979 declared: "The decision to go to alcohol is political, not technical. I have heard many studies about costs and economy, but we did not do those studies. We just went ahead and did it." See Charles Petit, "Alcohol Fuel Is Here," *San Francisco Chronicle*, 31 May 1979, p. 1.

[13]Interview with Ruy Miller Paiva, agricultural economist, IPEA, Rio de Janeiro, September 1979.

*Petrobrás*

Two of the most vocal *negativistas* were Shigeaki Ueki, the minister of mines and energy, and Petrobrás. That Ueki and Petrobrás took the same position is not surprising. Although Petrobrás is officially subsumed under the Ministry of Mines and Energy (MME), it is often acknowledged that the direction of influence operates in reverse. The state petroleum company is considered to be one of the most powerful entities in Brazil, one which can surely rival any government bureaucracy. Petrobrás is the largest corporation, public or private, operating in Brazil, and it is one of the world's fifty largest firms. An autonomous resource base and legal monopoly over the liquid fuels sector have given Petrobrás considerable influence over government policy in the energy domain.

In the early stages of *Proálcool*, Petrobrás officially supported the exploration of the alcohol alternative. The president of Petrobrás, General Araken de Oliveira, announced in June 1976 that "the potentialities and infrastructure of our company allow us to participate in the National Alcohol Program in a large way."[14] More specifically, the company decided to construct a pioneering alcohol distillery in Minas Gerais using manioc as its raw material. As we have seen, this decision was motivated principally by the firm's desire to maintain control over the liquid fuels sector. The manioc grown at the Minas Gerais project, however, became infected with a disease that sometimes occurs when the crop is cultivated on plantations. (Manioc is traditionally grown by independent planters on small farms rather than on large-scale plantations.)[15] The size of the Minas project was temporarily reduced, and Petrobrás's poor performance gave many the impression that the company had little interest in the alcohol program. In order to improve the firm's image, the Petrobrás

[14]Aluísio Raimundo, "Custa da troca de gasolina por álcool."
[15]Nira Silva, "Proálcool, uma ameaça a estrutura da Petrobrás," *Diário Comércio e Indústria*, 6 June 1978.

project was later revived using manioc supplied by small farmers near the distillery.

As alcohol production increased in 1976–78, *Proálcool* quickly lost its innocence. In June 1978, Petrobrás Vice President Paulo Vieira Belotti claimed that the alcohol program was threatening the company's refining structure. By then it had become apparent that alcohol production would soon create a gasoline surplus if alternatives for diesel and industrial fuel oil were not developed or refinery cracking ratios were not modified. The vice president claimed that Petrobrás's refinery cracking ratios were relatively inflexible in the short run and that alterations in refinery structures would be technically complicated and unduly expensive. Belotti asserted, moreover, that Brazil should not rely on the international gasoline market to realize its foreign exchange earnings from alcohol production.[16] Two months later, Belotti also argued that it was more expensive to produce alcohol than gasoline.[17]

There was a clear consensus among observers of the first phase of the alcohol program that Petrobrás had been a primary cause of *Proálcool*'s early delays. Some of the program's supporters interviewed in 1979 even referred to the giant enterprise as "enemy number one." Beyond issuing statements such as those mentioned above, it is not clear what specific actions Petrobrás took to block the progress of *Proálcool*. Petrobrás appears to have developed its *negativista* reputation principally for its sins of omission. By failing to give the program its support, Petrobrás condemned *Proálcool* to an uphill battle. An August 1978 statement by Petrobrás Vice President Belotti exemplifies the company's apparent attitude:[18]

[16]Ibid.

[17]Fatima Belchior, "Álcool gera controvérsias," *Folha de São Paulo*, 23 August 1978.

[18]Belotti is said by those who know him to have been a supporter of the alcohol program since its beginning. He was, in fact, involved in the development of the 1975 decree. But Belotti's subsequent move to Petrobrás

Petrobrás does not have to take any initiative whatsoever in the program, because it was not cited in the National Alcohol Program except as a purchaser of alcohol. *Proálcool* does not bother [*incômoda*] the company. . . . If alcohol is developed intensely, it will bother automobile owners much more, since they will have to adapt their motors to alcohol.[19]

### The Energy/Planning Coalition

The minister of mines and energy, Shigeaki Ueki, joined Petrobrás's efforts to keep *Proálcool* closely identified with the sugar industry. Ueki did so by downplaying the value of the alcohol option for Brazil's long-run energy mix. Ueki allied himself with Finance Minister Mario Henrique Simonsen to urge that alcohol be produced only when world sugar prices were low.[20] In 1977, the two ministers argued that it would become more profitable to export sugar than to produce alcohol if the world price of sugar reached $US 250 per metric ton (11 cents per pound). Ueki and Simonsen used their arguments to convince the informed public that *Proálcool* was a temporary measure to protect the sugar industry.

While sugar exports were seen as the first priority, Ueki and Simonsen said that the petrochemical industry should receive second priority in the allocation of alcohol. Motor fuel use, they argued, should receive only third priority. In making these recommendations, the two ministers claimed that they were advancing a "purely" economic argument. According to Finance Minister Simonsen:

We have already learned how to live with the oil crisis. And after 1980, the domestic production of petroleum will

apparently constrained the way in which he could express himself in the alcohol debate. One observer also mentioned that the same statement can be applied to Shigeaki Ueki, at the time minister of mines and energy.

[19]Belchior, "Álcool gera controvérsias."

[20]Milano Lopes, "Álcool carburante é agora 3? prioridade," *O Estado de São Paulo*, 4 December 1977.

inevitably increase, allowing petroleum imports to begin their declining phase. Thus, let's no longer talk about alcohol for motor fuel.[21]

Several days later, the prestigious *Estado de São Paulo* and the *Jornal da Tarde* blasted Ueki and Simonsen for their announcements:

With the utmost tranquility, the ministers of finance and mines and energy have launched a veritable torpedo against the National Alcohol Program.[22]

The *Jornal da Tarde* charged that Ueki and Simonsen were wrong to criticize the validity of the program, since it had been under way for several years. Not only had *Proálcool* generated much enthusiasm, but many public and private resources had already been committed to increase the production of alcohol. The *Estado* further charged that a national energy policy did not yet exist.[23] That interministerial conflict had reached an extremely high level was thus made vividly clear by the position of the two state officials.[24]

### CDE, CNAl, IAA, and the Financial Bureaucracy

Meanwhile, many of the distillery project proposals received by the IAA were eventually approved by the National Alcohol Council (CNAl). The task of CNAl was to select projects that were technically sound and met the council's objectives for the alcohol program. Although most projects were approved only

[21] Ibid.

[22] "A estranha ciclotimia dos nossos ministros," *Jornal da Tarde*, 6 December 1977.

[23] "Afinal, qual é a nossa política energética?" *O Estado de São Paulo*, 8 December 1977.

[24] In July 1978, Ueki reasserted his belief that Brazil should return to the world sugar market if prices increased. See Nira Silva, "Proálcool: definição no próximo governo," *Diário Comércio e Indústria*, 14 July 1978.

after great delays, the council accepted approximately 200 proposals between 1976 and 1978.[25]

The CNAl had no power over the actual financing of distillery expansion projects. Entrepreneurs needed to submit a second, financial proposal to the Banco do Brasil in order to receive loans at subsidized rates. According to Alberto Policaro, the Banco do Brasil's superintendent of credit for São Paulo, three factors were critical to the bank's financial evaluation.[26] The borrower had to be creditworthy, have assets valued at 125 percent of the loan (for the collateral or *guarantia*), and demonstrate that the specific project would be privately profitable at a rate acceptable to the bank. Once the Banco do Brasil approved a project, the proposal was then forwarded to the Central Bank for final approval.

Despite pressure from President Geisel and the CDE to speed *Proálcool* along, the Banco do Brasil and the Central Bank managed to block implementation of the financing plan. When the Banco do Brasil/Central Bank bottleneck first became apparent in October 1976, only eight projects had received financing out of the thirty-two approved by CNAl. To maintain confidence in the program, the CDE insisted publicly that *Proálcool* would be accelerated.[27] According to press accounts, at the tense CDE meeting called to deal with this problem, President Geisel at times raised his voice at the Banco do Brasil president, who was invited to attend.[28] Bank President Angelo Calmon de Sá explained that his institution was in no way obligated to give immediate attention to the alcohol projects. Financial analysis, he insisted, demanded time.[29] After the heated meeting, Planning Minister Reis Velloso announced

[25]Conselho Nacional de Pesquisas Tecnológicas (CNPq), "Avaliação Tecnológica do Álcool Etílico: Versão Preliminar," 1978, p. 98.

[26]Interview with Alberto Policaro, Banco do Brasil, São Paulo, August 1979.

[27]"Velloso diz que Plano do Álcool vai ser dinaminizado," *O Estado de São Paulo*, 28 October 1976.

[28]"Geisel está irritado com o atraso no Programa do Álcool como combustível. E decidiu apressá-lo," *Jornal da Tarde*, 28 October 1976.

[29]"Velloso diz que Plano do Álcool vai ser dinaminizado."

that collateral requirements would be eased and projects pending action would receive financing by the end of the year.[30]

During 1977, the Banco do Brasil approved projects at a more rapid rate, but still behind that of the CNAl. By May, some twenty-eight projects had been approved for financing out of the 112 passed onto the bank by CNAl.[31] The *Estado de São Paulo* claimed in June that the Banco do Brasil had approved only Cr$ 3 billion of the Cr$ 12 billion needed to finance projects certified by CNAl.[32] At the end of November 1977, however, the *Gazeta Mercantil* reported that only Cr$ 1.15 billion had been released by the bank, representing little more than 10 percent of the funding needed to reach the 1980 production goal.[33] Funding approvals by the Banco do Brasil and the Central Bank continued to lag far behind project approvals made by CNAl during 1978 and 1979 as well.

Why were the government's financial agencies unwilling to support the alcohol program fully? According to individuals close to the program, one reason was that the Banco do Brasil wanted to avoid issuing "bad loans." If a project became privately unprofitable and the entrepreneur defaulted on the loan, the Banco do Brasil would suffer the loss. Like any commercial enterprise, the bank, though state-owned, sought to minimize its risk for a given rate of return.

To the bankers, financing distilleries appeared to be far from a riskless business proposition. During the 1973–75 period of soaring world sugar prices, *usineiros* borrowed large sums of money from the Special Export Fund of the IAA for the modernization and expansion of plantations and mills. Since the industry remained deeply in debt, world sugar prices were

[30]Ibid.
[31]"Morosidade no Programa do Álcool," *O Estado de São Paulo*, 26 April 1977.
[32]"O indefinido Plano Nacional do Álcool," *O Estado de São Paulo*, 14 June 1977.
[33]"A confiança no Proálcool persiste," *Gazeta Mercantil*, 12 October 1977.

depressed, and the government's long-term commitment to the alcohol program seemed dubious, the Banco do Brasil had an incentive to exercise caution.[34]

There were reports in April 1978 that the Banco do Brasil had suspended its financing of agricultural projects associated with *Proálcool*. Angelo Calmon de Sá, who had become the minister of industry and commerce, explained that the bank, upon reaching its limit of agricultural financing, decided not to allocate funds for the expansion of sugarcane production.[35] At the same time, an interministerial working group recommended that sugarcane production in the Northeast increase at a slower rate and asked the Banco do Brasil and the IAA to restrict credit to that end.[36]

The Central Bank also gave the Banco do Brasil an incentive to approve *Proálcool* projects sparingly. In the early days of the program, the Central Bank refused to refinance the loans that the Banco do Brasil had already approved. As a result, the state commercial bank had to cover the projects with its own resources. In 1979, the Banco do Brasil's São Paulo credit superintendent, Alberto Policaro, noted that this conflict had been resolved by adapting project evaluation criteria to those of the Central Bank.[37]

The policy actions of the Central Bank, in turn, derived from its attempt to combat inflation:

> There is a tendency for the Central Bank to harden the criteria for project approval, which appears to be a maneuver to retard the liberation of resources within a broader policy of reducing the rate of growth of the money supply and inflation.[38]

[34]See Paulo Cesar de Araujo, "Dívida agrícola já preocupa o Governo," *O Estado de São Paulo*, 19 August 1977.

[35]Severino de Araujo Goes, "Calmon de Sá e o Proálcool," *Gazeta Mercantil*, 19 April 1978.

[36]"As dívidas do açúcar," *Gazeta Mercantil*, 19 April 1978.

[37]Interview with Alberto Policaro.

[38]CNPq, "Avaliação Tecnológica do Álcool Etílico."

That *Proálcool* financing was limited by the government's overall efforts to restrict credit was in evidence as early as mid-1977.[39] To impede credit approvals, numerous bureaucratic hurdles were erected. For example, the Banco do Brasil made the format of proposals demonstrating the financial validity of a given project quite distinct from that submitted to CNAl. Most entrepreneurs were apparently unfamiliar with the application procedure, and the bank took the opportunity to reject proposals that did not provide the required information.[40] Moreover, the bank's technocrats analyzed most proposals at an extremely slow pace. Often the pace of evaluation was sufficiently slow to invalidate the proposal itself: After several months, inflation had so distorted the analysis that the proposal had to be completely recalculated.[41] Entrepreneurs therefore insisted on submitting identical proposals to CNAl and the Banco do Brasil at the same time. As of mid-1979, these demands had not been met.[42]

## Outcome of the Affair

### *Production: 1976–78*

During Geisel's presidency, the CDE failed to determine whether alcohol production should be considered a long-run energy strategy or a short-run measure to protect the sugar industry during the years of low world sugar prices.[43] In some

[39]"Política monetária atrasa o Proálcool," *O Estado de São Paulo*, 17 August 1977. It is likely that the Central Bank's decision to harden the approval criteria for *Proálcool* was also motivated by the bank's assessment of the economic attractiveness of the alcohol option.

[40]Interview with Lázaro Lisboa, Banco do Brasil, S.A., São Paulo, August 1979.

[41]Ibid.

[42]See the request by Copersucar President Jorge Wolney Atalla for a *"projeto único"* in "Política monetária atrasa o Proálcool." That the demand had been made for years was reiterated by Copersucar executive Marco Gotlib in an interview, São Paulo, July 1979.

[43]See "Produção de açúcar ou de álcool," *O Estado de São Paulo*, 3 May 1977.

respects, the stalemate over this question did not matter. World sugar prices remained extremely low during the 1976–78 period, and exports continued to be unprofitable for the nation. The CDE, under President Geisel's leadership, therefore agreed periodically to increase the amount of sugarcane that could be converted directly into alcohol.

President Geisel himself issued the first of these decisions in May 1977. Producers were thereby authorized to convert 10 million metric tons of sugarcane into alcohol.[44] This decision permitted production to increase by more than 600 million liters above the already ambitious target for the year.[45] In October 1977, the *Gazeta Mercantil* reported that the forthcoming year's production would likely reach 1.6 billion liters, two and one-half times the 1976 level, and an amount nearly sufficient to supplement the gasoline supply by 10 percent.[46] Alcohol production, unlike *Proálcool*, was progressing according to plan.

Since world sugar prices remained low, the CDE again doubled the amount of sugarcane that could be legally transformed into alcohol during the 1978–79 harvest. Angelo Calmon de Sá, the minister of industry and commerce, predicted that this increase would enable alcohol production in 1978–79 to reach nearly 2.5 billion liters.[47] These moves demonstrated that President Geisel and his allies could influence the pace of alcohol production so long as world sugar prices remained low and sugarcane abundant.

The response of alcohol producers to the government's authorizations was resounding. During the 1977–78 harvest year, alcohol production doubled, and it then nearly doubled again during the following year.[48] By the end of 1978, alcohol

[44]"Geisel aprova nova política para o açúcar e o álcool," *O Estado de São Paulo*, 6 May 1977.

[45]"A confiança no Proálcool persiste."

[46]Ibid.

[47]"Álcool terá mais matéria-prima," *Gazeta Mercantil*, 12 May 1978.

[48]"Um grande aumento na produção de álcool," *Gazeta Mercantil*, 3 October 1978. According to the CENAL report, *Proálcool, Relatório Anual 1980* (Brasília: CENAL, 1981), alcohol production reached (in billions of

production had managed to reach significant levels, despite the obstacles erected by the Banco do Brasil and the Central Bank. Most of the increases were produced in distilleries annexed to sugar mills in São Paulo state. Although some of these mills and distilleries had been in place for years, many were financed by *usineiros* in anticipation of government financing. In fact, the *Gazeta Mercantil* reported at the end of 1977 that some twenty projects had already been in operation when *Proálcool* funds came through.[49]

### The National Alcohol Problem: 1978

By the second half of 1978, however, the National Alcohol Program began to be called the "National Alcohol Problem."[50] As distilleries produced increasing quantities of alcohol, the storage and distribution system became severely strained. Shortages of storage tanks, transportation infrastructure, and facilities to mix alcohol with gasoline became evident. The problem was particularly acute in the Northeast, where production had outstripped consumption.[51] At the same time, it was reported that alcohol production was not leading to the anticipated savings of foreign exchange, since equivalent amounts of crude oil were still being imported in order to produce nongasoline petroleum derivatives.[52] In the midst of these newly publicized problems, the *Estado de São Paulo* cautioned that the CDE's plan to double production was not viable.[53]

---

liters per harvest year): 1975–76, 0.6; 1976–77, 0.7; 1977–78, 1.5; 1978–79, 2.5; 1979–80, 3.4.

[49]José Roberto de Alencar, "Muito álcool, apesar do atraso," *Gazeta Mercantil*, 12 October 1977.

[50]"Polêmica: Programa (ou Problema?) Nacional do Álcool," *Jornal da Tarde*, 1 June 1978.

[51]"Sobra gasolina: que fazer do álcool?," *Diário Comércio e Indústria*, 1 June 1978.

[52]Ibid.

[53]"Inviável a meta aprovada para o álcool," *O Estado de São Paulo*, 26 May 1978.

By the end of 1978, the National Alcohol Program was rapidly approaching a crossroad. Without significant action to eliminate the bottlenecks created by the increasing production of alcohol, the government would have little choice but to decelerate the program. To move forward, major infrastructural investments would have to be made, automobile companies would have to produce alcohol-powered cars, and gasoline distributors would have to convert some of their pumps to pure alcohol. Moreover, if incremental alcohol production was to reduce petroleum imports, Petrobrás would have to change its refinery practices and, ultimately, its refining structures.

By mid-1978, it became clear that the future of the alcohol program would not be resolved by President Geisel.[54] The choice which would confront President Geisel's successor, General João Batista Figueiredo, would not be an easy one since there was substantial resistance to a deeper commitment to *Proálcool*. First, Petrobrás would surely oppose any government scheme that could ultimately diminish its control of the liquid fuels sector. With its established monopoly and impressive financial resources, Petrobrás and its managers had a great deal to lose. The state enterprise would not yield easily to any attempt to reduce its standing.

Second, *usineiros* could not necessarily be counted upon to support a vigorous expansion of *Proálcool*. The industry had always tried to maintain the sugar-alcohol identification, and its productive control of both sectors could be threatened by the development of autonomous distilleries. Third, the financial bureaucracy appeared unenthusiastic about allocating funds for such a venture. Fourth, the future success of *Proálcool* depended on the willingness of automobile manufacturers to produce alcohol-powered cars. Although the industry had been supportive of the first phase of the program, the government might be forced to cajole the manufacturers to produce the new alcohol engines.

[54]Silva, "Proálcool: definição no próximo governo."

Finally, certain government agencies continued to call attention to the seemingly forgotten social objectives of *Proálcool*. The stated income distribution goal was clearly being subordinated to other objectives during implementation of the program. More than 80 percent of production was taking place in São Paulo state, few manioc projects had been approved by CNAl, and the idea of constructing minidistilleries was not being promoted at all. While most agencies were not enthusiastic about pursuing the income redistribution objectives, the Ministry of Agriculture and the National Council of Technological Research (CNPq) continued to press the issue.[55]

Thus, as presidential-designate João Batista Figueiredo planned his administration's policies, observers wondered whether the program would be vigorously promoted or simply dropped. The wait-and-see game had begun.

### Explaining the 1976–78 Period

From haggling over the terms of the November 1975 decree, the mutual adjustment process between state officials soon turned to what would normally be labeled "policy implementation." But policy implementation is a gross misnomer for a good part of the interaction among these officials during the 1976–78 period. As we have seen, the original decree contained a hodgepodge of partly compatible and partly competing goals, such as protecting the sugar industry, producing a gasoline substitute, expanding the capital goods sector, redistributing income, and so on. Only one issue was firmly settled by the November 1975 plan: There would be established a formal alcohol program in order to encourage the conversion of substantially greater quantities of sugarcane into anhydrous alcohol. Many more questions, however, were left unanswered by the open-ended decree: Would alcohol eventually play a significant role in the liquid fuels sector?

[55]Marizete Mundim, "O futuro do Proálcool divide os ministros," *Folha de São Paulo*, 23 December 1978.

Would Petrobrás succeed in defusing the alcohol threat? Would alcohol be produced principally from sugarcane or from manioc? Having postponed the resolution of the competition and conflict which underlay these issues, state officials during the policy implementation phase struggled over the execution of a temporary expedient to bolster the sugar industry *as well as* over the future role of alcohol production in the Brazilian political economy.

Among the key issues contested through policy implementation was productive control. The Petrobrás investment in manioc production at their new plantation in Minas Gerais provides a priceless example of how an ostensible act of policy implementation was essentially a tactic to defend vigorously what was left of this state enterprise's legal monopoly in the liquid fuels sector. What is further notable is that, in so doing, Petrobrás radically transfigured the original idea of using manioc for alcohol production. Manioc, it will be recalled, was initially proposed by the Ministry of Agriculture in order to benefit small farmers in relatively disadvantaged regions. Although the Petrobrás practice of producing manioc on plantations proved agronomically mistaken, the key point is that manioc also became infected with the struggle over public and private enterprise property rights as well as over the secondary issue of Petrobrás's particular zone of productive control.

Disputes over the long-range future of the alcohol program similarly helped to create the Banco do Brasil/Central Bank bottleneck. As evidenced by the subsequent priority granted to *Proálcool* in 1980–81, the extensive delays in approving credits during 1976–78 cannot be attributed to bureaucratic rigidity alone. On the contrary, the great bureaucratic care bestowed on proposals for subsidized credit helped justify the apparent decision by high-ranking officials within the state financial system to slow down the alcohol program.

Since these actions were not explicitly justified in public, we must infer why the decision to go slow was made. One reason may have been the economic inefficiency of anhydrous alcohol as a gasoline substitute. The categorical remark, "let's no longer talk about alcohol for motor fuel," made in 1977 by Finance Minister Simonsen, together with the statement that sugar exports would become profitable as soon as world prices reached $US 0.11 per pound, suggests that efficiency concerns did come into play.

Aside from long-term efficiency considerations, short-term monetary management was also at issue. Throughout the late 1970s, credit subsidies were increasingly funded by creating money rather than by raising taxes or issuing public debt. At the same time, a growing percentage of agricultural credit was being provided by the Banco do Brasil instead of private commercial banks.[56] These trends worried monetary authorities, especially since they were also faced with 40 percent inflation and a growing trade deficit. Once they began to follow a more restrictive policy in 1977–78, monetary authorities were unenthusiastic about granting special treatment for a new source of credit demand. Since the primary mission of the Central Bank was to achieve macroeconomic stability, this institution could resist central decision makers' specific goals for the alcohol program with relative ease. Moreover, given the macroeconomic situation, the indebtedness of the *usineiros*, and the Central Bank's reticence to refinance loans for alcohol distilleries, the Banco do Brasil's delays could have been expected. The elaborately slow process of project evaluation could be further defended as prudent for such a quasi-commercial financial institution. It is also reasonable to suspect that the bank's resistance to President Geisel's personal intervention, even to his raised voice, was buoyed by the fact that alcohol was being produced without *Proálcool*.

Competition and conflict over alcohol production were thus accentuated by its protean nature as both a costly sugar industry bailout scheme and a potentially major source of

[56]For background, see João do Carmo Oliveira and Roberto Marcos da Silva Montezano, "Os limites das fontes de financiamento à agricultura no Brasil," *Estudos Econômicos* (August 1982):139–59.

liquid fuel. These struggles can be partly explained as an attempt to reduce the idea of alcohol production to its historical profile. If alcohol remained clearly subsidiary to sugar, the property rights of Petrobrás would be considerably less attenuated by *Proálcool*. Higher world sugar prices would simply eliminate this particular threat.[57] From his remarks we can infer that Mario Henrique Simonsen, another member of the *negativista* alliance, probably would have approved of Phase One—had he been sure that the current substitutability of sugar and alcohol in production and alcohol and gasoline in consumption would be forever preserved. If the ground had been less fertile for eventually turning alcohol into something spectacular—a possibility noted in Chapter 5—neither the struggle over authority nor that over policy would have been so intense.

As a sugar industry bailout scheme, alcohol was an old, simple, and small issue area. "Old" because the existing structure of authority could easily handle the temporarily increased conversion of sugarcane into alcohol. "Simple" because increased alcohol production did not involve a wide range of tightly coupled policy actions. "Small" because the amount of credit needed to finance expansions of annexed distilleries was relatively modest, despite an increasingly restrictive monetary policy in 1977–78. If conflict had been limited by the assurance that alcohol would remain an old, simple, and small issue area, central decision makers could have more easily controlled the policy-making process.

President Geisel did achieve limited control over the implementation of the alcohol program. By making it difficult for state agencies to oppose the idea of *Proálcool*, for instance, some projects eventually had to be approved by CNAl, the Banco do Brasil, and the Central Bank. Petrobrás, moreover, could not refuse to sell gasohol at its retail stations. Above all,

---

[57]However, the threat posed by top authorities' insistence that risk contracts for petroleum exploration be offered to multinationals clearly remained.

the Council for Economic Development could not oppose plans to raise the ceilings on the direct conversion of sugarcane into alcohol.

Limited central control over policy-making translated into substantial central control over alcohol production and private investments in distilleries. Why this turn of events is not paradoxical was explained in Chapter 3. So long as the conversion of sugarcane into alcohol was permitted during the period of low world sugar prices, the *usineiros* had every incentive to invest in annexed distilleries and raise alcohol production markedly from its minuscule base.

The equilibrium relationship between private investment, current policy, and policy expectations that prevailed during Phase One could be disturbed only by changes in the variables exogenous to the model presented in Chapter 4. By the end of 1978, for example, it was clear that the rapid disappearance of excess capacity in the sugar industry and in the marketing and consumption system would soon feed back upon the issue area's age, size, and complexity. As for enhanced conflict resolution, only clairvoyant observers, foreseeing the Iranian Revolution, might have expected the task environment to shift sufficiently for the *negativistas'* policy actions to be constrained. When the thin consensus over *Proálcool* became deeply frayed at the end of 1978, some groups even expected the whole idea of alcohol energy to be dropped by the incoming president. They were wrong.

CHAPTER

# 7

# Phase Two (1979):
# The New *Proálcool?*

In December 1978, the Iranian Revolution pushed the energy issue to the top of the new administration's policy agenda.[1] Until this new crisis, many government officials had regarded the world price of oil as stable and reduced the urgency of efforts to develop alternative energy options.[2] Since Iran had been the second largest supplier of petroleum to Brazil, government leaders were rapidly sensitized to the new political situation.[3] "Iran" therefore set in motion several processes that

[1]OPEC prices climbed 14.5 percent in December. See "Solução da Petrobrás para o problema: álcool," *Jornal da Tarde*, 23 December 1978.

[2]Over the preceding three years, the real price of OPEC oil had declined due to U.S. inflation and expanded Saudi Arabian oil production. See Robert Stobaugh and Daniel Yergin, "Energy: An Emergency Telescoped," *Foreign Affairs: America and the World 1979* (1980).

[3]"O álcool também no óleo diesel," *Gazeta Mercantil*, 31 January 1979.

brought the notion of a major alcohol program closer to reality.

## The Iranian Shock and Its Aftermath

### *A New Player: The Automobile Industry*

Above all, the Iranian Revolution helped to transform the relationship between the automobile industry and the government with respect to the alcohol issue. Automobile manufacturers seized upon the opportunities presented by the conjuncture of the Iranian crisis and the formation of the Figueiredo government to propel the alcohol program forward. Although the industry had been publicly supportive of the program during Phase One, executives insisted that alcohol-powered cars would not be produced until the supply of alcohol was assured. In the meantime, the automakers began to invest in the research and development of alcohol engines.[4]

During Phase One, auto executives seriously doubted that the government would ever implement the second phase of *Proálcool*. Delays in implementing the program did little to bolster the industry's confidence that the government's idealistic goals would be met. In fact, the enormous gap between the actual pace of the program and the "dreams" of technocrats such as Walter Bautista Vidal led many industry leaders to believe that *Proálcool* was nothing more than "Latin talk." Vidal, the official in charge of the Secretariat of Industrial Technology (an agency within the Ministry of Industry and Commerce), chose to promote the program so ardently that he gained a reputation among auto producers as a "clown."[5]

[4]Volkswagen could draw upon their experience producing alcohol engines during World War II. Interview with Georg Pischinger, Volkswagen do Brasil, São Paulo, July 1979.

[5]See, for example, the way in which Vidal characterized the alcohol program in "Primeira fase do programa está encerrada, afirma Batista [*sic*] Vidal," *Gazeta Mercantil*, 11 October 1978. Vidal claims to have taken on the

Without credibility, the government could hardly assure automakers that the alcohol fuel supply would meet the demand created by alcohol-powered cars.

The auto industry began to take the prospect of a significant alcohol program seriously in 1978. Due primarily to President Geisel's authorizations for the 1977–78 harvest, alcohol production had increased markedly by mid-1978. This trend did more to convince auto producers that alcohol could become a major substitute for gasoline than did any promise by government officials.

The importance of the automobile industry's support cannot be overestimated. Most of Brazil's goods move by truck, in part because the government has constructed highways rather than railroads to achieve national integration—the paved road system doubled between 1968 and 1974 alone.[6] Created in the late 1950s as part of the country's import substitution strategy, the automobile industry soon became a principal source of economic growth. As I emphasized in Chapter 4, the automobile later emerged as *the* symbol of the Brazilian economic miracle and a cherished status symbol in society.[7] With huge infusions of foreign investment from Europe and the United States, the output of the industry doubled between 1964 and 1970 and doubled again between 1970 and 1974.[8] Apart from

---

role of the dreamer in order to counteract the overly pessimistic pronouncements of the *negativistas* (interview with Walter Bautista Vidal, Stanford, California, May 1980). Once again, it is evident that care must be taken in ascribing the characteristics of public roles to the individuals who play those roles (see note 18 in Chapter 6). The observed behavior thus primarily reflects structural features of the political system rather than the peculiarities of the individuals involved.

[6]Instituto Brasileiro de Geografia e Estatística, *Sinopse Estatística do Brasil, 1977*, p. 406.

[7]One observer illustrated this point to me by explaining that his maid owns a Volkswagen beetle even though she has only one day off per week. On that day, she drives around São Paulo.

[8]James Kurth, "The Political Consequences of the Product Cycle: Industrial History and Political Outcomes," *International Organization* (Winter 1979):31.

its contribution to national income, the automobile industry, directly and indirectly, generates many jobs.[9]

An initial understanding between the automobile industry and the government was reached in August 1978, several months *before* the Iranian crisis. After a three-hour meeting, company presidents and Industry and Commerce Minister Angelo Calmon de Sá announced that alcohol-powered cars would constitute one-sixth of the industry's production in 1982.[10] Several commissions were established at the same time to accelerate the implementation of Phase Two.[11] The government/industry agreement suggests that by mid-1978 automobile producers viewed this phase as likely to be in the long-run interests of their businesses. A few weeks later, Fiat and Volkswagen announced that production could begin in less than two years.[12] At the same time, however, IAA President Amaury Santos Fassy stated publicly that alcohol production could not meet the increased fuel demand that would be generated by a fleet of alcohol-powered cars. Fassy also claimed that alcohol production probably would not reach 20 percent of the motor fuel supply until 1982.[13] Thus, many ambiguities persisted despite the government/industry agreement.

### *The Presidential Succession: 1978–79*

The enduring conflict between the Ministry of Mines and Energy (MME) and the Ministry of Industry and Commerce

[9]The Volkswagen plant in São Bernardo do Campo employed 40,000 people before the 1981 layoffs and is the largest Volkswagen factory in the world. The Brazilian company is the largest subsidiary of Volkswagen (Germany). Interview with Georg Pischinger.

[10]"Um sexto dos carros a álcool até 1982," *Folha de São Paulo*, 25 August 1978.

[11]Ibid.

[12]Pedro Lobato, "Pronto o Fiat-Álcool," *Gazeta Mercantil*, 4 September 1978; see also "A era do álcool já está aí, mas seus automóveis só daqui a dois anos," *Jornal do Brasil*, 5 September 1978.

[13]Marcia Cristina Barros, "Entraves para o carro a álcool," *Gazeta Mercantil*, 5 September 1978.

(MIC) surfaced once again at the first Brazilian energy congress in mid-December 1978. At the meeting, MME Minister Shigeaki Ueki announced that alcohol exports would take priority over internal consumption because they would enable Brazil to import two barrels of petroleum for every barrel of alcohol sold on the world market.[14] Ueki also informed the audience that 100 million liters of alcohol had already been sold to Europe at an undisclosed price.[15] MIC Minister Angelo Calmon de Sá strongly opposed the Ueki plan, charging that the alcohol program could not remain subject to "casual decisions" if Phase Two were to get under way.[16] At the same time, Calmon de Sá praised the automobile manufacturers for their willingness to produce alcohol engines.

In the climate of the Iranian-Revolution and the Geisel–Figueiredo transition, Ueki's announcement sharpened the conflict over the energy issue. The *Jornal da Tarde* published the following editorial in mid-December 1978:

> We are convinced that the first priority of the minister of mines and energy is the destruction of the National Alcohol Program, for this was not the first time that he introduced doubt and hesitation for all those who are ready to accelerate their investments to produce alcohol. With this, we are convinced that the national energy policy must begin to be coordinated by an organ that does not suffer from the paralyzing influences of the ministry and Petrobrás.[17]

On the other hand, Petrobrás Vice President Paulo Vieira Belotti announced his support for large-scale alcohol production as well as government subsidies for alcohol-powered

[14]"Prioridade para álcool é agora exportação, diz Ueki," *O Estado de São Paulo*, 13 December 1978.

[15]"Ueki nega ter mudado prioridade para álcool," *O Estado de São Paulo*, 14 December 1978.

[16]"Ueki e Calmon: dois destinos para o álcool," *Diário Comércio e Indústria*, 14 December 1978.

[17]"Programa nuclear e política energética," *Jornal da Tarde*, 14 December 1978.

cars.[18] Although such support probably did not pervade the Petrobrás establishment, Belotti's publicized remarks suggest that the events of December 1978 transformed the political environment within the state. The Ministry of Industry and Commerce, meanwhile, proposed that autonomous, rather than annexed, distilleries be given priority.[19] This step, if taken, would break the historical identification between sugar and alcohol production.

Policymakers moved cautiously during the first three months of 1979.[20] The ministers appointed by presidential-designate Figueiredo managed to reduce the appearance of conflict by working out certain accommodations with one another. Behind the scenes, the future ministers also conferred with respresentatives of the automobile industry. These discussions built confidence in the new administration's commitment to *Proálcool.* Automobile executives appreciated what they perceived to be the Figueiredo team's realistic approach to the alcohol program. Once the government's alcohol production targets were seen as credible, Volkswagen, the country's largest auto producer, announced in February 1979 that it would accelerate the development of alcohol-powered cars and set November of the same year as the target date for production.

Four policy actions bolstered the automobile industry's confidence as well as alcohol production. On 1 February 1979, the government increased slightly the price producers received

[18]"Belotti defende um preço subsidiado para o álcool," *Diário Comércio e Indústria,* 14 December 1978.

[19]"Uma nova orientação para o Plano do Álcool," *Diário Comércio e Indústria,* 21 December 1978.

[20]For example, proponents of the alcohol program asked Lamartine Navarro, one of the first operators of an autonomous distillery, to present a report on the economics of alcohol production from such a facility. In the report, Navarro argued that the government should establish clear definitions and objectives for the program and reduce the uncertainty that surrounded it. Otherwise, he argued, entrepreneurs would not enter the sector. See Lamartine Navarro, Jr., "Análise do Desenvolvimento do Plano Nacional do Álcool," São Paulo, January 1979.

for alcohol relative to sugar. The portion of a mill's capacity which could be legally used for alcohol production at annexed distilleries was increased by another 10 percent. A plan was announced to add alcohol to diesel fuel. Finally, Finance Minister Mario Henrique Simonsen asserted that sufficient financial resources would be allocated to accelerate the "rhythm" of alcohol production.[21] Although the specific resources had not been defined, the minister of industry and commerce assured the public that *Proálcool* would receive first priority in the government's credit budget.[22]

By early March 1979, the shape of the alcohol program under President Figueiredo became clearer. For example, it was announced that important responsibilities for *Proálcool* would be transfered to the Ministry of Mines and Energy. The MME was granted absolute control over planning the quantities, terms, and location for alcohol production, while the MIC retained only responsibility for the program's implementation.[23] This arrangement appeared to be awkward from the beginning, since alcohol policy affected the institutional interests of many state agencies.[24] The agreement did, however, indicate that some consensus favorable to *Proálcool* existed at the time of João Batista Figueiredo's inauguration on 15 March 1979.

In subsequent months, policymakers confronted issues triggered by the expansion of the alcohol program. A retail price for pure alcohol fuel had to be selected at a level that would encourage consumer purchases of alcohol-powered cars.[25] A plan for storage and distribution needed to be

[21]"Aumentado preço do álcool para produtor," *O Estado de São Paulo*, 1 February 1979.

[22]Ariosto Teixeira, "Mistura carburante diesel pode ter até 10% de álcool etílico," *Gazeta Mercantil*, 2 February 1979.

[23]"Proálcool passará para Minas e Energia," *O Estado de São Paulo*, 3 March 1979; "Proálcool: Secretaria Executiva," *O Estado de São Paulo*, 7 March 1979.

[24]"Uma missão difícil para o Ministro Camilo Penna," *O Estado de São Paulo*, 3 April 1979.

[25]"Proálcool: Secretaria Executiva."

developed and implemented to ensure that the alcohol produced reached the market. Alcohol pumps had to be installed
at filling stations. Subsidies would have to be created in order
to stimulate sales of alcohol-powered cars. Social issues
relating to the program would have to be faced, since it had
become increasingly apparent that *Proálcool* was concentrating
income rather than redistributing it.[26] Finally, an overall liquid
fuels policy had to be devised to ensure that alcohol production would actually reduce petroleum imports. But at the time
Jõao Figueiredo took office as president, his vision of an
overall Brazilian energy strategy did not appear to be particularly detailed.[27]

## Competition and Conflict in 1979

Two of the most vexing issues remained to be resolved as well.
The battle over the regulatory control of *Proálcool* was hardly
settled by the announcement of the MME's new role in the
program; the jockeying for power therefore continued. In May
1979, the new minister of industry and commerce, Camilo
Penna, asked those involved in the alcohol program whether a
complete institutional reform was needed. Penna set 4 June
1979 as the deadline for these memos, which were then to be
reviewed by the Council for Economic Development (CDE).[28]

The battle lines for the intense competition over productive
control were also drawn by May 1979. One contender was
Petrobrás. In opposition to the giant state enterprise's bid for
the control of alcohol production rallied a coalition of local
private capitalists, the multinational automobile companies,
and the Ministry of Industry and Commerce. This coalition
favored the private sector's control over alcohol production.

[26]"Como vai o Programa do Álcool? Vai bem, mas . . . ," *Jornal da Tarde*,
9 March 1979.
[27]"A política energética do General Figueiredo," *O Estado de São Paulo*, 20
March 1979.
[28]Luiz Artur Toribio, "Reflexões sobre o programa não incluem criação
da Álcoolbras," *Gazeta Mercantil*, 16 May 1979.

As part of its strategy, Petrobrás said it would create a new subsidiary, "Álcoolbras." This subsidiary would invest in sugarcane and manioc plantations, alcohol distilleries, and storage and distribution facilities.[29] Moreover, the Petrobrás plan called for Álcoolbras to be given a legal monopoly over the distribution of alcohol. In this way, Petrobrás tried to achieve productive control over the alcohol sector.[30]

In pressing its demands, Petrobrás could mobilize considerable political clout. As Brazil's largest corporation, with links to thirty-seven companies across numerous sectors, employing 43,000 people, and generating more profit per unit of sales than any other petroleum company in the world, Petrobrás dwarfed most public and private entities in the country.[31] Petrobrás's strong political position was further bolstered by its creation under the nationalist banner, *O Petróleo é Nosso* (The Petroleum Is Ours) in the 1950s.[32]

By the end of the 1970s, however, Petrobrás had come under intense political fire. Although it was created to explore and produce petroleum in Brazil, the declining world oil prices of the 1960s encouraged Petrobrás to import oil rather than to expend large sums on its unsatisfactory domestic exploration efforts. Beginning in 1970, in fact, Petrobrás greatly reduced its investments in exploration and production activities, causing drilling activity to fall sharply.[33] At the same time, Petrobrás began to diversify into retail gasoline sales, petrochemicals,

[29]Danubio Rodrigues, "Nova subsidiária: Álcoolbras," *O Estado de São Paulo*, 13 May 1979.

[30]"O monopólio do álcool nas mãos da Petrobrás?" *Jornal da Tarde*, 15 May 1979; "A Petrobrás pretende controlar também o álcool," *O Estado de São Paulo*, 22 May 1979.

[31]"Petrobrás, 25 anos. Poder e riqueza, mesmo com pouco óleo," *Exame* (25 October 1978):24.

[32]For a detailed history of the creation of Petrobrás, see John Wirth, *The Politics of Brazilian Development, 1930–1954* (Stanford: Stanford University Press, 1970), pp. 133–216. See also Peter Evans, *Dependent Development: The Alliance of Multinational, State, and Local Capital in Brazil* (Princeton: Princeton University Press, 1979), pp. 85–95.

[33]"Petrobrás, 25 anos," p. 32.

overseas exploration, the import-export business, minerals, and fertilizers.[34] The failure of Petrobrás to discover domestic petroleum deeply undercut the firm's political position especially in 1979, when the new round of OPEC price rises began to take their toll. Reduced investments in exploration and production, high profits, and diversification were considered to be unacceptable forms of state corporate behavior at a time when world petroleum prices and availability had become a crucial problem.[35]

Petrobrás was therefore extremely vulnerable to the ongoing debate over the "statization" of the economy. Opposition to further state encroachment into what some considered to be the territory of local private capital made the Petrobrás bid for a dominant role in alcohol production politically treacherous.[36] In fact, the coalition of local and multinational capital and the Ministry of Industry and Commerce rallied around the opposition to *estatização*. In challenging Petrobrás, these groups proposed the creation of an institution that would accelerate *Proálcool* by providing financial and technical support to interested private entrepreneurs. The initiative for the project was taken by the Zanini and Dedini groups, which together produced about 70 percent of the country's output of milling and distillery equipment. The other major force behind the idea was the minister of industry and commerce, Camilo Penna, who reportedly used the MIC to support the organizational efforts of the Zanini and Dedini groups.[37]

The idea of the new private institution, to be called "Investiálcool," evolved rapidly during May. In the words of its founders, Investiálcool would be an "agency for development" of the alcohol sector. Apart from lobbying for policies

[34]Ibid., pp. 28–29.

[35]"O monopólio do álcool nas mãos da Petrobrás?"

[36]President Figueiredo was on record as being in favor of reducing state involvement in the economy and preventing further *estatização*; see "Álcool-bras, mas sem controle da Petrobrás," *O Estado de São Paulo*, 15 May 1979.

[37]José Carlos Thomé, "Um 'pool' para o álcool," *Gazeta Mercantil*, 26 April 1979; Toribio, "Reflexões sobre o programa."

favorable to the expansion of the alcohol sector, Investiálcool would provide capital for those entrepreneurs who did not have sufficient equity to install a distillery on their own. The basic idea, of course, was to retain private control over an expanding alcohol sector by weakening Petrobrás's argument that its participation was necessary for a successful alcohol program.[38]

The ownership structure of Investiálcool resembled the increasingly prominent form of industrial organization in Brazil: the *tri-pé*.[39] Private local firms that supported the idea included the Dedini and Zanini groups, construction engineers, and the *usineiros*. Multinational capital was to be provided by the now extremely supportive automobile industry. ANFAVEA President Mario Garnero, in fact, blasted the idea of a Petrobrás subsidiary and the suggestion of state monopoly control over the distribution of alcohol.[40] State capital would be provided by Petrobrás, presumably under pressure from central decision makers.

The issue was resolved by top authorities by the end of May 1979. On 22 May, ANFAVEA President Garnero announced that the Petrobrás idea for a new Álcoolbras subsidiary had been rejected by President Figueiredo. Planning Minister Mario Henrique Simonsen and MIC Minister João Camilo Penna reportedly assured Garnero that there would be no state interference in the alcohol program, thus clearing the way for the creation of Investiálcool.[41] The Dedini group subsequently announced that Investiálcool would be created within a few days.[42]

---

[38]"Álcoolbras, mas sem controle da Petrobrás."

[39]In *Dependent Development*, Peter Evans explores the development of the *tri-pé* (tripod) form of industrial organization in Brazil.

[40]Toribio, "Reflexões sobre o programa."

[41]"A Álcoolbras já está fora dos planos do Governo?" *Jornal da Tarde*, 23 May 1979; and "Criação da Investiálcool e o papel do Petrobrás," *Jornal da Tarde*, 25 May 1979.

[42]"Investiálcool será criada nos próximos dias," *O Estado de São Paulo*, 24 May 1979.

The Figueiredo decision of May 1979 did not resolve conclusively the struggle over productive control. Investiálcool would support the creation of a new alcohol sector but not produce alcohol. The decision was nonetheless important, since it indicated that top authorities would rule in favor of private control despite strong resistance by Petrobrás. It also signaled that the deepest conflicts surrounding the alcohol program would have to be resolved at the highest levels of state—if at all.

## Paralysis of the Program

### *Temporary Equilibrium: May 1979*

While *Proálcool* was moving forward in some respects, it was paralyzed in others. On the positive side, government/industry understandings paved the way for the production of alcohol-powered cars. Producers agreed to forgo royalty payments to their home countries for alcohol engines, partly because much of the technology was developed in Brazil. ANFAVEA's Garnero also announced that the price of alcohol at the pump would be set lower than that of gasoline and that taxes on new alcohol-powered cars would be reduced to encourage car sales.[43]

On the other hand, the uncertainty generated by the fierce debate over the future of alcohol energy had blocked distillery project approvals. During the first five months of 1979, all projects were frozen within the IAA while few others were submitted, pending a clearer definition of the rules of the game.[44] Furthermore, no project passed through the Banco do Brasil's final contract phase for financing during this same period.[45]

[43]"A Álcoolbrás já está fora dos planos do Governo?"

[44]José Carlos Thomé, "Proálcool: inquietação e dúvidas com a in-definição das regras do jogo," *Gazeta Mercantil*, 17 May 1979.

[45]José Carlos Thomé, "Proálcool, com atrasos e dúvidas," *Gazeta Mercantil*, 21 May 1979.

Although *Proálcool* was obviously stalled during the policy debates of the early Figueiredo months, a few of the uncertainties were cleared up by the government's decision to end the short-lived Álcoolbras affair. The struggles over regulatory and productive control were not, however, fundamentally resolved, and the source of financing remained an open question. A new push was apparently required to move *Proálcool* off dead center.

### The June 1979 OPEC Price Boost

On 6 June 1979, the OPEC secretary-general announced that petroleum prices could climb that month by 37 percent, reaching $US 20 per barrel (up from $US 14.55).[46] In typical crisis style, the Figueiredo government responded by raising the energy issue to the highest level of political importance.[47] The same day, the Council for Economic Development met to raise the production target of the alcohol program to 10.7 billion liters in 1985. The CDE also set an investment goal of $US 5 billion for this period;[48] the source of these funds, however, was not identified.[49] The ambitious goal of 10.7 billion liters, nonetheless, was only expected to enable alcohol fuel to equal about 20 percent of gasoline demand in 1985.[50]

The seemingly paralyzed National Alcohol Council (CNAl) was abolished by top authorities in early June and a new, higher-level body with a similar name, the National Alcohol

[46]"A decisão que não podemos mais adiar," *Jornal da Tarde*, 7 June 1979.

[47]Planning Minister Simonsen said, "We either solve this problem or, certainly, we will not succeed in constructing any model of development or well-being for the Brazilian society. If we don't resolve the energy problem, we will have to return to the stone age." Quoted in Anamarcia Vainsencher, "Plano do Álcool: não da para esperar," *Isto É*, 13 June 1979.

[48]"O Proálcool: agora em novo ritmo," *Jornal da Tarde*, 7 June 1979.

[49]José Carlos Thomé, "Proálcool, no labirinto," *Gazeta Mercantil*, 18 June 1979.

[50]"CDE: álcool estabilizará o consumo dos derivados," *Folha de São Paulo*, 7 June 1979.

Commission (Comissão Nacional do Álcool—CNA), was created. This new group was to consist of the general secretaries of all the formerly represented ministries and was to add officials from the Ministries of Labor and Transportation and from the Armed Forces Chief of Staff. An executive commission (CENAL) was also created to give "technical and administrative support" to the new CNA. CENAL was to be chaired by the general secretary of the Ministry of Industry and Commerce.[51] Press reports suspected that the new CNA would likely implement the alcohol program more rapidly.[52]

### *Failure to Formulate an Energy Plan*

By June 1979, it had become even clearer that the alcohol program, as an isolated measure, would do little to reduce Brazil's petroleum imports. In the absence of other moves, Petrobrás would have to continue to import enormous quantities of crude petroleum in order to meet the demand for nongasoline derivatives, including diesel and industrial fuel oil.[53] Substitutes for these derivatives were sometimes mentioned, but no major development program was under way. During its 6 June meeting, the CDE did approve a few projects to develop methanol and coal into substitutes for diesel and fuel oil, respectively.[54] These actions did not convince many that President Figueiredo or his aides had an overall energy strategy in mind.[55]

News from the OPEC ministers meeting in Geneva at the end of June 1979 indicated that oil prices would surely reach $US

[51]"O Proálcool: agora em novo ritmo."

[52]"O Programa do Álcool entra em nova fase," *Jornal da Tarde*, 4 June 1979.

[53]"As verdadeiras dimensões do novo Programa do Álcool," *O Estado de São Paulo*, 8 June 1979.

[54]"Proálcool terá $US 5 bi até 85," *Diário Comércio e Indústria*, 7 June 1979.

[55]"Porque não podemos mais depender do petróleo," *Jornal da Tarde*, 25 June 1979.

20 per barrel, representing an increase of more than 35 percent. The OPEC action prompted President Figueiredo to create a new National Energy Commission (CNE) to develop and implement an integrated energy strategy. At the same time, Figueiredo portrayed these moves as elements of an *"economia de guerra"* or "war economy." By early July 1979, the energy issue had thus gained its highest political importance to date.[56] The *Estado de São Paulo* nevertheless complained that the president had failed to propose concrete measures in response to higher oil prices.[57]

For the CNE's first meeting in early July, Planning Minister Simonsen prepared a document entitled "Notes About an Energy Policy for Brazil."[58] The report defined Brazil's precarious energy situation and delineated a framework for national policy. During the hectic and confused months of July to September 1979, the Simonsen "notes" served as the government's principal energy policy document, although their credibility was weakened when the minister departed from his post in mid-August 1979.[59]

Simonsen defined three possible energy programs. The "basic" program called for an increase in domestic oil production, the substitution of 25 percent of the fuel oil supply by coal, an increase in the oil-exploration risk contracts with multinational oil companies, and a 10.7 billion liter goal for alcohol production by 1985. A second, more ambitious program would involve a 15 billion liter goal for alcohol production in 1985 as well as the further substitution of diesel and fuel oil. The third program was said to be an emergency plan, which Simonsen did not divulge to the public.

The planning minister's notes framed the liquid fuels

[56]"Falar, já se falou muito; agora é hora de agir," *Jornal de Tarde*, 5 July 1979.

[57]Ibid.

[58]"Plano Simonsen vai orientar novas opções sobre energia," *Jornal do Brasil*, 9 July 1979.

[59]Simonsen left the government during the shake-up that brought Antonio Delfim Netto to power as minister of planning.

problem clearly. Simonsen acknowledged that alcohol production might not lower petroleum imports without the
development of substitutes for diesel and fuel oil and the
modification of Petrobrás's refinery cracking ratios. Although
alcohol was said to be a technically inefficient substitute for
diesel oil, the Simonsen report claimed that the gasoline made
surplus by the alcohol program could be added to diesel fuel
without a critical loss of efficiency. Furthermore, government
support would be given to a research program to develop
methanol and vegetable oils as diesel substitutes. In the notes
Simonsen argued that this option, however, could not be fully
developed in the near future. Coal was seen as an attractive
substitute for fuel oil, and a plan to develop Brazil's coal
deposits in the south was under review.

Simonsen proceeded to raise the nagging question of financial resources for the expansion of alcohol production. The
minister of planning specifically recommended that funds be
obtained through foreign borrowing. Since interest rates on
these loans would be subsidized by the government's general
funds, an increase in the income tax might be necessary, he
argued, to finance the subsidization scheme. Because of the
shortage of funds, Simonsen did not want Petrobrás or
multinational firms to be excluded from entering the alcohol
sector.

## The "New" National Alcohol Program?

The so-called war economy and the salience of energy issues
spawned a flurry of activity around the "new" *Proálcool.*
ANFAVEA President Garnero, who had been appointed to the
National Energy Commission (CNE), pushed hard for the
immediate production of alcohol-powered cars. The deal that
had been struck between Garnero and the government provided strong incentives for consumer purchases of alcohol cars,
including a reduction in excise taxes and an expanded period
for buyers to repay their automobile loans (thirty-six months

instead of twelve).[60] Manufacturers were delighted with the incentives, since these would bolster sagging car sales. Adding fuel to the fire, Garnero announced in mid-August 1979 that alcohol-powered cars could constitute 100 percent of automobile production by June 1980.[61] At the same time, ANFAVEA made it clear that alcohol cars would be produced only at a rate commensurate with the expansion of the alcohol fuel supply. Whether carmakers would actually begin large-scale production therefore depended on the ability of the stalled alcohol program to get moving again.

As a favorable sign for the alcohol program, Investiálcool was gaining ground. The *tri-pé* arrangement that was designed to promote a new alcohol sector changed its name to "Brasálcool," and it received the official support and capital of Petrobrás.[62] The creation of Brasálcool in no way guaranteed that the alcohol sector would grow. It did, however, create hope that the collective efforts of interested groups might be able to break through the bureaucratic bottlenecks that had sometimes paralyzed the program.[63]

Despite all the commotion over energy, *Proálcool* did not take a dramatic step forward during the months following Simonsen's speech. New rules were made to limit bureaucratic delays involved in project approval,[64] but the new National Alcohol Commission failed to approve projects during its initial

[60]"Atenção: marcar passo!," *Veja* (22 August 1979):93.

[61]"Ano que vem só carro a álcool," *Diário Comércio e Indústria*, 10 August 1979.

[62]José Carlos Thomé, "Proálcool: Petrobrás já acertou sua participação na Brasálcool," *Gazeta Mercantil*, 20 July 1979. The accord among Brasálcool shareholders was established by the end of the month, and the objectives of the entity were clearly spelled out. Brasálcool would not actually engage in alcohol production, but it could fund up to 30 percent of private entrepreneurial ventures. See José Carlos Thomé, "Finalmente, o acordo entre os acionistas da Brasálcool," *Gazeta Mercantil*, 25 July 1979.

[63]It soon became apparent that the primary supporters of Brasálcool continued to be the Dedini and Zanini groups.

[64]Suely Caldas, "No Proálcool, projetos serão aprovados em três mêses," *Gazeta Mercantil*, 12 July 1979.

meetings.[65] Uncertainty continued to undermine *Proálcool*.

The pricing issue was raised once again, and it became a key point of contention between the *usineiros* and the government. Copersucar claimed that profits from alcohol production were not adequate and that the price of alcohol should be doubled in order to reach that of gasoline. Copersucar executive Márcio Gotlib further demanded that the sugar-alcohol parity co-efficient be adjusted again to reflect the "actual" relationship between the two products. By altering the technical parity, the producer price of alcohol would climb. Finally, producers wanted the 30 percent limit on the milling capacity that could be used for direct alcohol production to be removed as well.[66]

## Explaining 1979

To presidential-designate João Figueiredo, pushing *Proálcool* beyond Phase One must have seemed like an ideal strategy to broaden support for his forthcoming rule. With this single stroke, so it seemed, Figueiredo could reduce Brazil's dependence on increasingly expensive foreign oil, enhance the country's national security, safeguard the leading sector of the "economic miracle," provide new investment opportunities for the private sector, and inspire hope that the overall liquid fuels problem would be ameliorated over the next several years. The expansion of alcohol production and the marketing of alcohol-powered cars, moreover, would constitute a uniquely *Brazilian* response to the world energy crisis. For all these reasons, the idea of Phase Two could potentially attract a wide variety of allies. To illustrate how nonantagonistic this reformist strategy could be,[67] staunch advocates of the Brazilian

[65]Interview with Márcio Gotlib, São Paulo, June 1979.

[66]Ibid.

[67]On antagonistic and nonantagonistic routes to reform, see Albert O. Hirschman, *Journeys Toward Progress: Studies of Economic Policy-Making in Latin America* (New York: Norton, 1973), pp. 251–75.

model might be just as attracted to Phase Two as their critics who claimed that the country's recent industrialization constituted a wholesale adoption of foreign tastes and technologies. In a sense, the production of this renewable fuel and its consumption in special engines marketed only in Brazil would subvert imported patterns of production and consumption in order to save them.

The first major obstacle to this strategy of reform could have been the automobile industry itself. Once alcohol gained a 20 percent share of the motor fuel supply, either some adjustments would have to be made to standard gasoline engines or strictly alcohol-powered cars would have to be produced and sold. But a variety of factors should have made the automobile industry extremely skeptical of committing itself to Phase Two, especially before the second oil shock.

Simple political analysis would have revealed, for example, that whatever support there was for the less ambitious Phase One rested almost completely on the historic sugar/alcohol nexus. From the beginning, the financial bureaucracies appeared totally unsympathetic to the idea of granting the alcohol sector "special priority," while Petrobrás seemed likely to undermine any long-term commitment to alcohol fuel if given half a chance. It was even possible that if world sugar prices moved significantly upward, the *usineiros* and the IAA would join the *negativistas* in undermining any enduring commitment to alcohol production and consumption. Aside from these reasons for skepticism, the automobile companies probably had some doubts about how well their experimental results would match the performance of alcohol-powered cars in the real world. Faced with such vexing political and technological uncertainties, auto industry executives must have been uneasy about the prospect of defending their participation in Phase Two to higher authorities back home in Germany or the United States.

Because of the risks involved, it was almost certainly irrational for the automobile industry to make an irreversible commitment to the alcohol program before the Iranian Revolution succeeded in December 1978. Assuming that these investors were rational, how can we then account for the August 1978 agreement calling for the production of alcohol-powered cars? I would argue that since production was set to begin two years later, this first agreement had little operational significance; it therefore did not constitute an irreversible commitment to Phase Two. What made signing the agreement rational was that some action needed to be taken to keep the possibility of Phase Two alive once *Proálcool* was labeled the National Alcohol Problem—especially since the difficulties of further expansion became apparent during the presidential transition. ANFAVEA probably decided that a well-publicized agreement to produce alcohol-powered cars would be the best means to accomplish the urgent goal of bolstering the ongoing alcohol program.

Although an immediate commitment to produce alcohol-powered cars was premature, the auto industry's expressed interest in Phase Two was not disingenuous. In response to two surprising events, these firms would have rationally begun to draft contingency production plans by the end of the previous year. In 1977, the doubling of alcohol production demonstrated that this fuel could be produced in huge quantities. Meanwhile, automobile sales declined for the first year since domestic production had begun. Although we cannot ascertain how much the industry revised its expectations of the alcohol program as production grew, the downturn in car sales surely led the most bullish executives to lower substantially their long-run expectations for the Brazilian automobile market.

Previously bullish assumptions were challenged by the fact that the 1977 sales slump was directly linked to the restrictive monetary and fiscal policies which the government reluctantly imposed in order to narrow the country's trade deficit. Faced with a classic policy dilemma, the relevant authorities showed that they were willing to purchase greater external balance at the cost of slower growth.[68] This policy dilemma would become more serious, of course, if world oil prices further increased. Since the automobile industry would be on the leading edge of future attempts to restrict aggregate demand, even highly risk-averse executives by 1978 were probably willing to entertain the imaginative business strategy of producing alcohol-powered cars.

With news of the Iranian Revolution and the simultaneous rise in world oil prices, both ANFAVEA and members of the incoming Figueiredo administration must have clearly perceived the mutual benefits that could be derived from turning *Proálcool* into something spectacular. The subsequent events should remind us that investors as privileged as the automobile industry do not simply take political signals as given and adapt their expectations and decisions accordingly. The well-publicized, periodic advances in the target date for producing alcohol-powered cars deliberately generated important political signals. Apart from the diffuse support they may have engendered, these signals also demonstrated that the automobile industry would be an implicit and powerful coalition partner for other investors potentially interested in benefiting from an expanding alcohol sector.[69]

Despite the close cooperation between central decision makers and the automobile industry, the production of alcohol-powered cars would be risky. The growing size and complexity of the issue area during Phase Two, for example, would make an inconsistent policy set even more likely than during Phase One. The effects of the Iranian Revolution, on

---

[68] On the general issue of attaining internal and external balance, see W. M. Corden, *Inflation, Exchange Rates, and the World Economy* (Chicago: University of Chicago Press, 1977), pp. 7–18. For an argument that the tension between internal and external balance had grown considerably *before* the first oil shock, see Edmar L. Bacha, "Issues and Evidence on Recent Brazilian Economic Growth," *World Development* (January/February 1977): 47–67.

[69] But the automobile industry could be counted upon as a coalition partner only so long as the alternative of exclusively producing gasoline-powered cars did not become appealing.

the other hand, would enhance the ability of central decision makers to control implementation of the program. In weighing these offsetting tendencies, the automobile industry perhaps discounted as "old news" the signals generated by the policy implementation process during Phase One. The Figueiredo transition, the perceived realism of the incoming ministers, continuing increases in alcohol production, political instability in the Middle East, as well as other sources of upward pressure on oil prices, might have wiped the slate clean.

What probably provided the most powerful signal of all was the willingness of central decision makers to resolve the struggle for productive control. The landmark decision to block the formation of the Petrobrás subsidiary demonstrated that the alcohol program was sufficiently important to top authorities that even such extremely difficult choices would be made. The patterns of coalition formation that precipitated the Álcoolbras decision further brightened the prospects of Phase Two. Since alcohol had become *the* symbolic issue through which the struggle for expanded private enterprise property rights was being waged, one could easily surmise that central decision makers would use Phase Two of *Proálcool* to help regain the support of local capitalists generally.[70]

By May 1979, therefore, Phase Two was already linked to a variety of the regime's macropolitical objectives, including expanding the zone of private enterprise control, promoting

---

[70]There were a variety of reasons why the implicit renegotiation of what Peter Evans calls the "Triple Alliance" eventually centered around the alcohol program. First was the ability of both multinational and local capitalists to ally themselves under the banner of private enterprise property rights, so that the "international/national" fissure in the Brazilian model was suppressed. Second, Petrobrás, though historically preeminent among state enterprises, was in an especially vulnerable position due to its poor performance in producing oil in Brazil. Third, domestic energy production was likely to be one of the key growth sectors in the 1980s. The fourth reason was the impressive underlying support for the alcohol program due to its nonantagonistic profile. A final reason was the political perceptiveness of the Dedini and Zanini groups, which made great use of the idea that the alcohol program fought *estatização*.

national security, and preserving the Brazilian economic model. Support for the idea was further boosted by the June 1979 oil crisis. This shock to the task environment seems to have converted Mario Henrique Simonsen into an *otimista*. The minister of planning was the most influential economic policymaker at the time, and the signals he provided in his "notes on an energy policy" were loud and clear. The 10.7 billion liter production target indicated that the new *Proálcool* would be much more ambitious than the old one. The proposed investment of $US 5 billion, if implemented, would eliminate doubts about the most important of all production incentives. To resolve the conflicts exacerbated by the program's increasing size and complexity, key symbols of the regime's legitimacy were already being manipulated (as suggested by the declaration of a "war economy"). Moreover, CNAl was upgraded into the National Alcohol Commission, which would presumably join forces with a newly created National Energy Commission. Stronger signals at the policy formulation level could hardly have been generated.

By placing *Proálcool* on the front lines of the "war economy," Simonsen raised the possibility that alcohol production would become the central component of Brazil's energy strategy and that energy, in turn, would become the top priority of the Figueiredo government. But Simonsen's honest characterization of Brazil's energy predicament raised as many questions as it answered. His notes frankly recognized, for example, that gasoline was a single joint product of crude oil refining and that alcohol therefore could not substitute for an overall liquid fuels strategy. Although it was not a startling observation, this comment called attention to Petrobrás's long-standing claim that its refinery cracking ratios were inflexible. If this were true, incremental alcohol production would eventually create an excess supply of gasoline unless substitutes for diesel and fuel oil were produced in comparable quantities. Given the sketchiness of the plans for producing methanol and coal, the petroleum savings afforded by *Proálcool* would likely depend on Petrobrás's response to the anticipated decline in gasoline consumption. Since information about the inflexibility of the cracking ratios was provided by this noted foe of the alcohol program, no one could be sure whether Petrobrás might be forced to accommodate accumulating gasoline stocks by adjusting its refining facilities and practices.[71]

The year 1979, in sum, provided a variety of critical shocks to the policy-making process. By June, the system had only just begun to adjust to the Iranian Revolution, the cooperative efforts of the automobile industry and central decision makers, and the growing complexity of the issue area. Paradoxically, perhaps, the implementation of Phase One ground to a halt while the commitment to Phase Two was being formulated. This divergence between policy formulation and implementation cannot be fully accounted for by Cyert and March's insight that organizations attend to goals sequentially. This datum illustrates the short-run reaction of risk-avoiding state officials to an issue area that suddenly becomes new, complex, and large.

[71]Despite Petrobrás's protestations during Phase One, the company did reduce the output of gasoline per barrel of oil by importing heavier crudes, as discussed in Chapter 2.

# The
# Alcohol Boom
# (1980–81): An Unstable
# Equilibrium

### *Proálcool* Comes of Age

The quiet revolution that took place during the latter part of
1979 and throughout 1980 kept *Proálcool* at the forefront of
Brazil's efforts to achieve energy adjustment. Piece by piece,
barriers to the rapid development of alcohol energy fell by the
wayside. Evidence of substantial progress recorded in newspaper headlines and through less formal channels signaled
that the political support for *Proálcool* had gelled. By this time,
both public and private players were inclined to bank on their
favorable political assessments. Then, with the renewed tinge
of vulnerability provided by the 1980 Iran–Iraq War, threatening the petroleum exports of Brazil's predominant suppliers,
*Proálcool* could finally be termed irreversible.

## Project Approvals

Gradually, the conflict over regulatory control of the alcohol program diminished. By late 1979, the Ministry of Industry and Commerce had become identified as the principal locus of authority for the program. The domain of regulatory control was incomplete, to be sure: Questions of production goals, producer and consumer prices, finance, and marketing lay well outside the portfolio of MIC Minister Camilo Penna and his subordinates. Yet as the National Executive Commission for Alcohol (CENAL) gained prominence, set technical criteria, approved projects, and provided increasingly reliable information, potential producers grew more confident.[1] Many felt that now there was at least someone in the government to talk to.[2]

The existence of CENAL as an executive agent for the new, higher-level National Alcohol Council (CNA) improved the political and administrative capacity for rapid approval of projects. The increased pace of the decision-making process was due in part to the reduction of several hurdles that had slowed down approvals, at times to a halt. After 1979, only one technical project proposal had to be submitted to the non-financial bureaucracy, whereas potential producers had earlier been required to submit copies of their plans to both the CNAl and the IAA for approval. More important, the long battle for a unified proposal (*projeto único*) was finally won. Interested parties could therefore submit a proposal to financial agents, such as the Banco do Brasil, at the same time they delivered the technical proposal to CENAL. These seemingly minor admin-

[1]CENAL ruled on technical designs, the appropriateness of land for raw material production, distribution from proposed locations, project siting, and zoning. Interview with Marcos de Lima Fernandes, executive secretary, CENAL, Brasília, D.F., June 1981.

[2]Interview with Francisco H. de Barros, president, Brasálcool, São Paulo, June 1981.

istrative changes, together with a new positive political environment, enabled the technical project approvals process to be shortened from over six months to less than three.[3] The success of the Ministry of Industry and Commerce in changing these bureaucratic rules of the game both reflected and spurred ahead the growing political basis for *Proálcool*.[4] As telling evidence, approved distillery capacity increased by 2.7 billion liters per year in 1980, compared to an increment of only 935 million liters per year in 1979.[5]

*Finance*

At the same time, regulatory control over the financial bureaucracy was becoming increasingly centralized as Antonio Delfim Netto consolidated his power as minister of planning.[6] The political space for authoritative behavior in economic policy was broadened as the country's economic problems intensified, and Delfim succeeded in overcoming the fragmentation of power within the state. Delfim gained his tightest

[3]Interview with Fernando Toledo Pisa, Institute of Sugar and Alcohol, São Paulo, May 1981. CENAL President Marcos José Marques claimed in May 1980 that "project evaluation required only sixty days—clearly the least amount of time in the country for a work of such complexity." See "Presidente da CENAL desmente atraso no Programa do Álcool," *Folha de São Paulo*, 28 May 1980.

[4]In March 1980, Marques could claim that "the year had started well. In January and February, CENAL approved projects with a net capacity of 2.3 million liters/day." And he signaled that more than fifty other projects were under construction. See Glaucia da Mata Machado, "O sucesso do Proálcool depende da produção de 30 milhões de litros/dia," *Gazeta Mercantil*, 14 March 1980. CENAL announced in May that 271 projects had been approved since 1975, with a total capacity of 5.1 billion liters. See "Até agora, o Proálcool tem 271 projetos," *O Estado de São Paulo*, 10 May 1980. It is important to note that learning effects may have contributed to the quality of the proposals and hence the speed of the approval process. The establishment of several consulting firms to assist in the preparation of project proposals likely had a major effect on the process as well.

[5]CENAL, *Proálcool, Relatório Anual 1980* (Brasília: CENAL, 1981), p. 7.

[6]Delfim Netto took office in August 1979, when Mario Henrique Simonsen stepped aside.

grip on resource allocation through his leadership of the National Monetary Council (CMN).

By November 1979, inflation was expected to exceed 70 percent for the year—the highest level since 1964—and central decision makers became increasingly concerned with its control.[7] In January 1980, Delfim announced a "new economic package" in an effort to reduce the public's inflationary expectations to the 50 percent level. A tight money policy and the unconventional announcement—at the beginning of the year—of both the annual monetary correction (at 45 percent) and the cruzeiro's devaluation (40 percent) were the major elements of Delfim's New Year's package.[8]

Tight credit and a politicized monetary policy were two critical background variables that contributed to the alcohol boom of 1980.[9] In this context, the acceleration of financial contracts for *Proálcool* during 1980 was viewed with considerable interest by potential producers. As the competition for public financial resources intensified under the restrictive credit policy, the availability of subsidized finance under *Proálcool* signaled that the government's commitment to the sector was now strong. What better evidence could be shown for a deep political commitment than the willingness of the financial bureaucracy, for so long the prime bottleneck in the development of the alcohol sector, to provide finance even under such restrictive circumstances? Moreover, access to credit provided an exit for agricultural producers then engaged in privately unprofitable activities.

[7]Reginalda Heller, "Técnicos confirmam a previsão de 70% para inflação este ano," *Gazeta Mercantil*, 2 November 1979.

[8]Celso Ming, "Por que o governo pode ter de recuar," *Jornal da Tarde*, 17 January 1980; "Delfim explica prefixação de índicies," *O Estado de São Paulo*, 18 January 1980.

[9]The "monetary budget" of the Central Bank gained particular attention with the politicization of monetary policy throughout the year. See "Em estudo o orçamento monetário," *O Estado de São Paulo*, 6 February 1980; "A prioridade do controle monetário," *O Estado de São Paulo*, 23 January 1980; and Fabio Pahim, Jr., "Os problemas da economia neste semestre," *Jornal da Tarde*, 7 July 1980.

Several policy actions accelerated the financial contracting process. First, the concurrent submission of both financial and technical proposals reduced the distortions created by inflation. Fewer proposals were therefore rejected for this reason alone. Second, commercial banks, along with the National Bank for Economic Development (BNDE), were designated as financial agents for alcohol program credits. Long-standing customer relationships between applicants and these banks facilitated the prompt evaluation of "entrepreneurial capacity," an important criterion of the financial analysis.[10] Third, the special *Proálcool* credit program for agricultural working capital and investments was folded into the regular operations of the Banco do Brasil at the end of 1979, eliminating an administrative conflict that had slowed up an important element of the program.[11] Fourth, estimates of fixed investment costs, which served as a baseline for financing levels, were automatically increased in line with the monetary correction, insulating *Proálcool* from an inflation-generated reduction in the amount of credit provided in real terms. These measures stimulated the alcohol program by signaling that the government was willing and able to eliminate some of the barriers that had obstructed *Proálcool* since its creation in 1975.

The gradual acceleration of the number of projects actually receiving funding provided even stronger evidence of the program's underlying political support. Complaints about the slow process of financing approvals continued to abound in

[10]Interview with Francisco H. de Barros, June 1981. Even so, Barros claimed that the banks frequently delved into considerable technical detail in the appraisal process, often leading to a slowdown in contracting.

[11]"CMN aprova crédito imediato para a agricultura," *O Estado de São Paulo*, 22 December 1979. Additional restrictions had been applied to *Proálcool*'s low-interest-rate loans. Working capital financing was subsequently provided through the Banco do Brasil's rural credit account (*Carteira de Crédito Rural*) without restriction. Agricultural investment financing was also available from the Banco do Brasil through another program. Interviews with officials at the Banco do Brasil, Brasília, D.F., June 1981.

late 1979,[12] but by March 1980 announcements of recent Banco do Brasil contracts for *Proálcool* occurred regularly.[13] Although the change in credit allocation trends did not occur overnight, announcements of plans for greater *Proálcool* financing bolstered the favorable signs. By the end of 1979, CENAL announced that Cr$ 54 billion would be invested in *Proálcool* during the coming year.[14]

The clearest possible evidence of support for the alcohol program emerged in August 1980. *Proálcool* became an "open account" in the state's monetary budget; targets for annual increases in credit allocation were therefore no longer binding on the financial agents. These banks were advised that the Central Bank would refinance, at subsidized rates, all projects meeting stated technical and financial specifications.[15] Financing for agricultural working capital (for all crops) and for selected nonagricultural export projects were the only activities with a similar open-account status. Both political and price signals favoring a movement of resources toward the alcohol sector were thus loud and clear.

Confidence that the CMN's decision to grant *Proálcool* priority status would be a lasting one was strengthened by the development of the Energy Mobilization Fund, which was to be funded by excise taxes on petroleum products and new car sales. By citing the coffers of the energy fund, proponents of

[12]Only twenty new distillery projects were reported to have received contracts by October. See "Como evitar que o Proálcool acabe sendo um fracasso," *Jornal da Tarde*, 17 October 1979. For later complaints, see Milton F. da Rocha Filho, "Produtor começa a duvidar que Proálcool atinja sua meta," *Jornal do Brasil*, 5 November 1979.

[13]"Proálcool: BB contrata 10 bilhões," *O Estado de São Paulo*, 25 March 1980; "BB já liberou Cr$ 12 bilhões para Proálcool," *O Estado de São Paulo*, 20 January 1980; "BB já autorizou crédito de 23 bilhões para álcool," *O Estado de São Paulo*, 24 August 1980; "BB já financiou 30,73 bilhões para o Proálcool," *O Estado de São Paulo*, 21 November 1980.

[14]"Proálcool: Investimentos globais de Cr$ 54 bilhões em 1980," *Gazeta Mercantil*, 21 December 1979.

[15]See "Recursos para o álcool aumentarão 60% em 81," *O Estado de São Paulo*, 14 August 1980.

the program could back up their assurances that resources would not be lacking.[16] In reality, however, the allocation of credit for *Proálcool* was not directly constrained by the size of the Energy Mobilization Fund since the program was being financed through the monetary budget.[17] Nonetheless, the appearance of a tax-based source of funding for the credit scheme tended to temper conflict over the program. Such a lubricant may have been critical as monetary policy became increasingly politicized throughout the period.

Support for *Proálcool* was strengthened by continued interest in the program by international financial capital. Rumors of external loans for *Proálcool* circulated as early as October 1979. Upon returning from Europe, for example, Central Bank President Ernane Galveas announced that nine European and American banks would provide $1 billion in loans for *Proálcool* before January 1980.[18] The fundraising success of Galveas had two principal effects: The announcement conveyed to potential alcohol producers and consumers that resources for the program would likely be ample; moreover, high-ranking state officials learned the *Proálcool* provided a useful device to attract much-needed international financial capital. The strong appeal of an innovative energy adjustment scheme must have pleased the international bankers at a time when they were becoming increasingly uneasy about Brazil's economic prospects. With oil prices over $US 30 per barrel, the year 1980 would obviously be a difficult one for the Brazilian current

[16]David Renault, "Consumo de gasolina subsidia o Proálcool," *O Estado de São Paulo*, 6 July 1980; "Álcool: Fixada Meta de 14 bilhões de litros em 87," *O Estado de São Paulo*, 4 December 1979; "Proálcool terá US$ 2,4 bilhões até 85," *O Estado de São Paulo*, 3 January 1980; and Solange Morgado, "Cr$ 85 bilhões para a energia," *Gazeta Mercantil*, 25 February 1981.

[17]Funds collected from the Energy Mobilization Fund were transferred to the monetary budget, but this fact did not represent an operational constraint. Interviews at the Banco do Brasil, Brasília, June 1981.

[18]"Empréstimo de $US 1 bilhão vai ser aplicado no Proálcool," *O Estado de São Paulo*, 9 October 1979; and "Colin confirma US$ 1 bilhão para Proálcool," *O Estado de São Paulo*, 12 October 1979.

account. Providing $US 1 billion in credits ostensibly for *Proálcool* was a convenient mechanism for banks to extend a major balance of payments loan to Brazil. Hard and fast guarantees on the flow of the counterpart cruzeiros were by no means established.[19]

The international financial and political support of the World Bank also appeared on the horizon in September 1980 with a report that the organization would lend up to another $US 1 billion on even more favorable terms.[20] Alcohol's prestige value was growing by leaps and bounds, and both public and private players were taking note.[21] Negotiations dragged on for nearly a year, however, and an agreement for a $US 250 million loan was not signed until June 1981.[22]

### Prices and Output

Jurisdiction over producer and consumer prices for alcohol had long been a matter of controversy. Despite considerable efforts to retain their authority, both the IAA and MIC lost in the struggle for control of this important element of the program. By 1980, power over price setting had been usurped by Planning Minister Delfim Netto, reducing the jurisdictional disputes surrounding the alcohol program. Conflict was limited to setting the actual prices for producers and consumers.

Apart from the pace of project approvals by CENAL and the financial bureaucracy, the principal issue over which state officials and producers negotiated was the price for alcohol.

[19]Interview with José Saavedra, vice president, Morgan Guaranty Trust Company of New York, São Paulo, May 1981.

[20]"BIRD ofereceu US$ 1 bilhão para o Proálcool," *O Estado de São Paulo,*" 18 December 1980.

[21]When the tentative agreement had been reached, MIC Minister Penna claimed: "The most demanding organization in the world is giving all positive signals to the progress of the program." See "Carro a álcool: Penna é contra corte na produção," *O Estado de São Paulo*, 16 May 1981.

[22]For evidence of less tangible benefits from *Proálcool*'s international status, see José Antonio Severo, "A expectativa de novos projetos," *Gazeta Mercantil*, 31 July 1980.

Large producers such as the Ometto family frequently proclaimed that entrepreneurial interest would be small if prices for alcohol were not raised.[23] Delfim raised these prices only moderately every six months; the effects of these pricing decisions on output depended on whether the planning minister had successfully called the producers' bluff.

Direct negotiation did not, of course, take place between state officials and the numerous and unorganized consumers. Instead the pump price for hydrated alcohol was used to signal consumers that it would be profitable to buy alcohol-powered cars or to convert their gasoline engines to the new fuel. State officials soon learned, however, that their range of flexibility was relatively narrow—bounded on the upside by alcohol's lower fuel efficiency and on the downside by the need to discourage wasteful consumption.[24] During 1980, the pump price of hydrated alcohol varied between 40 and 65 percent of the price of gasoline.[25] Such variation took place against a

[23]Producers sought a parity between alcohol and gasoline prices on the expectation that the latter would grow faster than the domestic price of sugar, which was the traditional reference point for setting producer alcohol prices. See Milton F. da Rocha Filho, "Produtor começa a duvidar que Proálcool atinja sua meta"; letter to the editor by João Guilherme Sabino Ometto, "Os empresários e o Proálcool," *Jornal da Tarde*, 24 December 1979; and "O que há de errado no Proálcool?" *Jornal da Tarde*, 17 March 1980.

[24]The lower bound became apparent by May 1980. See "Comercialização do álcool é irregular em SP," *Folha de São Paulo*, 15 May 1980. See also Paulo Ludmer, "Os problemas de suprimento," *Gazeta Mercantil*, 9 June 1980; and "O motivo para o álcool aumentar," *Jornal da Tarde*, 15 January 1981.

[25]Prices in 1980 were (in Cr$/liter):

| Date | Hydrated Alcohol | Gasoline | Alcohol/Gasoline |
|------|------------------|----------|------------------|
| 12/10/79 | 11.40 | 22.60 | 58.4% |
| 3/19/80 | 11.40 | 26.00 | 43.8% |
| 4/24/80 | 11.40 | 28.00 | 40.7% |
| 5/19/80 | 18.20 | 28.00 | 65.0% |
| 5/29/80 | 18.20 | 30.00 | 60.7% |
| 6/26/80 | 18.20 | 34.50 | 52.7% |
| 7/31/80 | 18.20 | 38.00 | 47.9% |
| 9/27/80 | 24.70 | 38.00 | 65.0% |
| 10/3/80 | 24.70 | 45.00 | 54.9% |
| 12/4/80 | 27.50 | 51.00 | 53.9% |

SOURCE: CENAL, *Proálcool, Relatório Anual 1980* (Brasilia: CENAL, 1981), p. 35.

backdrop of rapidly escalating consumer prices for liquid fuels; gasoline prices more than doubled in 1980.[26] This element in Delfim's scheme to alter relative prices made consumers uneasy about the future price and availability of gasoline. Heightened sensitivity to fuel prices made the price of pure alcohol at the pump an especially strong signal of the state's policy intentions in the liquid fuels sector. Rising gasoline prices also served to reduce gasoline consumption markedly.[27] Excess gasoline supplies became a factor in the cool but ongoing debate over the desirability of *Proálcool*; they also constrained government price-setting behavior as well.[28]

The uneven execution of the consumer pricing policy was due more to these troubling considerations than to the fragmentation of authority over the issue. Delfim's grip on the state's price-setting apparatus resolved the question of power in this domain.[29] Wary consumers, however, could not be sure whether buying an alcohol-powered car would become an obsolescing bargain. MIC Minister Penna's claim that hydrated alcohol prices would always remain below 65 percent of the price of gasoline did increase the public's confidence that alcohol cars, as well as the program itself, represented a good deal for themselves and for Brazil.[30] Higher prices by midyear,

[26]Flávio Rogerio Troyano, "'Inflação é corretiva,' diz Delfim," *Gazeta Mercantil*, 4 October 1979. Part of the problem was created by the November 1979 devaluation. See "Petrobrás: inevitável nova alta da gasolina," *O Estado de São Paulo*, 12 February 1980.

[27]Petrobrás President Ueki told the CNE in February 1980 that they should not delude themselves of the fact that surplus gasoline was being created and exported. See "CNE desvia parte da TRU para energia," *Jornal do Brasil*, 6 February 1980. News of a fall in gasoline consumption crossed the headlines frequently. See "O consumo interno foi 23, 4% menor que em janeiro de 79," *O Estado de São Paulo*, 16 February 1980; and "O consumo em fevereiro caiu 18%," *O Estado de São Paulo*, 8 March 1980.

[28]See Chapter 2.

[29]See Laercio Silva, "Cals cai para 5? nas decisões sobre energia," *Jornal do Brasil*, 10 February 1980. This assessment was confirmed by many observers, both inside and outside the government, during interviews in May–June 1981.

[30]See, for example, "Os novos preços do álcool," *Jornal da Tarde*, 30 April 1980; "Figueiredo aponta álcool como solução," *O Estado de São Paulo*, 25 May 1980; and "Álcool vai custar 60% do preço da gasolina," *Jornal do Brasil*, 15 January 1981.

however, which were imposed to reduce wasteful consumption of hydrated alcohol, raised consumers' suspicions. The problem intensified when the performance of alcohol engines disappointed their owners in late 1980 and 1981.[31]

A resurgence of the Brazilian national security ideology accompanied the concentration of power under Delfim. Worried by the fading image of the economic miracle, the military-dominated National Petroleum Council (CNP) assumed an increasingly important role in *Proálcool*. Liquid fuels policy had long been the darling of security-conscious military planners, and the economic difficulties of the 1979–81 period motivated the CNP to take charge of setting annual alcohol production quotas.[32] Actions by the CNP removed these important policy decisions from the portfolio of MIC and the IAA and thereby facilitated the integration of alcohol production and consumption. The parallel processes of authority concentration and military activism thus favored the alcohol program in yet another domain.[33]

An important signal provided by short-run production policy was transmitted in mid-1980 when world sugar prices jumped markedly upward for the first time since 1974. By the time international sugar prices reached $US 800 per metric ton in July 1980,[34] sugar production had become by far a socially profitable export activity. Although the IAA informally relaxed sugar production quotas in order to attend to the export market, the alcohol program was not noticeably affected by

[31]The issue surfaced by May 1980, especially for converted engines. See Glaucia da Mata Machado, "A polémica sobre conversão de motores em São Paulo," *Gazeta Mercantil*, 7 May 1980. As more alcohol cars joined the fleet, the debate intensified: "Consumo do motor a álcool deve ser limitado," *O Estado de São Paulo*, 18 January 1981.

[32]"CNP fixa cotas para nova safra de álcool," *O Estado de São Paulo*, 24 September 1981.

[33]Petrobrás was notably excluded from decisions involving alcohol production levels.

[34]"Produção de açúcar crescerá mais que a do álcool em 1980/81," *Folha de São Paulo*, 1 July 1980.

this turn of events. Two years earlier, an entirely contrary scenario could easily have been imagined. At that time, broad political support for *Proálcool* was clearly contingent upon the comforting alternative of abandoning alcohol production in the event that world sugar prices resurged. *Proálcool* thus survived its moment of truth in mid-1980, providing immense evidence that the underlying political basis for the program was sound.[35]

Long-run production policy was determined at the highest levels of state. The annual production target for 1985 signaled the top political priority the alcohol program was being granted; it also defined the magnitude of the opportunities presented by the burgeoning sector. Once the 10.7 billion liter goal was taken seriously, it provided a catalyst for action. As evidence, Brasálcool President Francisco de Barros claimed publicly in September 1979 that more than 200 distilleries would be needed to reach the goal.[36] In January 1980, the *Estado de São Paulo* claimed that sixty new distilleries per year would be necessary to reach the desired goal.[37] By March 1980, it had become apparent that most of the expansion would be generated through the construction of autonomous distilleries, inviting entrepreneurs outside the established sugar industry to invest in the alcohol sector.[38]

The source and consistency of the distant production goal contributed to the strength of this policy as a signaling device. Its origin in Simonsen's notes and its endorsement by Delfim and the National Energy Commission (CNE) contributed to the perception that *Proálcool* rested on firm political ground.

[35]These events probably increased the credibility of the *otimistas*, who had assured the public that high sugar prices would not prejudice *Proálcool*. See "Álcool: altos preços do açúcar não prejudicam Proálcool," *Gazeta Mercantil*, 7 July 1980.

[36]Luis Artur Toribio, "A assistência diversificada da Brasálcool," *Gazeta Mercantil*, 19 September 1979.

[37]"O programa energético agora em novo ritmo," *O Estado de São Paulo*, 22 January 1980.

[38]Machado, "O sucesso do Proálcool."

Moreover, the consistency with which the specific goal was enunciated over time added to its credibility, especially since the objective was ambitious but not inconceivably achieved.[39] Nonetheless, even more ambitious targets were suggested by the program's proponents from time to time, perhaps to prevent favorable information from appearing stale.[40]

Several other policy decisions aided alcohol production. First, in December 1979 President Figueiredo approved an MIC proposal that nullified the policy limiting the production of alcohol at annexed distilleries.[41] Second, throughout 1980 the special problems of incorporating new lands for sugarcane and alcohol production climbed their way up the bureaucratic agenda. Since lands in the western part of São Paulo state were generally owned by small ranchers and farmers, autonomous distilleries could be supported only through a cooperative form of organization or by selling out to a large producer. To assist these smaller groups, in June 1980 the CMN authorized financial agents to provide 90 percent of the necessary capital for *Proálcool* industrial projects proposed by cooperatives or similar producer associations. For all other projects, only 80 percent of the required funds would continue to be provided.[42]

---

[39]Confidence in the program was probably enhanced by MIC Minister Penna's consistent statements throughout 1980 on the objectives and limitations of *Proálcool*. He frequently asserted that alcohol production would serve only to meet incremental gasoline demand. See, for example, "Proálcool não é solução para o problema energético," *O Estado de São Paulo*, 30 December 1979.

[40]See "Proposta a duplição da meta do Proálcool até 85," *Folha de São Paulo*, 24 November 1979. Acting alone, MIC announced a 14 billion liter goal for the 1987–88 harvest year: "Álcool: fixada a meta de 14 bilhões de litros em 87," *O Estado de São Paulo*, 4 December 1979; moved it up one year by May 1980: "Governo poderá aumentar as metas de produção de álcool," *O Estado de São Paulo*, 28 May 1980; and moved it up by another year after the Iran–Iraq War began: "Álcool: as exportações foram suspensas. É uma medida para garantir nossas estoques," *Jornal da Tarde*, 30 September 1980.

[41]"Álcool: fixada a meta de 14 bilhões de litros em 87."

[42]"CMN aprova elevação do teto ao Proálcool," *Folha de São Paulo*, 12 June 1980.

Third, by year's end both the Banco do Brasil and the BNDE became engaged in special financing packages for infrastructure in frontier areas.[43] These financial efforts were bolstered by the guidance of Brasálcool President Francisco de Barros, whose agency provided technical and managerial assistance, as well as needed capital, for cooperative ventures in the state of Mato Grosso.[44]

## Marketing

Many potential bottlenecks lurked in the long chain from distillery storage tanks to automobile engines. A successful marketing scheme had to ensure that alcohol production did not outstrip the capacity of the distribution system or the demand for hydrated fuel. To achieve this goal, the interests and actions of alcohol producers, liquid fuel distributors, automobile manufacturers, and consumers needed to be mutually consistent. Alcohol producers sought confidence that their market would be accessible, distributors demanded profit incentives, and consumers as well as carmakers had to be assured that fuel would be available to power alcohol engines.[45]

Dedicated to the nation's security, broadly defined, the generals of the CNP managed the marketing system. The council guaranteed alcohol producers that it would serve as marketer of last resort in the event fuel distributors were unwilling to buy their product. Petrobrás Distribudora and multinational fuel retailers were instructed to cover the

[43]Interview with Banco do Brasil officials, Brasília, June 1981.

[44]Although Brasálcool maintained a low profile after its creation in 1979, the organization was nevertheless instrumental in assisting project development. For evidence of these accomplishments, see Brasálcool, "Relatório descritivo das condições de acesso a empreendimentos álcooleiros localizados na região nordeste do Estado de Mato Grosso," São Paulo, 1981.

[45]MIC Minister Camilo Penna was apparently acutely aware of this delicate balance. See "A garantia de álcool para os carros," *Jornal da Tarde*, 20 March 1981.

transportation costs of moving alcohol from distilleries to mixing centers (in the case of anhydrous alcohol) and then to their retail locations. The price structure regulated by the CNP would reward these firms with a healthy profit for their services. In addition, the CNP succeeded in making available Petrobrás's pipelines for alcohol shipment.[46]

Persuading the multinational car companies to produce alcohol cars was unnecessary. Engineers at Volkswagen, General Motors, Ford, and Fiat had been busily at work improving upon alcohol engine technology ever since the accord between the government and ANFAVEA was signed in September 1979 for 250,000 alcohol-powered cars during the first year of production.[47] The 41-day strike of metallurgical workers in the

[46]The CNE decided in January 1980 to require that hydrated alcohol be sold through the pumps which traditionally contained one of the two grades of gasoline. See "O trabalho da CNE e a política energética," *Jornal da Tarde*, 10 January 1980. CENAL president Marques reported in March 1980 that more than 300 stations sold alcohol fuel, "permitting mobility throughout the whole country." See Machado, "O sucesso do Proálcool." That conflict persisted in this element of the system is evident from subsequent reports. See Marizete Mondim, "Governo terá que se envolver na produção de álcool," *Folha de São Paulo*, 8 March 1980; and "CNP congela cotas de álcool de 6.150 postos," *O Estado de São Paulo*, 19 March 1981. In November 1980, Petrobrás was asked to invest in strengthening the national alcohol storage system. See "Governo determina a estocagem de álcool," *O Estado de São Paulo*, 2 November 1980.

[47]"Um acordo com as fábricas para a produção de carros a álcool," *Gazeta Mercantil*, 11 September 1979. The accord was signed later in the month by Figueiredo and ANFAVEA at the presidential palace. The level of production depended on the tough problem of coordinating the introduction of a commodity whose supply and demand were inelastic. Officials had to exercise caution in order to avoid disappointing new car buyers or causing stocks to grow too large. See "O motivo para o álcool aumentar," *Jornal da Tarde*, 15 January 1981; "Consumo do motor deve ser limitado"; and "Álcool: MIC esclarece a limitação," *O Estado de São Paulo*, 31 January 1981. Because of the difficulties in maintaining this balance, the production quota for alcohol cars became a somewhat charged bargaining point. See "Redução na produção de carros a álcool? O governo é contra," *Jornal da Tarde*, 28 April 1981. Handling the issue in this way tended to undermine the appearance of a coherent policy, particularly because it generated public fears of an excess demand for alcohol fuel. See "Penna contesta críticas ao programa," *O Estado de São Paulo*, 5 May 1981; and Celso Ming, "O que o consumidor precisa saber," *Jornal da Tarde*, 13 May 1981.

São Paulo area during April and May 1980, however, caused the target to be revised downward by 50,000 units.[48] Production figures would ultimately depend on consumer acceptance of the final link in the complicated alcohol fuel chain.[49]

*Productive Control*

Its identification with the turning of the tide against *estatização* kept *Proálcool* within the orbit of local private capital. Although Petrobrás reduced many of its obstructionist tendencies, the giant state oil monopoly did not make major investments to change its refinery cracking ratios. Decisions taken at high levels, however, encouraged Petrobrás to change its blend of crude oil imports.[50] Petrobrás thus appears to have retained its *negativista* image,[51] but it had at least given up the struggle for productive control.[52]

The question of permitting joint ventures between local private, state, and multinational enterprises was raised occasionally, only to be settled by assertions that the alcohol sector would remain in the control of local private capital for nationalistic and "security" reasons.[53] From time to time, however, state officials rumored that foreign capital was eager to enter the sector—apparently as a threat to speed up

[48]"Haverá menor produção de veículos a álcool," *Folha de São Paulo*, 16 May 1980; and "Anunciada a redução na meta de carros a álcool," *O Estado de São Paulo*, 16 May 1980.

[49]In February 1980, the conversion of ordinary gasoline engines into alcohol engines was legalized so long as the work was performed by certified auto shops. See "Autorizada conversão de carros particulares," *Folha de São Paulo*, 29 February 1980.

[50]For evidence that such changes took place, see Chapter 2.

[51]In May 1981, Ueki used the occasion of reported excess gasoline supplies to suggest that the quota for the production of alcohol-powered cars be reduced. See "Carro a álcool: Penna é contra corte na produção," *O Estado de São Paulo*, 16 May 1981.

[52]See "Ueki: Petrobrás vai ficar só no petróleo," *O Estado de São Paulo*, 17 January 1980.

[53]See "Nacionalismo e o Proálcool," *O Estado de São Paulo*, 9 April 1980.

investments by local private capital.[54] Conflict over productive control thus lurked in the background but failed to interfere with the maturation of *Proálcool* during 1980.

## Toward an Unstable Equilibrium

### *Turning the Corner in Mid-1980*

In the May–September 1980 period, the National Alcohol Program gained considerable strength.[55] Projects were approved apace by CENAL and funded at a substantially increased clip by the Central Bank's financial agents. Administrative arrangements for determining prices, production, and distribution had been made. Once the metallurgical strike had ended, alcohol-powered cars were ready to roll off the assembly line. Then two events, one gradual and the other sudden, ignited producer and consumer participation in *Proálcool*. The risky attempt Delfim initiated in January to contain inflation appeared to be failing, as reports of price increases pushed various inflation indices well beyond recent levels. With the monetary correction having been earlier fixed at a rate below what was now observed to be the actual inflation rate, those with liquid wealth dove for cover by purchasing consumer durables and land. Conditions were thus ripe for a record boom in car sales. The sudden event of September 1980—the Iran–Iraq War—stimulated interest in alcohol cars in particular.

---

[54]See, for example, "Governo analisará capital externo no programa do álcool," *O Estado de São Paulo*, 30 March 1980; "Capital externo fora do Proálcool em 80," *O Estado de São Paulo*, 9 April 1980; "Capital externo não deve interferir no Proálcool," *O Estado de São Paulo*, 17 September 1980; "Estrangeiras no Proálcool? Por enquanto, não," *Jornal da Tarde*, 14 January 1981; and "Debatido o interesse do capital externo no álcool," *O Estado de São Paulo*, 27 May 1981.

[55]For a representative status report, see José Antonio Severo, "A expectativa de novos projetos," *Gazeta Mercantil*, 21 July 1980.

Just before the war began, Brazil imported approximately 41 percent of its petroleum from Iraq and 12 percent from Iran.[56] This supply concentration was due, in part, to the special relationship that existed between Iraq and Petrobrás's exploration subsidiary, Braspetro. Nine months earlier, that relationship had deteriorated when Brazil was forced to rescind a contract for the development of Iraq's Majnoon oil field, which had been discovered by Braspetro. But in return Brazil was guaranteed oil supplies from the field.[57] With the war, that guarantee lost its credibility and the alcohol-car boom was on.[58]

Alcohol-powered car sales jumped from 20,785 in August to 29,585 in September, 40,718 in October, 53,481 in November, and dropped slightly to 49,481 in December.[59] The original target of 250,000 units was reached.[60] In the words of the president of Volkswagen's advertising agency, "the public bought the idea."[61] Monthly consumption of hydrated alcohol in 1980 grew from less than 3000 cubic meters in January to more than 91,000 cubic meters by December.[62]

[56]Figures are for 1979. See Conselho Nacional de Petróleo, *Anuário Estatístico 1980, Complemento 1979* (Brasília: CNP, 1980), p. 3. Some 630,000 barrels per day were being imported from Iraq in March. See "As importações de petróleo podem atingir US$ 12 bilhões," *O Estado de São Paulo,* 2 March 1980.

[57]See "A humiliação brasileira em Majnoon," *O Estado de São Paulo,* 11 January 1980; and "Ueki acha que foi bom perder Majnoon," *Jornal da Tarde,* 11 January 1980.

[58]See S. Stefani, "Álcool: o susto da guerra provocou o 'boom'," *Relatório da Gazeta Mercantil,* 28 November 1980.

[59]Patrick Knight, "Brazil's Alcohol Car Boom Misfires," *London Times,* 1 September 1981.

[60]Some 254,016 units were sold, including trucks. See CENAL, *Proálcool, Relatório Anual 1980,* p. 39.

[61]Interview with Alex Periscinoto, director, Alcántara Machado Periscinoto Comunicações, Ltda., São Paulo, May 1981.

[62]These increases were sufficient to reduce the absolute consumption of anhydrous alcohol by November. See CENAL, *Proálcool, Relatório Anual 1980,* p. 26.

## Cycling Up in 1980

Encouraged by consumers' purchasing behavior, potential alcohol producers stepped up their proposals to CENAL.[63] Moreover, the fact that *Proálcool* had become an open account in the monetary budget encouraged investors to believe that credit for alcohol-related investments and working capital would be plentiful. The resulting surge of late 1980 provided what appeared to be irreversible momentum.

That success breeds success was reconfirmed as booming alcohol-powered car sales ratified *Proálcool*'s image as the Brazilian exit from energy vulnerability. Headlines boasted impressive statistics on accumulated distillery project approvals and productive capacity. More than 100 distilleries were approved on technical criteria by CENAL in 1980;[64] 53 more projects received the commission's blessing during the first four months of 1981 alone.[65] The approval of one huge project, a joint venture between the Ometto family and dominant urban capitalists such as Atlântica-Boa Vista, Votorantim, and Dedini, hinted that alcohol might become big business even for entrepreneurs historically detached from agriculture.[66] With a planned productive capacity of 800,000 liters per day, nearly eight times the size of the standard unit,

[63]The process, of course, was circular. Consumers would not have bought alcohol cars if they believed that future alcohol production would be unavailable or insufficient to keep the effective price of alcohol below that of gasoline.

[64]"Aprovados 115 projetos de destilarias em 1980," *O Estado de São Paulo*, 20 December 1980.

[65]CENAL, "Proálcool, Relatório Mensal, April 1981," p. 1. CENAL proclaimed in March 1981 that 255 projects were approved as part of *Proálcool* since 1975: "Próalcool já contratou 255 projetos," *O Estado de São Paulo*, 17 May 1981.

[66]"CENAL aprova projeto de destilaria da Bodoquena," *O Estado de São Paulo*, 15 April 1981. On the activities of these "*grupos bilionarios*," see Peter Evans, *Dependent Development* (Princeton: Princeton University Press, 1979), chap. 3.

the Destilaria Bodoquena symbolized for many the ambition of the National Alcohol Program.[67]

Many new projects were located in areas that did not previously produce sugarcane. In western São Paulo state, for example, small-scale farmers and ranchers formed producer cooperatives of sufficient scale to justify investments in autonomous distilleries and sugarcane plantations. In 1980 the opportunity to partake in the emerging alcohol boom was difficult to turn down, especially for those in the relatively unprofitable ranching industry.[68] Projects from frontier zones in the state of Mato Grosso frequently entered CENAL's docket as well.[69] One major reason was that investment finance for ordinary agricultural commodities was hard to find, whereas for *Proálcool* "all projects were attended to" by credit officials.[70] In 1980, some 83 of the 115 approved projects were autonomous distillery complexes.[71] During the following four months, all but eleven projects approved for funding were autonomous distilleries.[72] By April 1980, the number of approved projects was divided evenly between annexed and autonomous units.[73]

The move toward autonomous distilleries was encouraged by new financial terms. Autonomous projects presented after 17 December 1980 were to receive four years of grace during

[67]Other large alcohol "poles" were planned by the investment banking firm Brasilinvest in conjunction with Moneiro Aranha (a major private firm), Petrobrás, and two French concerns. See "Brasilinvest vai implantar pólo álcooleiro na Bahia," *O Estado de São Paulo*, 25 July 1980; and "Pólo de álcool sai em 3 anos," *O Estado de São Paulo*, 24 March 1981.

[68]Interviews at the Banco do Brasil, Brasília.

[69]Special problems relating to infrastructure, labor, and soil conditions plagued these and other projects. See "Destilarias da Nordeste enfrentam dificuldades," *O Estado de São Paulo*, 1 March 1981.

[70]This was the opinion of my informants at the Banco do Brasil, Brasília. For public information on this point, see "Proálcool gastou 30 bilhões em 1980," *O Estado de São Paulo*, 13 March 1981; "Cr$ 52,83 bilhões para o Proálcool," *O Estado de São Paulo*, 23 April 1981.

[71]CENAL, *Proálcool, Relatório Anual 1980*, p. 7.

[72]CENAL, "Proálcool, Relatório Mensal, April 1981," quadro I.

[73]Ibid., quadro V.

which interest, principal, and taxes on financial operations did not have to be paid.[74] The moderate tightening of the financial terms for all *Proálcool* projects, which went into effect on that date, appeared to be a small deterrent to the buoyancy of the program in the context of generally increased restrictiveness.[75] But the much longer lead times for these projects to reach full capacity placed in some doubt the ability of the country to reach its 1985 goal.[76]

## Clouds on the Horizon

At the same time, however, *Proálcool* generated new doubts and sources of opposition. Newspapers reported that sugarcane was transforming the interior, taking over whole regions, displacing the cultivation of other crops, and proletarianizing the former permanent labor force.[77] Conflicts among agricultural policy objectives, such as export promotion, food production, and energy generation, figured prominently in the

[74]Interview with officials in the departments of industrial and rural credit, Banco do Brasil, São Paulo, May 1981. See also "Governo quer ampliar Proálcool," *O Estado de São Paulo*, 30 January 1981.

[75]Interviews at Banco do Brasil, Brasília; and see David Renault, "Financiamento para álcool ainda atrai," *O Estado de São Paulo*, 1 February 1981. Additionally, encouragement for mini- and microdistilleries grew in 1980. See "Decreto regulamenta as microdistilerias," *O Estado de São Paulo*, 5 February 1981.

[76]See Celso Ming, "Álcool, ainda é bom negócio?" *Jornal da Tarde*, 13 May 1981; and "O Proálcool pode atingir as suas metas. Se houver interesse dos empresários," *Jornal da Tarde*, 19 May 1981. That production could approach the ambitious goal was impressive in itself and was not taken to indicate the failure of the program.

[77]Miguel Angelo Filiage, "Proálcool: os desertos verdes," *Jornal da Tarde*, 12 December 1979, traces the history of Sertãozinho, São Paulo. This feature article emphasized the enlargement of the "bóia-fria" (day labor) work force due to the seasonal labor requirements of sugarcane cultivation. A report of the National Council of Technological Research (CNPq), issued in 1979, was highly critical of the social effects of the alcohol program. See also Olga Khan, "A expansão da cana," *Gazeta Mercantil*, 26 February 1980; and "SP entra no ciclo do álcool carburante," *O Estado de São Paulo*, 29 June 1980.

intensifying debate.[78] Various policies, such as zoning, were contemplated to reduce the negative consequences of sugarcane's expansion in São Paulo.[79]

Other problems, touching the direct interests of alcohol consumers, raised concern even during this period of unparalleled popularity. Fears that the alcohol-car boom would exhaust fuel supplies were kindled by some press reports but soothed by proclamations from the *otimistas*.[80] Reports that a barrel of alcohol would command up to $US 70 on the export market worried those consumers suspicious of a turn in government policy toward generating export revenues, even at the political cost of deflating the domestic alcohol boom.[81] Limited flexibility in refinery cracking ratios reportedly led to

[78]Professor Fernando Homem de Melo of the University of São Paulo has consistently raised these issues in both the academic literature and the press. See, for example, his "A agricultura nos anos 80: perspectiva e conflitos entre objetivos de política," *Estudos Econômicos* (May/August 1980):57–101; "Em discussão este desafio: como produzir mais energia e mais comida," *Jornal da Tarde*, 13 December 1979; and "Proálcool versus Pronan," *Folha de São Paulo*, 13 July 1980.

[79]See "Ministério pode começar a controlar expansão da cana," *O Estado de São Paulo*, 23 February 1980; "Produção de álcool: um limite para São Paulo," *Jornal da Tarde*, 13 January 1981.

[80]See, for example, "Aumento do consumo do álcool carburante chega a 2000% em 12 messes," *Jornal do Brasil*, 21 May 1981; Celso Ming, "Álcool, ainda é bom negócio?" The discussion often centered on the alcohol-car quota and generated considerable dispute. See "Redução na produção de carros a álcool? O Governo é contra," *Jornal da Tarde*, 28 April 1981; "Carro a álcool: Penna é contra corte na produção," *O Estado de São Paulo*, 16 May 1981; and Mateus Kacowicz, "O que se fez para garantir o álcool," *Gazeta Mercantil*, 2 May 1981.

[81]Much publicity was given to the external accounts. See, for example, "Um prejuizo de 440 milhões de dólares," *Jornal da Tarde*, 29 January 1981; "Uma solução para a inflação do Proálcool," *Jornal da Tarde*, 22 January 1981; "Rigor para garantir a qualidade do álcool," *O Estado de São Paulo*, 25 March 1981. Reports of alcohol exports received editorial criticism: "Peturbação álcoolica," *Jornal do Brasil*, 3 April 1981. Penna assured the public that domestic demand had first priority: "Exportação de álcool depende do consumo," *O Estado de São Paulo*, 27 January 1981; but the export option was treated seriously on the editorial pages: "O reajuste para o álcool," *O Estado de São Paulo*, 31 January 1981.

the accumulation of gasoline stocks and to gasoline exports at discount prices. These reports suggested that *Proálcool* was failing to save as much foreign exchange as had been expected. For the politically alert consumer, excess demands for alcohol, excess supplies of gasoline, and high prices for alcohol exports signaled that policy toward the alcohol sector could take a large swing. All these problems could become much more prominent if world oil prices stabilized and the crisis atmosphere in the Middle East were dispelled.

Despite these continuing doubts and difficulties, *Proálcool* rested at an unstable equilibrium for nearly a year. But at the same time, the precariousness of this equilibrium increased as the country's macroeconomic circumstances deteriorated. Recognizing that the previously announced year-on-year monetary correction and series of exchange rate devaluations had failed to curb inflationary expectations, Delfim modified his economic program drastically in November 1980. Orthodox economic policy, absent from Brazil for fifteen years, characterized the new package.[82] Control of prices and interest rates was to be reduced, public deficits suppressed, and both the monetary correction and the exchange rate were once again to become functions of the inflation rate, rather than (supposedly) vice versa.[83]

With the stroke of Delfim's pen, uncertainty levels in the Brazilian economy greatly intensified. Recessionary policies soon began to create the largest economic downturn in public memory. Their probable effects on inflation were, however, unknown.[84] As interest rates soared,[85] commercial credit

[82]The declaration of the "new salary law," mandating nominal wage adjustments somewhat greater than inflation for the lowest-paid workers was a notable exception.

[83]"O que Delfim mudou," *Jornal da Tarde*, 5 November 1980; and José Carlos C. Morães, "Em 80, crescimento alto com inflação," *O Estado de São Paulo*, 4 January 1981.

[84]Celso Ming, "A inflação continuará alta. Só é difícil prever quanto," *Jornal da Tarde*, 5 January 1981.

[85]Celso Ming, "Porque o dinheiro ficou mais caro," *Jornal da Tarde*, 13

became practically unavailable even for long-standing bank customers and many profit opportunities dried up.[86] Although investment credits for alcohol production remained plentiful, *Proálcool* did not escape unscathed from Delfim's new tack. In the same month, November 1980, the planning minister branded the program inflationary.[87] He argued that "despite all the investment we are making, we are not increasing the mileage of our vehicles at all. That is, we are simply substituting alcohol for gasoline."[88] The only justification for the program, asserted Delfim, was the maintenance of employment in the automobile industry.

Delfim repeated his charge a month later, saying that "everyone wants their car, everyone wants *Proálcool*, but no one wants inflation."[89] A few days later, the *Jornal da Tarde* wondered in print whether Delfim's remarks were an announcement, a warning, or a lesson in economics. Suspicion was raised: "If [the announcement] was a preparation for a future decision, it would be good for the minister to say what he intends soon."[90] MIC Minister Camilo Penna challenged his colleague immediately thereafter, contending that *Proálcool* created inflationary pressures only during the period before projects reached their full capacity. Penna also reiterated his view that the program was not supposed to be miraculous; it

November 1980; "A absurda alta das taxas de juros," *Jornal da Tarde*, 17 February 1981; and José Antonio Ribeiro, "Custo dos empréstimos dobrou em doze messes," *O Estado de São Paulo*, 17 May 1981.

[86]See "A contração do crédito e os negócios," *O Estado de São Paulo*, 14 February 1981.

[87]"Delfim: o álcool é inflacionário," *Jornal da Tarde*, 27 November 1980.

[88]Ibid.

[89]"Uma solução para a inflação do Proálcool," *Jornal da Tarde*, 2 January 1981.

[90]"O Proálcool e outros geradores de inflação," *Jornal da Tarde*, 5 January 1981.

was just intended to substitute for incremental gasoline demand.[91] Despite these efforts, the press acknowledged with increasing frequency, the notion that *Proálcool* generated inflation.[92]

Over the next few months, orthodox macroeconomic ideas gained a tight grip on the beliefs of state officials and private elites.[93] The money supply, domestic credit, the monetary budget, and public subsidies therefore became key referents in Brazil's much-transformed economic policy debate. More concretely, subsidies for agricultural working capital, minimum prices, and exports were identified as principal sources of inflation.[94]

By early May, the system of open accounts in the monetary budget had become the prime focus of attention. Before the month was out, Central Bank President Carlos Langoni announced that this system would be eliminated within a year

---

[91]"Próalcool: Camilo Penna contesta Delfim," *Jornal da Tarde*, 6 January 1981. See also "Álcool vai custar 60% do preço da gasolina," *Jornal do Brasil*, 15 January 1981, where Penna stressed the security value of alcohol production.

[92]See "O Proálcool, inflacionário," *O Estado de São Paulo*, 6 January 1981; Homem de Melo, "Proálcool inflacionário," *O Estado de São Paulo*, 11 January 1981.

[93]For the foreign dimension, see "O apoio dos banqueiros a nova política econômica. O motivo: está de acordo com o FMI," *Jornal da Tarde*, 15 April 1981.

[94]See "Expansão dos empréstimos alcança 56%," *O Estado de São Paulo*, 26 November 1980; "Emitidos mais Cr$ 70 bilhões," *O Estado de São Paulo*, 1 January 1981; Julian Chacel, "Dificuldades para desaquecer economia," *O Estado de São Paulo*, 4 January 1981. The money supply growth target was established at 50 percent when inflation at the beginning of 1981 was 110 percent. See Johnson Santos, "Os riscos do orçamento monetário," *O Estado de São Paulo*, 7 January 1981; "Os técnicos leem a integra do orçamento. E ficam assustados," *Jornal da Tarde*, 7 January 1981; "Governo divulga o orçamento monetário," *Jornal da Tarde*, 9 January 1981; "A contração do crédito e os negócios," *O Estado de São Paulo*, 7 March 1981; "As dificuldades do controle monetário," *O Estado de São Paulo*, 20 March 1981; Milano Lopes, "Governo reconhece pressão, mas nada fará para reduzir os juros," *O Estado de São Paulo*, 22 March 1981; "Cr$ 1 trilhão, os gastos com subsídios," *O Estado de São Paulo*, 19 April 1981; Fabio Pahim, Jr., "A dívida interna cresce: para financiar os subsídios," *Jornal da Tarde*, 12 May 1981.

and all subsidies would then have to be financed through the Treasury with what he called "noninflationary resources."[95]

During the debate, credit demands for agricultural working capital, marketing the year's bumper coffee crop, and promoting exports received primary blame. *Proálcool* appeared to stay in the eye of the hurricane, prompting the *Estado de São Paulo* to remark on 21 May 1981 that there was "finally coherence in the alcohol policy."[96] But just three weeks later the headline "PROÁLCOOL: NEW PROJECTS SUSPENDED" dominated page one of the *Jornal da Tarde*.[97]

## Explaining the Boom

By the end of 1979, the Brazilian politico-economic system was in extraordinarily deep trouble. On top of the substantial increases in oil prices announced by OPEC earlier in the year, the country was suddenly faced with a radical change in U.S. monetary policy which would soon drive up Brazil's interest payments to unprecedented levels. Brazil therefore could not cushion the impact of the second oil shock by accumulating cheap debt as it did in the 1974–79 period. Moreover, if international banks greatly raised their estimates of the risks associated with loans to public and private Brazilian entities, even expensive credit might be difficult to obtain. Given the worsening international economic scene, by year's end it was fully apparent to all concerned that the government had to work miracles in order to achieve some acceptable combina-

[95]"Em 82, fim das contas em aberto," *O Estado de São Paulo*, 13 May 1981; "O Governo vai rever suas contas?" *Jornal da Tarde*, 18 May 1981; Claudia Safatle, "Efeitos da austeridade monetária," *Gazeta Mercantil*, 20 May 1981. The problem was exaggerated in the short run by the decline in tax receipts caused by the recession: "Subsídios atingirão Cr$ 900 bilhões," *O Estado de São Paulo*, 24 May 1981; "O governo, já quase sem dinheiro," *Jornal da Tarde*, 27 May 1981; "As emissões serão criteriosas," *O Estado de São Paulo*, 2 June 1981; "Como o governo pagará suas contas," *Jornal da Tarde*, 3 June 1981.

[96]"Álcool, afinal a coerência," *O Estado de São Paulo*, 21 May 1981.

[97]*Jornal da Tarde*, 16 June 1981.

tion of internal and external macroeconomic targets. In these extraordinary times, "Delfim Netto entered the Planning Ministry with an apparent carte-blanche from the military establishment and the Brazilian entrepreneurial elite. He had to do something spectacular."[98]

Although Delfim Netto was much more concerned with macroeconomic policy than with energy policy, his command of the economic policy-making process was instrumental to the rise of the alcohol boom. In particular, Delfim's seemingly uncontested control over all important economic policy decisions inspired confidence that the kind of interagency conflict experienced through mid-1979 now would be resolved. We cannot know whether authority over the economic policy-making process would have become so concentrated if the planning minister had not been known for his political agility and presidential ambitions. The concentration of authority under Delfim does suggest, however, that the political constraints which ordinarily limit central control over policy-making can be suppressed during extraordinary times. The striking adaptation of authority patterns to threatening circumstances is often noted, as in the case of effective central economic planning by the United States government during World War II.[99]

For a while, Delfim's heterodox macroeconomic policies inspired hope, both at home and abroad, that Brazil would be able to improve its external balance without suffering the steep declines in income that had occurred in Argentina and Chile. As part of this heterodox adjustment strategy, Brazil needed to retain the confidence of the international banking community. When this community joined the coalition of supporters of the alcohol program, the favorable implementation of Phase Two

[98]Edmar L. Bacha, "Vicissitudes of Recent Stabilization Attempts in Brazil and the IMF Alternative," in *IMF Conditionality*, ed. J. Williamson (Cambridge, Mass.: M.I.T. Press for the Institute for International Economics, 1983), p. 323.

[99]See Charles E. Lindblom, *Politics and Markets: The World's Political-Economic Systems* (New York: Basic Books, 1977), pp. 166–67.

by the Brazilian financial bureaucracies was therefore assured.[100] Now the alcohol program could satisfy not only the objectives outlined in Chapter 7 but also the goal of maintaining macroeconomic stability through continued access to international credit markets. Alcohol seemed to reconcile so many ordinarily competing goals of the regime that state officials all down the line could not rationally oppose any measure that would speed up implementation of the alcohol program.

As the *negativista* alliance collapsed, a continuous stream of positive signals was generated by the policy implementation process. From the vantage point of early 1980, changes in only two exogenous variables—the task environment and resource availability—appeared capable of upsetting the status quo. Since both oil prices and the current account deficit were on the rise, there seemed to be little reason to expect that central decision makers' enthusiasm for the alcohol program or their control over the state apparatus would diminish. Concerns about the availability of financial resources for distilleries were assuaged in early 1980 by the increasing amounts of credit reported to be flowing to the sector, by the open account status attained in August 1980, by the reports of loans offered by international private banks and the World Bank for the program, and by the apparent use of tax revenues to finance the construction of distilleries.

Thus, by the time of the Iran–Iraq War, political signals had become uniformly favorable and potential producers began to respond accordingly.[101] What remained to be completed was

[100]Why did the international banking community join forces with the *otimistas?* Probably for a variety of reasons, some of which were surely associated with intrabank politics. Those bankers who wanted to lend more money to Brazil could presumably point to the alcohol program as evidence that it was still the "country of the future."

[101]These investors were in effect joining an extremely strong coalition consisting of central decision makers, the automobile industry, the *usineiros*, private international bankers, and the World Bank. In a sense, new investors in alcohol distilleries were expecting to benefit from the privileged position of these groups.

the link between production and consumption. These strongly favorable signals were greatly amplified by the Iran–Iraq War. Sales of alcohol-powered cars benefited greatly from this well-timed external shock as well as from the inflation-induced consumer portfolio shift from financial to real assets. Moreover, as consumer investments in alcohol-powered cars increased, the remaining potential buyers likely revised upward their estimates of favorable future policies. The cycle of reinforcing positive expectations was complete.

This cycle was bound to be broken, however, at least temporarily. The instability of the boom derived in part from the difficulty of the coordination problem in such a complex system of production, marketing, and consumption in which investments had to be made in each link of the chain. But the inherent instability of the program must be understood as an outgrowth of the very conditions that made possible the alcohol boom. The perceived stability of policy was reinforced by the program's status as an open account, its uniqueness as an energy strategy, and the exclusion of Petrobrás from participation. As resource availability diminished following the implementation of orthodox stabilization measures, the political signals of support for *Proálcool* became stronger simply because the program appeared to withstand the politicization of monetary policy. Demands for credit increased accordingly, as investors tried to take advantage of the alcohol boom before it was too late. The positive cycle of monetary policy politicization and demand for *Proálcool* credits was not, however, indefinitely sustainable. At a minimum, small adjustments in credit policy would be necessary.

*Proálcool* also undermined itself because by 1980 the liquid fuels sector could no longer be treated as several independent issue areas, each corresponding to a derivative of petroleum. Although Planning Minister Simonsen had outlined an overall energy plan, the only component which could conceivably come to fruition in a few years was the alcohol program's 1985 targeted output of 10.7 billion liters. Substitutes for diesel fuel were in the purely experimental stage and promised to be extremely expensive. The production of coal as a substitute for industrial fuel oil required large investments, particularly in infrastructure to transport the material to the energy-consuming Center-South. The rapid accumulation of gasoline stocks during 1981 made it generally apparent that alcohol could not constitute a successful energy strategy on its own. The excess supply of gasoline and excess demand for alcohol eventually induced the CNP to eliminate the effective relative price differential between these two fuels. This change in instrument settings at a time of stabilizing world oil prices was extremely significant, particularly because of the inefficiency of political signals for consumers—the most ordinary of investors. Fears of insufficient alcohol fuel supplies were further heightened once credits for distilleries were suspended in June 1981.

# CHAPTER 9

# Denouement
# and Equilibration

## Cycling Down in 1981

*Justification for the Announcement*

The official reason given for the suspension of the credit element of *Proálcool* was that the government needed time to determine the inflationary consequences of the program. All proposals under review by the financial agents were at first affected by the decree. Two weeks later, however, contracts were allowed for projects submitted to CENAL before December 1980.[1] Both long-standing *otimistas* and former *negativistas* claimed publicly that the suspension was only temporary.[2] But

[1]For a useful summary of the evolution of these policies, see "Reabertas contratações de projetos do Proálcool," *O Estado de São Paulo*, 13 August 1981.

[2]"Proálcool ainda sob restrições," *O Estado de São Paulo*, 19 June 1981.

temporary decisions emit signals with long-lasting consequences. The public's slow accumulation of confidence in the program was suddenly shaken. "The doubts of *Proálcool*" returned as the main theme of newspaper headlines for several months after the brusque announcement of June.[3]

Although the economic inefficiency of alcohol production was the underlying cause of *Proálcool*'s vulnerability, it took the conjuncture of economic events of mid-1981 to prompt an attack by the most powerful of economic policymakers. First, as world oil prices stabilized around $US 34 per barrel, the call for a war economy appeared somewhat less compelling. Second, accelerating inflation emerged as a principal problem, to be dealt with in part by reducing drastically the role of subsidies in the steered economy. Continuing funding for *Proálcool* was therefore automatically on the agenda of the National Monetary Council, especially when the demand for project financing exceeded authorities' expectations. Third, further delays in stabilizing the economy became untenable when the country's creditors refused to finance the ongoing current account deficits in the same manner as they had in 1974–79.

The vulnerability of *Proálcool* to a policy reversal was heightened by its increasingly transparent failure to solve the energy problem. By midyear, many policymakers and others realized that substituting for gasoline contributed but modestly to energy security.[4] It was also clear that the problem of "balancing the barrel" would go unresolved until Petrobrás

[3]Celso Ming, "O verdadeiro problema: falta de planejamento," *Jornal da Tarde*, 16 June 1981; "O preço da falta de uma política energética," *O Estado de São Paulo*, 18 June 1981; "Proálcool: agora, mais dúvidas," *O Estado de São Paulo*, 26 June 1981; "Para restaurar a credibilidade no Proálcool," *Gazeta Mercantil*, 12 August 1981.

[4]See, for example, David Renault, "Esforço para recuperar Proálcool," *O Estado de São Paulo*, 28 June 1981; Mateus Kacowitz, "Revisão nas prioridades energéticas," *Gazeta Mercantil*, 24 August 1981; and "CENAL admite revisão no plano do álcool," *O Estado de São Paulo*, 20 August 1981.

made large investments to alter its refinery cracking ratios.[5] Since gasoline exports did not command a high price at the time, the government decided to let the public burn the surplus gasoline instead. As one indication of this policy, gasoline and alcohol retail prices rose much more slowly in 1981 than did those for diesel fuel.[6] These signals seemed to indicate that *Proálcool* was not, after all, the exit to the oil crisis.

## Some Consequences

Consumer confidence in the alcohol program deteriorated markedly during 1981. One reason was that many owners of alcohol-powered cars were unexpectedly faced with poor fuel efficiency and prices for alcohol that were not so favorable when compared to gasoline. Monthly car sales peaked in November 1980 at 53,481 units and then declined to 16,035 cars in March, to 5,126 in June, and to 2,720 in July.[7] Although collapsing sales figures overstate the extent of consumer dissatisfaction with their end of the alcohol chain, the euphoria was certainly gone.[8]

Much of the related political debate in late 1981 focused on the production goal and on alcohol exports, in addition to the financing issue itself. Doubts about the feasibility of the 10.7 billion liter goal for 1985 raised before the announcement of 16 June were confirmed by reports of the stalled approvals and

---

[5]See Chapter 2 for a discussion of this problem.

[6]"Álcool e gasolina, abaixo da inflação," *Jornal da Tarde*, 19 October 1981; José Roberto de Alencar, "Gasolina: postos abertos nos fins de semana, saída para o estoque alto," *Gazeta Mercantil*, 12 September 1981.

[7]Industry-wide sales dropped 40 percent in 1981 over the preceding year, according to S. Stefani, "Veículos: mercado interno 40% menor," *Gazeta Mercantil*, 27 June 1981. CENAL officials tried, however, to picture the resulting situation as more desirable than the period of the alcohol car boom. See "Reabertas contratações de projetos do Proálcool."

[8]Interestingly, foreign journalistic accounts quickly turned on the alcohol program. For an example, see "Brazil's Alcohol-Car Binge Dries Up," *Wall Street Journal*, 15 October 1981.

contracting process.[9] By August, the slowdown in the program was acknowledged publicly even by its most ardent *otimistas*.[10]

CENAL suggested a new timetable in which 11.5 billion liters of alcohol would be produced in the distant 1988–89 harvest year.[11] At the same time, alcohol exports were again suggested as an option to rid the country of surplus fuel and to earn foreign exchange. With improvement of the country's external balance a leading objective at the time, the IAA lifted its restrictions on alcohol exports in June for the first time since the outbreak of the Iran–Iraq War. These sales commanded up to $US 90 per barrel on the world market.[12] By September, alcohol exports were projected to be about 250 million liters for the year.[13]

The so-called review of *Proálcool* apparently ended after two months, when CENAL announced in mid-August that project contracts would be reopened. Projects approved by CENAL in 1981 became eligible for financing, although it was announced that the resources would be released only in 1982.[14] At the same time, CENAL said that the resources officially allocated to the program had been increased.[15] Since many such promises never materialized during Phase One of the program, an announcement that resources would be available only in the

[9]David Renault, "Dúvidas sobre a meta de produção de álcool," *O Estado de São Paulo*, 16 August 1981.

[10]"Cenal admite revisão no plano do álcool," *O Estado de São Paulo*, 20 August 1981; "Proálcool, desacreditado e desacelerado," *Gazeta Mercantil*, 22 August 1981; "O impasse do álcool: com a retração de vendas o governo decide diminuir o ritmo do programa do álcool, abalando mais a confiança do consumidor," *Veja*, 26 August 1981.

[11]Walter Clemente, "Os prazos do álcool," *Gazeta Mercantil*, 26 August 1981. The previous goal was 10.7 billion liters in 1985.

[12]Tania Nogueira Alvares, "Contratos de exportações liberados esta semana," *Gazeta Mercantil*, 25 June 1981.

[13]"Quanto o Brasil deve exportar de álcool este ano," *Jornal da Tarde*, 10 September 1981.

[14]"Reabertas contratações de projetos do Proálcool."

[15]Ibid.

following year did little to sustain producers' interest in the program.[16]

The experience of late 1981 was a case of *déjà vu* for those who had followed the program since its beginning. Not only were project financings suspended, but CENAL failed to approve new distilleries for months.[17] Only in September did the commission decide to include four new projects in the program.[18] Despite the stream of unfavorable news—including the lower production goal, the financing suspension, alcohol exports, and lower car sales—some *otimistas* tried to assure the public that the program would continue to be a government priority.[19]

Other *otimistas*, such as Newton Chiaparini, the new president of ANFAVEA, instead expressed pessimism about the future of *Proálcool*. "The euphoria of the market for alcohol-powered cars," he declared, "will never return."[20] The auto

[16]An increased credit budget for *Proálcool* was periodically announced with the stipulation that the resources would not be released until 1982. See "Saiu mais dinheiro para a Proálcool," *Jornal da Tarde*, 1 September 1981; "O Proálcool garantirá projetos já aprovados," *O Estado de São Paulo*, 2 September 1981; "Recursos de 87 bilhões para o programa em 82," *O Estado de São Paulo*, 5 September 1981; and "Proálcool terá recursos de 115 bilhões este ano," *O Estado de São Paulo*, 28 October 1981.

[17]Graça Seligman, "Proálcool: os recursos adicionais ainda não estão no BB," *Gazeta Mercantil*, 11 September 1981; Paulo Ludmer, "Proálcool: Relatório da CENAL mostra dois mêses sem projetos aprovados," *Gazeta Mercantil*, 10 September 1981.

[18]Paulo Ludmer, "Proálcool: CENAL anuncia o enquadramento de quatro projetos," *Gazeta Mercantil*, 17 September 1981. In October, eight projects were canceled: "Proálcool teve 8 disistências só em outubro," *Gazeta Mercantil*, 10 November 1981. Concurrently, *usineiros* wondered publicly whether they would continue to plant sugarcane; see Ludmer, "Relatório da CENAL."

[19]See, for example, "Incentivo para veículo a álcool não será ampliada," *O Estado de São Paulo*, 29 August 1981.

[20]"O impasse do álcool." In this article *Veja* concluded that "there is no sign in the short run that indicates how *Proálcool* could exit from the difficult waters it entered in the beginning of the year." In explaining the decline of consumer confidence in the program, this important weekly newsmagazine emphasized the following factors: Since the beginning of the year, alcohol prices rose by 321 percent, while gasoline prices increased only 231 percent; a

industry's pessimistic expectations about the long term were influenced not only by the stream of negative political signals. Of immediate concern was the size of their inventory of alcohol-powered cars, which had reached 30,000 units at a time when monthly sales of these vehicles failed to exceed 3000.[21] The accumulation of so many unsold cars could not have occurred at a worse time. Working capital credit became extremely expensive after November 1980 due to the contractionary monetary policy that Delfim Netto imposed after the apparent failure of his extremely risky macroeconomic strategy of 1980.[22] The high real interest rates that resulted led automobile companies and dealers to sell alcohol-powered cars at a discount—reversing the situation of the previous year when some consumers were willing to pay a premium (under the table) to acquire these special Brazilian vehicles.[23]

## Revitalization of *Proálcool*: 1982–84

### A Change of Direction

By March 1982, the stream of negative news about the future of the alcohol program had begun to change direction. Early in

---

variety of statements were made by government officials to the effect that the government could not necessarily guarantee an adequate supply of alcohol fuel; the performance and corrosion of alcohol engines disappointed consumers; the enormous Bodoquena distillery, owned jointly by the most privileged investors among local private capitalists, was "on the edge of death"; the minister of industry and commerce proposed to cut alcohol-powered car production from 360,000 vehicles to 200,000 units; and it became common knowledge that producing alcohol was more expensive for the country than the alternative of importing petroleum and refining it into gasoline.

[21] Ibid.

[22] "The liquidity crunch picked up toward the end of 1980 to acquire unheard-of proportions halfway through 1981. At the height of the crunch, in the second quarter of 1981, the money stock in real terms was made nearly 30 percent lower than a year before." See Edmar L. Bacha, "Vicissitudes of Recent Stabilization Attempts in Brazil and the IMF Alternative," in *IMF Conditionality*, ed. J. Williamson (Cambridge, Mass.: M.I.T. Press for the Institute for International Economics, 1983), pp. 331–32.

[23] "O impasse do álcool."

the month, government officials announced that a variety of new measures designed to stimulate consumer purchases of alcohol-powered cars were under consideration.[24] The possibility that the alcohol program would be revitalized at a time when world oil prices were steadily falling appears to have raised more than a few eyebrows.[25] But Planning Minister Delfim Netto argued that an expansion of alcohol production, though the costs of production were greater than the value of alcohol in world prices, would improve the country's trade balance. Whereas less than one year earlier Delfim was particularly interested in reducing the expansion of the alcohol program in order to combat inflation, he was now explicitly willing to risk higher inflation in order to compress imports in the short run.

The new measures designed to revitalize the alcohol program were announced by the end of the month.[26] State officials promised that the consumer price of alcohol would not exceed 59 percent of the consumer price of gasohol for at least the next two years. This wedge between fuel prices, if actually preserved, would reduce the costs of operating alcohol-powered cars by about 20 percent relative to the costs of operating gasoline-powered cars. A more surefire benefit was offered through tax policy. The tax on industrial products (IPI), essentially an excise tax paid when purchasing a vehicle, would be reduced for alcohol-powered cars and raised for gasoline-powered autos. These two measures would make

[24]See "Proálcool: Luz amarela, preços do óleo ameaçam avanço do programa," *Veja*, 10 March 1982; and "Plano da indústria para o *Proálcool*," *Jornal da Tarde*, 9 February 1982.

[25]"Proálcool: Luz amarela." "At the same time petroleum is becoming cheaper, the economic authorities are preparing to continue justifying heavy investments in the National Alcohol Program, which will swallow 153 billion cruzeiros this year. That amount is equivalent to one-third of the taxes received by the Treasury in 1981 from the tax on industrial products (IPI)."

[26]"A subida da montanha: baixas vendas levam o Governo dar novo incentivos para o carro a álcool," *Veja*, 31 March 1982. The special credit terms for alcohol-powered cars, namely the 36-month repayment period, as well as the reduced annual road tax (TRU), remained in force.

the acquisition cost of an alcohol-powered Volkswagen 1300 about 5 percent cheaper than a gasoline-powered model. To sweeten the deal further, the automobile industry extended the warranty period for alcohol cars (first-generation alcohol engines suffered from corrosion), and a number of accessories would be added to alcohol-powered cars free of charge.[27] Upon announcing these new measures, MIC Minister Penna said he expected 150,000 alcohol-powered cars to be sold during 1982 (though only 7000 had been sold before March).

These extremely lucrative incentives were greated with cautious interest by consumers. Sales of alcohol-powered cars increased by 2000 in April and May, and by 5000 in June and July. Sales of alcohol-powered cars for the year reached 21,400 units in August and 23,000 units in September. To be sure, the price and other incentives made alcohol-powered cars more attractive during 1982. But despite these strong incentives, monthly alcohol-powered car sales in September 1982 were only half as large as they were in December 1980.[28] This moderate expansion was welcomed by the automobile industry and some government officials. Although policies had to be extremely favorable in order to induce such an expansion, it was hoped that these incentives would not generate another alcohol boom.[29]

### The Liquidity Crisis and Its Consequences

The September 1982 Mexican payments crisis set off a chain reaction of events that, among other effects, generated a steady

[27]The value of the accessories was said to drive a further 2 percent wedge between the acquisition cost of the two types of cars.

[28]Data are from "Carro a álcool: sem engasgos, *Veja*, 20 October 1982. The relatively weak effect of the new, stronger incentives perhaps indicates that the earlier demise of *Proálcool* reduced the efficiency of political signaling for potential investors in alcohol-powered cars.

[29]A 30 percent share of automobile sales was the unofficial goal. See "Carro a álcool, caminho de volta," *Veja*, 12 May 1982; and David Renault, "MIC avalia demanda de álcool até 1985," *O Estado de São Paulo*, 3 October 1982.

stream of extremely favorable political signals for alcohol production and consumption. Following the highly charged negotiations between Mexico and its creditors, Brazil found its access to international capital markets suddenly restricted. This change in the asset preferences of money center and, especially, regional banks soon upset the precarious situation that had allowed Brazil to run current account deficits of about $US 10 billion per year. Before the Mexican crisis, Brazil was able to finance these substantial current account deficits with surpluses on the capital account, hence avoiding a deep recession.[30] Once credit flows ebbed, Brazil's immediate economic prospects deteriorated rapidly. By November 1982, Brazilian authorities were essentially forced to ask the International Monetary Fund for emergency financial assistance.

During this same period, the powerful National Monetary Council (CMN) announced that the main thrust of government economic policy would be to reduce the current account deficit. Among the few specific targets announced by the CMN was a $US 1 billion reduction in petroleum imports. Although the exact policies were not elaborated, consumers could easily infer that gasoline prices would soon climb steeply. The sharpest increases came a few months later, in February 1983, following a 30 percent maxidevaluation of the cruzeiro. This drastic measure, taken in the midst of ongoing negotiations with the IMF, plainly indicated that gasoline would become increasingly expensive, if available at all. Many consumers must have drawn this same conclusion even *before* the maxi-devaluation. By January 1983, alcohol-powered cars already constituted 59 percent of total monthly sales.[31] The renewed popularity of these cars greatly outstripped the industry's earlier expectations.

---

[30]The capital account surplus was also made possible by an extremely restrictive domestic monetary policy which raised cruzeiro interest rates to levels that could more than compensate for the expected cruzeiro exchange rate depreciation. For those entities that could borrow abroad, it would be cheaper to do so.

[31]*Journal of Commerce*, 1 June 1983.

Consumer interest was stimulated by positive signals about the alcohol program in addition to negative news about the price and availability of gasoline. First among these positive signals must have been evidence that alcohol production continued to meet demand. In March 1983, for example, *Veja* reported that 5.4 billion liters of alcohol were produced in the previous harvest year and that production was expected to reach 6.6 billion liters in the current year.[32] The phenomenal response by potential investors during the alcohol boom was already bearing considerable fruit. Due to the supply response as well as to the decrease in alcohol consumption during the bust period, the stocks of this alternative fuel continued to grow. At the end of 1982, stocks were reportedly about 3.5 billion liters.[33]

Surplus alcohol was a severe problem for those who had to store the fuel,[34] but for consumers these reports relieved the fears that had punctured the alcohol boom of 1980–81. Apart from hearing about huge current surpluses, consumers also learned that the government would offer new inducements to build distilleries, thereby raising expectations that supply would at least continue to meet demand.[35] With the external payments situation deteriorating, alcohol soon appeared to be a more secure source of motor fuel than gasoline—reversing the situation that had prevailed a year earlier. The benefit of a relatively assured supply greatly magnified the operating and capital cost advantages of alcohol-powered cars.

[32]"Em curto-circuito," *Veja*, 2 March 1983.

[33]"Sete anos de Proálcool," *O Estado de São Paulo*, 16 November 1982.

[34]"Proálcool: queixas dos empresários," *Jornal da Tarde*, 14 April 1983; Fatima Turci, "Indefinação compromete o Proálcool," *O Estado de São Paulo*, 8 November 1983; and Wilson Thimóteo, "Excesso de álcool no mercado causa problemas de estocagem," *Jornal do Brasil*, 23 April 1984.

[35]In July 1982, alcohol distilleries became excempt from the tax on industrial products. It should be noted, however, that credit subsidies were reduced substantially during this period in order to restrain inflation. These reductions affected all agricultural activities, and the alcohol sector remained relatively unscathed during 1983–84 by the government's efforts to reduce credit subsidies in accordance with IMF conditions.

*The 1983–84 Recession and the*
*Equilibration of Proálcool*

These favorable incentives were further reinforced as the IMF stabilization program went into effect. In June 1983, for example, Delfim announced a ten-point austerity program designed to satisfy the IMF's conditions. This package included provisions for raising the price of oil derivatives by 43 percent and for reducing rural credit subsidies by 50 percent.[36] During this same period, Petrobrás's demands for extended credit terms from its petroleum suppliers were meeting stiff resistance. Reports that the company could not easily finance its petroleum imports created a general fear of gasoline rationing.[37]

Consumers might have feared the effects of restraints on credit subsidies mandated by the IMF agreement. But *Proálcool* was reportedly exempt from the drastic curbs on such spending. This positive signal complemented several others. For example, 280 distillery projects were said to be in operation, the government was spending Cr$ 3 billion on an advertising campaign to boost sales of alcohol-powered cars, and alcohol fuel surpluses continued to mount. At the same time, alcohol reportedly comprised 26 percent of the gasohol fuel supply— well above the technically efficient 20 percent level.[38] Moreover, the most astute consumers might have recognized that the world sugar price had fallen to historically low levels and that the government might therefore encourage the *usineiros* to produce more alcohol at the expense of sugar.

As a result of these extremely strong political and price signals, about 75 percent of the automobiles sold in 1983 were

[36]Economist Intelligence Unit, *Quarterly Economic Review of Brazil*, no. 2 (1983):2.

[37]"Racionamento: as razões de especulação," *Visão*, 25 July 1983.

[38]There was, however, some speculation about the possibility of an eventual supply shortage. Projections of future alochol demand led the automobile industry to express a desire to slow down the growth of the alcohol car fleet. See "As incertezas estão de volta ao Proálcool," *Exame*, 29 June 1983.

powered by alcohol engines.[39] Investor interest in alcohol distilleries also revived during this critical period. By November 1983, CENAL had approved 452 distillery projects (194 annexed and 258 autonomous) with a combined capacity of over 10 billion liters per year. Investment credits, while less subsidized than during earlier periods and unavailable for many other activities, were available for the alcohol sector. The provision of these financial resources was apparently linked, at least in part, to World Bank loans for the alcohol program.[40] Although there was no assurance that working capital would be made available at subsidized rates for alcohol production, potential investors could probably expect that the cost and availability of working capital would be at least as attractive for alcohol production as for any other agricultural activity. To reassure the skeptical on this point, Petrobrás appeared willing to finance working capital needs and to purchase surplus stocks of alcohol.[41]

By the end of 1983, Brazil was fully committed to alcohol production and consumption. Some 500 distilleries had been approved by CENAL, at least half of which were in operation. According to a variety of sources, the government had already invested about $US 5 billion in the program. More than 1.5 million alcohol-powered cars had been sold. Some 95 percent of the automobiles being produced were equipped with alcohol engines. About 17 percent of the 1983 monetary budget was said to be allocated to the alcohol sector.[42] These

[39]Economist Intelligence Unit, *Quarterly Economic Review of Brazil*, no. 1 (1984):1.

[40]See "500 milhões de dólares para o Proálcool," *Jornal da Tarde*, 9 September 1983; and "Proálcool devesa ter mais Cr$ 135 bilhões," *O Estado de São Paulo*, 4 February 1984.

[41]*Petrobrás News*, November 1983. Petrobrás's management must have understood by then that their privileged position would be best preserved by joining the chorus, which frequently described the alcohol program as a "national victory." In taking this line, Petrobrás also claimed credit for the success of *Proálcool*. See *Petrobrás News*, March 1984.

[42]"Proálcool: uma vitória brasileira," *Índice Semanal*, 17 September 1984.

trends seemed immune from the continuing decline in real world oil prices. The *otimistas*, which now apparently included Petrobrás as well as the state financial apparatus, could with justification declare that *Proálcool* was entering its third and mature phase.

### Explaining the Collapse and Resurgence of *Proálcool*

*Cycling Down as a High-Probability Event*

The cycling down of the alcohol program in 1981 was not due primarily to an exogenous shock. Instead the program's success during 1980 undermined the same conditions that had given rise to the rapid movement of private resources into alcohol production and consumption. We have seen, for example, that the strongest signal of political support for *Proálcool* had been the continuation of its status as an open account at a time when credit subsidies were coming under intense scrutiny. This signal, given the environment within which it was transmitted, was in good measure responsible for the unexpectedly large number of proposals to build new alcohol production complexes. The resulting demand for credit could not be sustained forever if the monetary authorities were to achieve their increasingly urgent objective of reducing the rate of increase in the money supply. For this reason, the decision to withhold new alcohol credits was likely to occur at some time.

The second major reason why the first alcohol boom undermined itself was the suddenness and magnitude of consumer enthusiasm for alcohol-powered cars. Although this response to contemporaneous political and price signals encouraged ranchers and others to invest in alcohol production complexes, the extremely rapid growth in alcohol consumption created a dynamic mismatch between supply and demand. Given the substantial lead times needed before autonomous distillery complexes would become operational, it soon appeared that projected supplies could not accommodate the rate of increase in the alcohol-powered car fleet which characterized the September 1980–February 1981 period. Not only state officials were worried about the possibility of a shortfall in alcohol supplies. Consumers appear to have begun to adjust their expectations accordingly before the boom was even six months old.

What made this situation a pressing problem for policymakers was the rapid accumulation of gasoline stocks during the 1980–81 period. To some extent, this undesired inventory buildup was the direct counterpart of the rapid increase in alcohol consumption. But the demand for gasoline also fell as a consequence of the 1981 economic slowdown and the rise in gasoline prices at the pump. Since gasoline demand slowed more quickly than the demand for diesel or industrial fuel oil, in the absence of further changes in refinery cracking ratios at Petrobrás (or extensive international trade in petroleum products) this trend necessarily produced an excess supply of gasoline. As we have seen, Petrobrás had warned of this possibility for years. Although there is no evidence to prove that Petrobrás intentionally allowed gasoline stocks to accumulate, news of this growing problem signaled to state officials and investors that the alcohol program could not by itself significantly reduce expensive petroleum imports.

Faced with a potential excess demand for alcohol and an immediate excess supply of gasoline, the National Petroleum Council raised the price of alcohol relative to gasoline. This measure was imposed to decrease the growth rate of the fleet of alcohol-powered cars. However, perhaps to the CNP's surprise, this move helped puncture the alcohol boom. In light of news about occasional deep-discount gasoline exports, excess gasoline stocks, and a potential shortage in alcohol supplies, the adjustment in relative prices emitted a powerful political signal. As atomistic investors with close substitution possibilities, consumers were probably more sensitive to such adverse signals than were the other players in the game. The resulting decline in alcohol car sales gave an obvious push to the syndrome of cycling down.

To sum up, investor interest in alcohol distilleries was partly predicated on the alcohol program's open account status, while consumer demand for alcohol-powered cars was partly based on alcohol prices at the pump which more than compensated for the relative fuel inefficiency of alcohol engines. Because these two specific policies were designed to signal deep political support for alcohol production and consumption, changes in these policies could not be used to fine-tune the demand for credit or the demand for alcohol-powered cars.

The growth in alcohol production and consumption would have been a smoother process if consumers had not been strategic players in this game. To gain the cooperation of these atomistic investors who faced close substitution possibilities was an unrealistically ambitious task. Could consumers' strategic role have been eliminated? The automobile industry conceivably had the technological knowledge to develop an engine that could be powered by a gasohol fuel mixture containing, say, 30 to 60 percent alcohol and the rest gasoline. If only this (hypothetical) gasohol-powered car had been marketed instead of allowing consumers to choose between alcohol and gasoline cars, these investors would not have been in a position to ignite or defuse an alcohol boom. Among other benefits, the automobile industry could have avoided the costs of carrying 30,000 unsold alcohol-powered cars in 1981. More important, a controlled expansion of the country's commitment to alcohol production and consumption might have been possible under this scenario.

### The Second Alcohol Boom

By August 1981, almost everyone's expectations about the future of *Proálcool* were deeply pessimistic. Since world oil prices appeared to have peaked, few people had reason to expect that enough political support for the program could be generated to fashion another expansion of alcohol production and consumption. Yet the equilibrium prevailing at the end of 1981 was not dynamically stable. The unexpected rush of resources into alcohol production during the 1980–81 boom had already begun to yield marked increments in output during the 1981–82 harvest year. Meanwhile the projected increases in alcohol consumption failed to materialize. The demand shortfall was due mostly to the lack of consumer interest in alcohol-powered cars; but it was also due to high gasohol prices and the recession-induced decline in personal income. By March 1982, these trends forced policymakers to deal with an alcohol surplus.

At the same time, Delfim Netto and other central decision makers were coping with a variety of other threatening problems. While the domestic economy was rebounding somewhat from the sharp 1981 recession, the external picture remained bleak. Most advanced industrial countries were still following disinflationary macroeconomic policies. The unprecedented real interest rates which resulted from the highly restrictive credit policies of the time placed enormous pressure on Brazil's current account. Furthermore, the effects of the recession on world commodity prices and on the demand for Brazilian exports greatly limited the country's ability to run a trade surplus. In this setting, the military regime was also beginning to experience a serious political challenge. Popular support for democratization seemed to be gaining strength, while the government was planning to allow direct elections in November for state governors and for the federal Congress. A top priority for the military and Delfim in 1982 was clearly to stem the decline in their system of rule.

Reinvigorating sales of alcohol-powered cars would simultaneously address this macropolitical problem and reduce the surplus of alcohol fuel. Greater car sales would help the automobile industry rebound from the recession, with positive effects on income and industrial employment in the politically vulnerable Center-South. Furthermore, middle-class consumers would benefit directly from the favorable tax and credit treatment offered to buyers of alcohol-powered cars and from the newly lowered relative price of alcohol.

It is striking how slowly consumers responded to these extremely favorable incentives. Apart from the structural impediments to efficient signaling in such situations (as explained in Chapter 4), the earlier demise of the alcohol program must have contributed to their skepticism. In any case, the events of 1982 certainly provide one of the clearest demonstrations of the relative importance of political signals. While price incentives remained roughly constant, changing political signals led consumers increasingly to favor alcohol-powered cars. Since potential investors in alcohol distilleries adapted their own behavior accordingly, thanks to the credit made available by the government, Brazil became increasingly committed to alcohol production and consumption over this period of declining world oil prices.

In many respects, the second alcohol boom was an artifact of the deep political and economic crisis which Brazil endured in the 1982–84 period. After November 1982, the most immediate economic priority was to create a surplus on the trade account that could cover as much of the service account deficit as possible. In this environment, long-run efficiency calculations, based on fundamental exchange rates such as those discussed in Chapter 2, were practically irrelevant. The inflationary effects of financing distillery expansions through subsidized credit, however, were of continuing concern. *Pro-álcool* slipped through the constraints on credit subsidies imposed by the IMF for much the same reasons as it escaped the politicization of monetary policy in 1980–81. This privileged program continued to satisfy a variety of contradictory objectives of the regime, including promoting national security, strengthening local private capital, maintaining access to international credit markets, and enhancing political support from the middle class. Beyond these considerations, the World Bank, presumably an ally of the IMF, provided nearly one-half billion dollars in loans to finance distillery construction. In light of all these reasons to press on, Brazil's deepening commitment to increasingly inefficient alcohol production and consumption appears to have been politically rational, as well as privately profitable.

CHAPTER

# Conclusion

## On the Analysis of Politico-Economic Systems

*Obstacles to an Integrated Social Science*

Already fifteen years have passed since Albert O. Hirschman, in his introductory essay to *A Bias for Hope*, called upon political scientists and economists to forge a more integrated social science by exploring politico-economic interactions in the small.[1] In light of the impetus Hirschman's work has given to the growth of the political economy field in recent years, it is curious that the kind of research program adumbrated in this classic essay remains largely underexplored. Political scientists continue to emphasize "the politics of economic issues," often

---

[1]Hirschman, "Introduction: Political Economics and Possibilism," in *A Bias for Hope: Essays on Development and Latin America* (New Haven: Yale University Press, 1971), pp. 1–37.

at the aggregate level, and have tended to neglect opportunities to study "the finer features of the economic landscape."[2] Meanwhile, academic research by economists still reflects deeply ingrained habits of thought which prescribe treating policy as exogenous to models of the resource allocation process. An integrated social science may therefore still be only a distant possibility.

Given the methodological strictures of mainstream economics, economists are inclined to treat policy as an exogenous variable in a model of a market system so long as it is arguably useful to do so. Whether a given modeling strategy is considered useful is, of course, defined by the economics profession itself. In this book, I have consistently taken mainstream economists on their own terms. By grounding the analysis of the politicized market economy in current theories of microeconomic optimization, I have argued that in these systems sector-specific policy, policy expectations, and private investment decisions must be treated as mutually determined endogenous variables. This microanalytic approach has permitted me to introduce regime goals, segmentation, and situational factors (such as an issue area's age, size, and complexity) as exogenous variables in the model of the politicized market economy. Although these are unfamiliar variables in economic models, the structure of the argument is perfectly consistent with—and significantly inspired by—the modeling precepts of contemporary economic theory. For certain problems, therefore, it is possible that mainstream economists will be led by the rationality of their own research program to forge an integrated micropolitical economy.

Barriers to the development of an integrated social science by political scientists are perhaps more diffuse than those hindering such forays by economists. Despite the absence of a dominant paradigm in political science, there is a marked tendency for political economists to focus their analytic efforts

---

[2]Ibid., p. 8.

on the policy-making process rather than on the continuing interplay between market and political forces. Among the many reasons for this tendency is the "macro bias" within the discipline: It is much more common for political scientists to examine either macroeconomic policy—and sometimes outcomes—or microeconomic policies and outcomes across a wide range of sectors than to analyze historical sequences within one or a few sectors.

When specific sectors are examined, political scientists rarely build politico-economic models that can be used to interpret and abstract from a historical sequence. Model building tends to be a research strategy employed almost exclusively by statistically oriented political scientists and by theorists dealing with formal aspects of public choice. These political scientists seldom use their modeling talents to analyze historical cases in depth. Theoretical progress along the lines elaborated by Hirschman would be furthered by narrowing the professional distance between formal and historical political science.

### Uses and Limits of Modeling

Semiformal politico-economic modeling is not necessarily a component of Hirschman's own research strategy. But for those of us who lack Hirschman's genius for unraveling intimate politico-economic interactions, the logical exercise of model building is likely to be an extremely valuable research technique. Developing the model of the politicized market economy, for example, greatly extended my capacity to analyze Brazil's National Alcohol Program. And through a lengthy iterative process, the analysis of the case also led me to amend the model in a wide variety of important respects. The extent to which this iterative process pushed the analysis forward was a frequent source of surprise and motivation throughout the writing of this book.

In his introduction to *A Bias for Hope*, Hirschman assembled and illustrated several heuristic devices that he often uses to guide his own politico-economic analysis.[3] Interesting as these ideas are, such devices do not provide the kind of guidance most of us need to carry out this kind of research program. For broad guidance on modeling politico-economic systems, we can fortunately draw on the more general conceptual work of Charles E. Lindblom, as I have done in the present study.[4] It is extremely useful, for example, to distinguish analytically among three mutual adjustment processes which are intertwined in real-world politico-economic interactions. One is the mutual adjustment of top political authorities and their supporting organizations. Another is the mutual adjustment of state officials (including top authorities) to each other. A third is the mutual adjustment of state officials and market agents (such as investors) to one another.

This essentially microanalytic approach focuses attention on the objectives pursued by participants in each of these processes as well as on the devices they all can employ to control each other.[5] The actions of policymakers and market agents are then usefully viewed as a by-product of this vast system of mutual controls, embedded in a specific historical context. The massive commitment of resources to alcohol production and consumption in Brazil, for example, was a by-product of several forces: central decision makers' attempts to strengthen their authority to rule (by almost nonantagonistically reforming, at the margin, the production and ownership patterns of

[3]Including, for example, his well-known use of the concept of "blessings in disguise." See Hirschman, "Introduction," pp. 13–14.

[4]Lindblom, *Politics and Markets: The World's Political-Economic Systems* (New York: Basic Books, 1977), and *The Policy-Making Process*, 2d ed. (Englewood Cliffs, N.J.: Prentice-Hall, 1980). Although the *problématiques* of Lindblom and Hirschman overlap in many respects, their work is seldom woven together in the ways I am suggesting here. For an early comparison of their approaches, see Albert O. Hirschman and Charles E. Lindblom, "Economic Development, Research and Development, and Policy Making: Some Converging Views," *Behavioral Science* (April 1962):211–22, reprinted in Hirschman, *A Bias for Hope*, pp. 63–84.

[5]Lindblom, *Politics and Markets*, pp. 17–62, and *The Policy-Making Process*, pp. 43–55.

the Brazilian model); the substantial resolution of interagency conflict when the regime was faced with an extremely threatening task environment; and the valuation of alternative investments by both ordinary and privileged investors.

One distinct advantage of Lindblom's schema is that it can be used to integrate and thereby extend the elaborate conceptual devices social scientists have developed to understand each of these three mutual adjustment processes in specific contexts. Concepts explaining how regimes and organizations function, how investment projects are valued in a context of idiosyncratic exchange, and how mutual adjustment takes place when communication between decision makers is primarily indirect, for example, can provide powerful insights into complex social interactions, such as those which characterize politicized market economies. In this study, I have tried to show how these analytic tools can be combined in a logically consistent way to illuminate an important politico-economic research problem.

The integration of these specialized concepts permitted the derivation of "new facts" about resource allocation in a steered economy. I have shown, for example, why political signals are often a critical component of the incentive structure facing private investors in these systems. Furthermore, I have derived the proposition that political signaling tends to be most inefficient under the following circumstances: for ordinary investors; in new, complex, and large issue areas; during normal times; in countries where top authorities pursue intensely contradictory regime goals and where policy-making authority over each issue area tends to be diffused among many competing state agencies. In general, the logical relationships stipulated between these and other variables helped us explore the likely joint outcomes of the three mutual adjustment processes, delineated above, for qualitative values of the exogenous variables.

This short-term equilibrium model guided my interpretation of the National Alcohol Program by suggesting various ways in which diverse phenomena—such as capacity constraints in the alcohol production and consumption systems, the vulnerability of public enterprise property rights, and conditions in world credit markets—each systematically affected the mutual adjustment of central decision makers, other state officials, and market agents. The predictive power of this kind of model is limited. The effects of simultaneous changes in exogenous variables such as technological complexity and the state's task environment often introduce conflicting tendencies. For example, the growing size and complexity of the alcohol issue area in 1979 (which raised conflict) was accompanied shortly thereafter by an increasingly threatening task environment (which enhanced conflict resolution). In the absence of knowledge about the relative strength of such conflicting tendencies, it is impossible for such a model to produce unambiguous results.[6] Quantitative knowledge of this nature can only be derived, if at all, from an intimate acquaintance with the policy-making process in a given politico-economic context.

The model developed here, moreover, can only take us a limited distance because of its short-run character. The variables included in the model are, in reality, always changing value. Investments made by privileged investors, for example, constrain the likelihood of future policy reversals. Production increases usually reduce excess capacity in an activity; approaching capacity constraints can alter a sector's age, size, and complexity. Reports of excess commodity supplies and demands provide information to state and market decision makers which, by a variety of channels, modify these agents' rational choices. Events in international goods and financial markets, moreover, can similarly disturb equilibrium tendencies, especially in an open economy such as Brazil's.

Realizing that any situation is at most a short-run equilibrium, one can use a static model to identify the forces most likely to upset current conditions. Looser constraints on the

[6]This is, of course, a problem inherent in the comparative static method.

Brazilian balance of payments, for example, would likely undermine the ongoing expansion of the alcohol sector. A weakening of the sense of economic crisis could lead policy-makers in the finance or planning ministries to price foreign exchange at a level commensurate with the fundamental rates estimated in Chapter 2. If world oil prices remain steady or fall below their current real levels, alcohol production and consumption would appear significantly inefficient. As a large issue area currently absorbing a substantial portion of public credit, *Proálcool* would become extremely vulnerable to a policy reversal—especially after the inflow of World Bank credit ceases. The extent of the reversal, however, would be cushioned by the magnitude of the irreversible investments made in this sector by privileged and ordinary producers and by perhaps a million individual consumers. These investments, embellished by the normative framework of economic nationalism and other values, have institutionalized the alcohol sector. Decreases in the current capacity to produce and consume alcohol, therefore, would likely occur only after considerable time.

## Patterns of Resource Allocation

Three stylized facts stand out among the many intricate features of the history of the National Alcohol Program in Brazil: the undisputed legitimacy of *Proálcool* as a scheme to protect the *usineiros* from the effects of collapsing world sugar prices; the struggle launched during Phase One against the idea that alcohol production was or should become an explicit energy strategy; and the dramatic growth of alcohol production and consumption after 1979. These elements of *Proálcool* were analyzed in their historical context in Part II. Here I would simply like to suggest how these stylized facts might illustrate certain basic patterns of resource allocation in the Brazilian steered economy.

### Circularity in the Steered Economy

In Brazil, producers of political products who experience dislocations or imbalances (as did the *usineiros* in 1975) automatically achieve privileged access to state officials. In some cases, access is institutionalized through an administrative agency whose mission is to regulate supply and demand for their products (as did the IAA for sugar and alcohol). Another avenue of access, though not a mutually exclusive one, leads directly to central decision makers. This channel is open primarily for those producers of political products who embody the developmental vision of top authorities or who for other reasons occupy a strategic position in the politico-economic system. These channels of access are among the mechanisms that select pressing problems from the vast array of issues which could conceivably be attacked by policymakers.

Structured differential access to policymakers, however, only begins to capture this source of bias in the steered economy.[7] In broad terms, a variety of economic, organizational, political, and ideological features jointly transform dislocations experienced by producers of political products into pressing problems for state officials. As we have seen, these interrelated factors raised the probability that *Proálcool* would have been created even without the oil shocks.

Some familiar generalizations can be drawn from this sequence. State agencies charged with policy-making authority over a political product, such as the IAA, usually enjoy administrative and ideological resources that enhance the legitimacy of their continued intervention. These agencies can often act in concert with highly organized producer groups,

---

[7]The concept of structured differential access is developed in Joseph La-Palombara, *Interest Groups in Italian Politics* (Princeton: Princeton University Press, 1964).

such as Copersucar, which often command their own political, economic, and ideological resources.[8]

Political commitments by top authorities to the development of a specific sector create a relationship of mutual dependence between these political elites and the privileged producers on whom they rely to exemplify their legitimating politico-economic vision. To typify such a vision is, of course, a valuable ideological resource in itself. The *usineiros*, we saw, mobilized these resources extremely effectively in 1975 and beyond.

In a general way, these selection mechanisms are common to all market-oriented systems.[9] What broadly distinguishes the Brazilian steered economy from many other market-oriented systems is the cumulative effect of fifty years of state-led development and twenty years of authoritarian rule. Because the military attempted to legitimate their rule to a large extent by transforming the economy and benefiting certain social groups directly (including local private capitalists and the middle class), sector-specific policy-making became central to both the economy and the polity. As a consequence, microeconomic allocation decisions became intimately bound up with struggles over fundamental politico-economic institutions. Contradictions in the system of rule therefore had a pervasive effect on the allocation of resources in the twilight of authoritarian rule.

[8]Some would say that the IAA and Copersucar "structurally reflect the socially constructed reality" of state intervention in the sugar sector. See John W. Meyer and Brian Rowan, "Institutionalized Organizations: Formal Structure as Myth and Ceremony," *American Journal of Sociology* (September 1977):340–63, who argue that powerful organizations attempt to build their goals and procedures directly into society as institutional rules.

[9]See Lindblom, *Politics and Markets*, pp. 170–221, and *The Policy-Making Process*, pp. 71–121. For more country-specific discussions, see Samuel H. Beer, *Britain Against Itself: The Political Contradictions of Collectivism* (New York: Norton, 1982); Francis G. Castles, *The Social Democratic Image of Society* (London: Routledge & Kegan Paul, 1978); Michael Pertschuk, *Revolt Against Regulation: The Rise and Pause of the Consumer Movement* (Berkeley: University of California Press, 1982).

## Obstacles to Economic Change

The asymmetric treatment of old and new political products by policymakers was vividly illustrated during the debate that preceded the announcement of the National Alcohol Plan in November 1975. That the controversy over the idea of converting large quantities of sugarcane into alcohol fuel raged only *after* it was justified as an energy strategy stands out as a remarkable historical fact. Both public and private players who participated in the formulation and implementation of *Proálcool* seemed to be acutely aware of its potential if the sugar/alcohol nexus were severed.

The intensity of the struggle over *Proálcool* during Phase One illustrates how a proposed expansion of a certain line of economic activity can become linked to struggles over fundamental institutions. One reason why this linkage is easily made, apart from the centrality of sector-specific policy-making to the economy and polity, is because change at the margin of a politico-economic system is relatively nonantagonistic. The promotion of alcohol fuel production, for example, was a much less antagonistic means to expand the scope of private enterprise property rights and to enhance the political position of the military regime than, to take an extreme case, privatizing Petrobrás.

One notable feature of the process by which the struggle over authority was resolved is that it took so long. Not until mid-1979 was Petrobrás defeated in its bid for productive control. The struggle over regulatory control persisted a short while more. This delay may reflect a tendency for complex organizations to follow paths of minimal resistance in selecting issues to be taken up over the course of time. Such a tendency appears to be especially severe in one of the world's most complex organizations: a mature developmental state that has successfully institutionalized a variety of competing visions of legitimate state action.

A persistent struggle over authority and policy can certainly impair confidence in future policy and thereby obstruct economic change. This constraint was not binding, however, during Phase One. So long as the *usineiros* believed that policy would be generally favorable while sugar prices remained depressed and so long as President Geisel could raise the ceilings on the conversion of surplus sugarcane into alcohol, investments in annexed distilleries were made and put to use. In this way, alcohol production initially prospered under the rubric of precedents, institutions, commitments, and entitlements governing policy over one of the oldest political products in the Brazilian steered economy. In this case, what might ordinarily have been an obstacle to change actually facilitated change, since rapidly growing alcohol production during Phase One helped trigger events leading to the severance of the sugar/alcohol nexus, the alcohol booms, and the institutionalization of alcohol as a commodity in its own right.

### Coalition Formation and Privileged Political Products

Although alcohol production could initially be smuggled in under the protective cover of the sugar/alcohol nexus, a more direct route to the institutionalization of this new commodity was required once production levels began to strain the inherited consumption system. For technological and political reasons, the automobile industry's decision to participate in the alcohol program was seminal. Since automobile engines soon needed to be modified for alcohol consumption to expand rapidly, this industry could certainly block the transition to Phase Two. Yet the political characteristics of the auto industry's initiative and its consequences are of more general significance.

As some of the most privileged investors in the Brazilian steered economy, the automobile companies could easily join with central decision makers in support of Phase Two. Faced with an unraveling economic miracle, top authorities could not afford to jeopardize either the production of automobiles or the ability of the middle class to own and operate these high-status durable goods. Once aware of the industry's willingness to manufacture alcohol-powered cars, members of the incoming Figueiredo administration seem to have quickly grasped the mutual benefits of successfully launching Phase Two.

The early entry of the automobile industry set in motion a variety of processes that brought the formulation and implementation of Phase Two to fruition. This move by the foreign-owned automobile companies enabled those who wanted to propel the alcohol program forward to do so by linking the issue to the struggle between public and private enterprise property rights. With respect to the alcohol issue, the complex struggle within the Triple Alliance was simplified into a two-sided game precisely when Petrobrás was acutely vulnerable to such a strategy. Forced to choose between mutually exclusive competing claims, central decision makers blocked Petrobrás from achieving productive control over the alcohol sector. This difficult decision signaled that central decision makers were willing to seize upon the alcohol program as a strategy to reform their system of rule. The nearly simultaneous jump in oil prices reinforced the increasingly favorable expectations of policy toward *Proálcool*, especially because the military was historically committed to a secure energy supply. When international financial institutions granted *Proálcool* their seal of approval and appeared willing to provide Brazil with continued access to foreign loans as a result, the financial bureaucracy joined the *otimista* coalition, too.

This coalition-building process transformed alcohol into one of the most privileged political products in the Brazilian steered economy. It may be that such a privileged status is necessary to the emergence and institutionalization of a new political product that is both complex and large in a politicized market economy beset with contradictory regime goals and tendencies toward the segmentation of policy-making authority.

Because alcohol became such a privileged product, private resources were skewed into the production and consumption of this commodity. Formally, this transfer of resources occurred when ordinary producers and consumers expected the current highly favorable policy set to be dynamically stable. From a different angle, we may view the rush of resources into this sector as part of a process of implicit coalition building.

Faced with rising market uncertainty in the early 1980s, the ranchers of western São Paulo and other ordinary producers had an increasing incentive to invest in political products. Shifting into alcohol production, it is true, would widen their exposure to strategic uncertainty. But by investing in this sector, these ordinary producers could form an implicit alliance with some of the most privileged investors in the Brazilian political economy. As a result, these producers could possibly bear a wide-open exposure to strategic uncertainty as efficiently as the *usineiros* and the automobile industry. The magnitude of the shift of private resources into alcohol production after 1979 suggests the importance in a politicized market economy of this form of nonbargaining mutual adjustment or implicit coalition building for skewing the allocation of resources toward certain privileged activities.[10]

## Reorienting the Theory of Economic Policy

Having used the model of the politicized market economy and the history of the alcohol case to identify several stylized facts about the pattern of resource allocation in the Brazilian steered economy, I would now like to turn to the evaluative questions posed in Chapter 1. In the introduction, I argued that the determinants of resource allocation in politicized market economies are so dimly understood that social scientists cannot yet claim to know the effects of pervasive state microeconomic intervention on economic welfare. To begin the evaluative discussion, we may ask whether the alcohol case

[10]The same politico-economic pressures which Peter Evans identified in his studies of bargaining over the organization of capital are thus of general significance for nonbargaining mutual adjustment as well.

sheds any light on the relationship between microeconomic intervention and efficient or socially profitable resource allocation.

## Efficiency and Control

The social profitability analysis of Chapter 2 indicated that during Phase One the production of anhydrous alcohol and its consumption as gasohol was an inefficient way to utilize domestic resources. The sugar industry bailout scheme, sponsored by central decision makers and legitimated by a multiplicity of political, organizational, and ideological factors, is one clear example of how some privileged investors can use the state to transfer the costs of an economic dislocation to others.

On the other hand, the high levels of unresolved conflict that impaired the implementation of certain components of *Proálcool* during Phase One appear to have had a positive function. In particular, the financial bureaucracy's slow pace in approving state-subsidized credits for alcohol distilleries, despite intense pressure from President Geisel, served to minimize the country's commitment to what was at the time an economically inefficient gasoline substitute. Moreover, the bureaucracy's tactics were partly successful in forcing the *usineiros* to mobilize their own resources for alcohol production. This evidence suggests that high levels of unresolved conflict can enhance the efficiency of resource allocation.

The relationship between efficient resource allocation and policy effectiveness—which I have defined narrowly as the ability of central decision makers to achieve their sector-specific policy objectives—was more ambiguous during Phase Two. According to the analysis presented in Chapter 2, producing and consuming hydrated alcohol never became an efficient use of domestic resources. But three caveats prevented us from concluding that Phase Two was economically irrational. Between the Iranian Revolution and mid-1981, future world oil prices were subject to an extreme degree of uncertainty. Furthermore, the effects of the world recession, extraordinarily high interest rates, and the deterioration in Brazil's terms of trade on the fundamental equilibrium cruzeiro/dollar exchange rates were difficult to quantify. My estimates in Chapter 2 allowed for a sharp real depreciation of the cruzeiro. Substantial uncertainty, nonetheless, attached to these figures for 1981–83.

Fundamental equilibrium exchange rates, in any event, were probably of minor significance for project evaluation during the crisis period of 1982–84. To strengthen Brazil's external position and ability to bargain with international financial institutions, top economic policymakers were committed at that time to generating a substantial trade surplus regardless of the long-term costs of this strategy. In sum, then, Phases One and Two present a complex and ambiguous relationship between the efficiency and effective central control of resource allocation. A firm basis on which to assess extensive micro-economic intervention must therefore be sought elsewhere.

A politicized market economy can be evaluated, in part, by the privileged problems selected for attack by public and private decision makers. We have seen that alcohol production, for example, became a privileged problem in Brazil because its promotion contributed simultaneously to the solution of a wide variety of pressing problems faced by the military regime. Strengthening private enterprise property rights, fostering economic nationalism, assuring middle-class access to private transportation, hedging market uncertainty for sugar producers and the automobile industry, and maintaining access to international credit markets were among the objectives that ultimately *biased* the resource allocation system in favor of alcohol production and consumption. Whether this bias is acceptable or not depends upon whether this constellation of goals should or should not receive greatest priority.

The efficiency of political signals also stands out from this study as a determinant of economic welfare. When signaling efficiency is impaired, attempts to control private investment behavior can claim substantial public resources. In Phase Two of the alcohol program, for example, tremendous credit subsidies were offered to induce investment in alcohol production. Since these subsidies were essentially financed through inflationary monetary policy, the public-at-large paid some price for the extreme signaling inefficiency of *Proálcool*. Apart from raising the costs of control in these circumstances, inefficient signaling can create a severe obstacle to the short-term adjustment of commodity supplies and demands. In the alcohol case, for instance, successive attempts to match supplies and demands emitted powerful political signals that contributed to the cycle from boom to bust to boom in the 1980–84 period. Most participants in the game would likely have preferred a steady expansion of alcohol production and consumption over the cycling pattern actually experienced.

In raising doubts about policy effectiveness, this study challenges certain powerful habits of thought which are expounded most succinctly by the "theory of economic policy."[11] The terminology associated with this tradition has practically achieved the status of ordinary language in the social sciences. Policymakers are said to specify the "targets" of policy and the "settings" on the available "policy instruments" in light of what is known about the structure of the economic system. The widespread influence of this approach is attributable to both its Keynesian affinities and to the ease with which its concepts are translated into mathematical models. Policy instruments become exogenous variables or parameters, instrument settings become the values of these variables, and targets become the endogenous variables. This setup has led many economists to infer that the state's ability to control the private economy is necessarily a positive function of the number of policy instruments it employs.

Strident challenges to the idea that there is necessarily a

---

[11]The *locus classicus* is Jan Tinbergen, *On the Theory of Economic Policy* (Amsterdam: North-Holland, 1954). For an extension, see William C. Brainard, "Uncertainty and the Effectiveness of Policy," *American Economic Review* (May 1967):411–25.

positive relationship between "instruments" and "control" have recently entered the mainstream professional literature on macroeconomic policy.[12] Nevertheless, the theory of economic policy still underlies many writings about microeconomic intervention, including those of political scientists. Even as perceptive a student of sector-specific policy as Peter Katzenstein has asserted that "the instruments which policy-makers command largely determine whether stated objectives can be achieved in the process of policy implementation."[13]

Unlike the critics of macroeconomic policy effectiveness, I do not challenge the theory of economic policy at the microeconomic level in order to turn it on its head. Instead I have tried to show that policy effectiveness depends in large measure on the macropolitical structure of nation-states, as well as on a variety of situational factors. Certain features of the politico-economic system in authoritarian Brazil, for example, sometimes impaired state control over private investment decisions, perhaps primarily because this system of rule has lacked the institutional mechanisms that apparently exist in Japan and France to facilitate state/market coordination.

In working toward stable democratic rule, Brazil's president-elect, Tancredo Neves, pledged that his administration would "reorganize the state," accelerate economic growth, and fight inflation. During this momentous period of transition and consolidation, his successor and Brazil's other new leaders would be wise to dedicate no small measure of their ingenuity to the design of politico-economic institutions that can best serve their vision of a developed and democratic Brazil.

[12]See, for example, Robert E. Lucas and Thomas J. Sargent, "After Keynesian Macroeconomics," in *After the Phillips Curve: Persistence of High Inflation and High Unemployment*, Conference Series Number 19 (Boston: Federal Reserve Bank of Boston, 1978), pp. 49–72.

[13]Katzenstein, ed., *Between Power and Plenty: Foreign Economic Policies of Advanced Industrial States* (Madison: University of Wisconsin Press, 1978), p. 297. The theoretical status of this comment is difficult to determine. As a premise, it is certainly mistaken. As an empirical generalization based on the limited set of countries examined in *Between Power and Plenty*, the comment may be perfectly valid.

# Appendix 1

*Costs of Production per Metric Ton of Sugarcane Collected: 1978-79 Harvest, São Paulo and Paraná*

| Input | Technical Coefficient | Price per Unit (Cr$) | Cost (Cr$/mt) |
|---|---|---|---|
| *Fixed costs* | | | |
| Maintenance and Supervision | | | |
| Labor | 0.00142 | 6652.22 | 9.44 |
| Maintenance Costs | N.A. | N.A. | 0.64 |
| Tax, Insurance, etc. | N.A. | N.A. | 1.09 |
| Capital Depreciation[a] | | | |
| Buildings | N.A. | N.A. | 6.06 |
| Installations | N.A. | N.A. | 0.05 |
| Machines | N.A. | N.A. | 7.46 |
| Trucks | N.A. | N.A. | 5.53 |
| Other Equipment | N.A. | N.A. | 0.83 |
| Interest on Fixed Capital and Unused Land | N.A. | N.A. | 33.30 |
| Land | N.A. | N.A. | 36.36 |
| Total Fixed Costs | N.A. | N.A. | 100.66 |
| *Variable Costs* | | | |
| Production—first cut | | | |
| Labor (man-days) | 0.06652 | 95.97 | 6.38 |
| Machines (per day) | 0.06017 | 165.78 | 9.97 |
| Transport (km) | 0.18822 | 6.68 | 1.26 |
| Animals (per day) | 0.00005 | 407.60 | 0.02 |
| Seeds (mt) | 0.04201 | 289.59 | 12.16 |
| Fertilizers (mt) | 0.00302 | 3063.87 | 9.25 |
| Soil Correctives (mt) | 0.00367 | 203.77 | 0.75 |
| Pesticides (kg) | 0.05482 | 65.97 | 3.62 |

| Input | Technical Coefficient | Price per Unit (Cr$) | Cost (Cr$/mt) |
|---|---|---|---|
| Production—second and third cuts | | | |
| Labor (man-days) | 0.07107 | 103.94 | 7.39 |
| Machines (days) | 0.04545 | 171.39 | 7.79 |
| Transport (km) | 0.00884 | 6.11 | 0.06 |
| Animals (days) | 0.00023 | 385.18 | 0.09 |
| Fertilizers (mt) | 0.00386 | 3395.20 | 13.11 |
| Pesticides (kg) | 0.05174 | 80.66 | 4.17 |
| Interest on Working Capital | N.A. | N.A. | 6.15 |
| Collection and Harvest | | | |
| Labor (man-days) | 0.19442 | 117.40 | 22.82 |
| Machines (hours) | 0.00994 | 415.79 | 4.13 |
| Transport (km) | 0.92191 | 4.58 | 4.22 |
| Collection/Carrying | | | |
| Machines (hours) | 0.03154 | 190.12 | 6.00 |
| Transportation to Mill (km) | 3.46837 | 6.78 | 23.52 |
| Total Variable Costs | N.A. | N.A. | 142.86 |
| Total Private Costs per Metric Ton, | | | |
| Excluding Capital Subsidy | N.A. | N.A. | 243.52 |

SOURCE: Copersucar, *Aspectos Econômicos, 1978/80* (São Paulo: Copersucar, 1980), p. 82. Reprinted from M. Barzelay and S. R. Pearson, "The Efficiency of Producing Alcohol for Energy in Brazil," *Economic Development and Cultural Change* (October 1982):136. © 1982 by University of Chicago Press.

NOTE: Costs are calculated in terms of September 1978 prices (Cr$); yield assumed to be 65 metric tons per hectare; N.A. = not applicable.

[a]The social opportunity cost of capital is estimated at 12 percent a year.

# Appendix 2

Costs of Production for Direct Alcohol per 1000 Liters: 1978–79
Harvest, São Paulo and Paraná

| Input | Technical Coefficient | Price per Unit (Cr$) | Cost (Cr$/1000 Liters) |
|---|---|---|---|
| *Fixed Costs* | | | |
| Maintenance | | | |
| Labor (man-months) | 0.01160 | 4828.72 | 55.99 |
| Material | N.A. | N.A. | 124.39 |
| Administration | | | |
| Personnel (man-months) | 0.02569 | 9593.62 | 246.46 |
| Taxes, Insurance | N.A. | N.A. | 22.57 |
| Miscellaneous | N.A. | N.A. | 81.52 |
| Capital Depreciation | | | |
| Buildings | N.A. | N.A. | 55.27 |
| Machines and Equipment | N.A. | N.A. | 309.30 |
| Other Installations | N.A. | N.A. | 38.44 |
| Interest on Fixed Capital[a] | N.A. | N.A. | 652.83 |
| Land | N.A. | N.A. | 0.54 |
| Total Fixed Costs | N.A. | N.A. | 1587.31 |
| *Variable Costs* | | | |
| Operations | | | |
| Chemicals (kg) | 9.98120 | 6.27 | 62.56 |
| Labor (man-months) | 0.02838 | 6142.35 | 174.32 |
| Electricity | 178.57625 | 0.61 | 108.86 |
| Fuel/Lubricants | 156.90060 | 0.29 | 46.02 |
| Maintenance | | | |
| Personnel | 0.02177 | 5735.41 | 124.86 |
| Material | N.A. | N.A. | 305.73 |
| Working Capital | N.A. | N.A. | 156.76 |
| Total Variable Costs | N.A. | N.A. | 979.11 |

| Input | Technical Coefficient | Price per Unit (Cr$) | Cost (Cr$/mt) |
|---|---|---|---|
| Total Private Costs per 1000 Liters, Excluding Subsidy to Capital | N.A. | N.A. | 2566.42 |

SOURCE: Copersucar, *Aspectos Econômicos, 1978/80* (São Paulo: Copersucar, 1980).

Reprinted from M. Barzelay and S. R. Pearson, "The Efficiency of Producing Alcohol for Energy in Brazil," *Economic Development and Cultural Change* (October 1982):137. © 1982 by University of Chicago Press.

NOTE: Costs are calculated in terms of September 1978 prices; N.A. = not applicable.

[a]The social opportunity cost of capital is estimated at 12 percent a year.

# Bibliography

## Published Books and Journal Articles

Akerlof, George A. "The Market for Lemons." *Quarterly Journal of Economics* (August 1970):488–500.

Allison, Graham. "Conceptual Models and the Cuban Missile Crisis." *American Political Science Review* (September 1969):689–718.

Arrow, Kenneth J. *The Limits of Organization.* New York: Norton, 1974.

Bacha, Edmar L. "Issues and Evidence on Recent Brazilian Economic Growth." *World Development* (January/February 1977): 47–67.

———. "Notes on the Brazilian Experience with Minidevaluations, 1968–1976." *Journal of Development Economics* (December 1979): 463–81.

———. "Selected Issues in Post-1964 Brazilian Economic Growth." In *Models of Growth and Distribution for Brazil*, edited by Lance Taylor et al. New York: Oxford University Press, 1980.

———. "Vicissitudes of Recent Stabilization Attempts in Brazil and the IMF Alternative." In *IMF Conditionality*, edited by John Williamson. Cambridge, Mass.: M.I.T. Press for the Institute for International Economics, 1983.

Bacha, Edmar L., and Taylor, Lance. "Foreign Exchange Shadow Prices: A Critical Review of Current Theories." *Quarterly Journal of Economics* (May 1971):197–224.

Baer, Werner. *The Brazilian Economy: Its Growth and Development.* Columbus, Ohio: Grid Publishing, 1979.

Barzelay, Michael, and Pearson, Scott R. "The Efficiency of Producing Alcohol for Energy in Brazil." *Economic Development and Cultural Change* (October 1982):121–44.

267

_____. "The Efficiency of Producing Alcohol for Energy in Brazil: Reply." *Economic Development and Cultural Change* (July 1985): 857–63.

Beer, Samuel H. *Britain Against Itself: The Political Contradictions of Collectivism.* New York: Norton, 1982.

Bergsman, Joel. *Brazil: Industrialization and Trade Policies.* London: Oxford University Press, 1970.

Brainard, William C. "Uncertainty and the Effectiveness of Policy." *American Economic Review* (May 1967):411–25.

Bryant, Ralph. *Money and Monetary Policy in Interdependent Nations.* Washington, D.C.: Brookings Institution, 1980.

Calabresi, Guido, and Melamed, A. Douglas. "Property Rules, Liability Rules, and Inalienability: One View of the Cathedral." *Harvard Law Review* (April 1972):1089–1127.

Cardoso, Fernando Henrique. "On the Characterization of Authoritarian Regimes in Latin America." In *The New Authoritarianism in Latin America*, edited by David Collier. Princeton: Princeton University Press, 1979.

do Carmo Oliveira, João, and da Silva Montezano, Roberto Marcos. "Os limites das fontes de financiamento à agricultura no Brasil." *Estudos Econômicos* (August 1982):139–59.

Castles, Francis G. *The Social Democratic Image of Society.* London: Routledge & Keegan Paul, 1978.

Coase, Ronald. "The Problem of Social Cost." *Journal of Law and Economics* (October 1960):1–44.

Collier, David, ed. *The New Authoritarianism in Latin America.* Princeton: Princeton University Press, 1979.

Corden, W. M. *Trade Policy and Economic Welfare.* Oxford: Clarendon Press, 1974.

_____. *Inflation, Exchange Rates, and the World Economy.* Chicago: University of Chicago Press, 1977.

Cyert, Richard M., and March, James G. *A Behavioral Theory of the Firm.* Englewood Cliffs, N.J.: Prentice-Hall, 1963.

Dahl, Robert A. *Dilemmas of Pluralist Democracy.* New Haven: Yale University Press, 1982.

Dahl, Robert A., and Lindblom, Charles E. *Politics, Economics, and Welfare.* Chicago: University of Chicago Press, 1976.

D'Inção e Mello, Maria Conceição. *O Bóia Fria: Acumulação e Miséria.* Petrópolis: Editora Vozes, 1975.

Evans, Peter. *Dependent Development: The Alliance of Multinational, State, and Local Capital in Brazil.* Princeton: Princeton University Press, 1979.

_____. "Reinventing the Bourgeoisie: State Entrepreneurship and Class Formation in Dependent Capitalist Development." In

*Marxist Inquiries*, edited by Michael Burawoy and Theda Skocpol. Chicago: University of Chicago Press, 1982.

Fama, Eugene F., and Miller, Merton H. *Theory of Finance*. New York: Holt, Rinehart and Winston, 1972.

Fendt, Robert, Jr. "The Crawling Peg: Brazil." In *Exchange Rate Rules*, ed. John Williamson. New York: St. Martin's Press, 1981.

Fishlow, Albert. "Origins and Consequences of Import Substitution in Brazil." In *International Economics and Development: Essays in Honor of Raul Prebisch*, edited by Luis Eugenio DiMarco. New York: Academic Press, 1972.

_____. "Some Reflections on Post-1964 Brazilian Economic Policy." In *Authoritarian Brazil*, edited by Alfred Stepan. New Haven: Yale University Press, 1973.

Flynn, Peter. *Brazil: A Political Analysis*. Boulder, Colo.: Westview Press, 1978.

Foxley, Alejandro. "Stabilization Policies and Their Effects on Employment and Income Distribution: A Latin American Perspective." In *Economic Stabilization in Developing Countries*, edited by William R. Cline and Sidney Weintraub. Washington, D.C.: Brookings Institution, 1981.

Grissa, Abdessatar. *The Structure of the International Sugar Market and Its Impact on the Developing Countries*. Paris: Development Centre of OECD, 1976.

Hahn, Frank. "Reflections on the Invisible Hand." *Lloyds Bank Review* (April 1982):1–21.

Hirschleifer, J. *Investment, Interest, and Capital*. Englewood Cliffs, N.J.: Prentice-Hall, 1970.

Hirschman, Albert O. *Exit, Voice, and Loyalty: Responses to Decline in Firms, Organizations, and States*. Cambridge, Mass.: Harvard University Press, 1970.

_____. *A Bias for Hope: Essays on Development and Latin America*. New Haven: Yale University Press, 1971.

_____. *Journeys Toward Progress: Studies of Economic Policy-Making in Latin America*. New York: Norton, 1973.

_____. "The Turn to Authoritarianism in Latin America and the Search for Its Economic Determinants." In *The New Authoritarianism in Latin America*, edited by David Collier. Princeton: Princeton University Press, 1979.

_____. *Essays in Trespassing: Economics to Politics and Beyond*. Cambridge: Cambridge University Press, 1981.

Hirschman, Albert O., and Lindblom, Charles E. "Economic Development, Research and Development, and Policy Making: Some Converging Views." *Behavioral Science* (April 1962):211–22.

Homem de Melo, Fernando. "A agricultura nos anos 80: perspectiva e conflitos entre objetivos de política." *Estudos Econômicos* (May/August 1980):57–101.

Homem de Melo, Fernando, and Gianetti da Fonseca, Eduardo. *Proálcool, Energia, e Transportes.* São Paulo: FIPE, 1981.

Horwitz, Morton J. *The Transformation of American Law, 1780–1860.* Cambridge, Mass.: Harvard University Press, 1977.

Hudson de Abranches, Sergio H. *The Divided Leviathan: State and Economic Policy Formation in Authoritarian Brazil.* Ann Arbor: University Microfilms, 1978.

Katzenstein, Peter J., ed. *Between Power and Plenty: Foreign Economic Policies of Advanced Industrial States.* Madison: University of Wisconsin Press, 1978.

Keohane, Robert O. "U.S. Foreign Economic Policy Toward Other Advanced Capitalist States: The Struggle to Make Others Adjust." In *Eagle Entangled: U.S. Foreign Policy in a Complex World,* edited by Kenneth Oye, Donald Rothchild, and Robert J. Lieber. New York and London: Longman, 1979.

Knight, Frank H. "Economics." In Knight, *On the History and Method of Economics: Selected Essays.* Chicago: University of Chicago Press, 1956.

———. *The Economic Organization.* New York: A. M. Kelley, 1967.

Kurth, James. "The Political Consequences of the Product Cycle: Industrial History and Political Outcomes." *International Organization* (Winter 1979):1–34.

LaPalombara, Joseph. *Interest Groups in Italian Politics.* Princeton: Princeton University Press, 1964.

Lindblom, Charles E. *The Intelligence of Democracy.* New York: Free Press, 1965.

———. *Politics and Markets: The World's Political-Economic Systems.* New York: Basic Books, 1977.

———. *The Policy-Making Process.* 2d ed. Englewood Cliffs, N.J.: Prentice-Hall, 1980.

Lucas, Robert E. "Econometric Policy Evaluation: A Critique." In Lucas, *Studies in Business-Cycle Theory.* Cambridge, Mass.: M.I.T. Press, 1981.

Lucas, Robert E., and Sargent, Thomas J. "After Keynesian Macroeconomics." In *After the Phillips Curve: Persistence of High Inflation and High Unemployment.* Conference Series Number 19. Boston: Federal Reserve Bank of Boston, 1978.

Luce, R. Duncan, and Raiffa, Howard. *Games and Decisions.* New York: Wiley, 1957.

Machlup, Fritz. "Equilibrium and Disequilibrium: Misplaced Concreteness and Disguised Politics." In Machlup, *International Payments, Debts, and Gold.* New York: Scribner's, 1964.

Malan, Pedro S., and Bonelli, Regis. "The Brazilian Economy in the Seventies: Old and New Developments." *World Development* (January/February 1977):19–46.

da Mata, Milton. "Crédito rural: caracterização do sistema e estimativas dos subsídios implícitos." *Revista Brasileira de Economia* (July/September 1982):215–45.

Meyer, John W., and Rowan, Brian. "Institutionalized Organizations: Formal Structure as Myth and Ceremony." *American Journal of Sociology* (September 1977):340–63.

Morgenstern, Oskar. "Thirteen Critical Points in Economic Theory: An Interpretation." *Journal of Economic Literature* (December 1972):1163–89.

Muth, J. "Rational Expectations and the Theory of Price Movements." *Econometrica* (July 1961):315–35.

Nelson, Richard R., and Winter, Sidney, G., Jr. *An Evolutionary Theory of Economic Change*. Cambridge, Mass.: Harvard University Press, 1982.

O'Donnell, Guillermo A. *Modernization and Bureaucratic-Authoritarianism*. Berkeley: Institute of International Studies, 1973.

Perrow, Charles. *Complex Organizations: A Critical Essay*. 2d ed. Glenview, Ill.: Scott, Foresman, 1979.

Pertschuk, Michael. *Revolt Against Regulation: The Rise and Pause of the Consumer Movement*. Berkeley: University of California Press, 1982.

Quadros da Silva, Salmão L. "O crescimento da lavoura canavieira no Brasil na década de 70." *Revista Brasileira de Economia* (January/March 1983):39–54.

Ross, Stephen A. "The Determination of Financial Structure: The Incentive-Signalling Approach." *Bell Journal of Economics* (Spring 1977):23–40.

Schelling, Thomas C. *Micromotives and Macrobehavior*. New York: Norton, 1978.

Schumpeter, Joseph A. *Capitalism, Socialism, and Democracy*. New York: Harper & Row, 1950.

Sen, Amartya. "The Profit Motive." *Lloyds Bank Review* (January 1983):1–20.

Serra, José. "Three Mistaken Theses Regarding the Connection Between Industrialization and Authoritarian Regimes." In *The New Authoritarianism in Latin America*, edited by David Collier. Princeton: Princeton University Press, 1979.

Schattschneider, E. E. *The Semisovereign People*. Hinsdale, Ill.: Dryden Press, 1975.

Shonfield, Andrew. *Modern Capitalism: The Changing Balance of Public and Private Power*. London: Oxford University Press, 1965.

Shubik, Martin. *Game Theory in the Social Sciences: Concepts and Solutions.* Cambridge, Mass.: M.I.T. Press, 1982.

Silberberg, Eugene. *The Structure of Economics.* New York: McGraw-Hill, 1978.

Simon, Herbert A. *Administrative Behavior.* 3d ed. New York: Free Press, 1976.

_____. *Sciences of the Artificial.* 2d ed. Cambridge, Mass.: M.I.T. Press, 1981.

Stepan, Alfred. *The Military in Politics: Changing Patterns in Brazil.* Princeton: Princeton University Press, 1971.

_____. "The New Professionalism of Internal Warfare and Military Role Expansion." In *Authoritarian Brazil,* edited by Alfred Stepan. New Haven: Yale University Press, 1973.

_____. *The State and Society: Peru in Comparative Perspective.* Princeton: Princeton University Press, 1978.

_____, ed. *Authoritarian Brazil.* New Haven: Yale University Press, 1973.

Stobaugh, Robert, and Yergin, Daniel. "Energy: An Emergency Telescoped." *Foreign Affairs: America and the World 1979* (1980): 563–95.

Szmrecsányi, Tamás. *O Planejamento da Agroindústria Canavieira do Brasil (1930–1975).* São Paulo: HUCITEC, 1979.

Timmer, C. Peter, Falcon, Walter P., and Pearson, Scott R. *Food Policy Analysis.* Baltimore: Johns Hopkins University Press, 1983.

Tinbergen, Jan. *On the Theory of Economic Policy.* Amsterdam: North-Holland, 1954.

Weber, Max. *Economy and Society.* Edited by Guenther Roth and Claus Wittich. Berkeley: University of California Press, 1978.

Williamson, John. *The Exchange Rate System.* Cambridge, Mass.: M.I.T. Press for the Institute for International Economics, 1983.

Williamson, Oliver L. *Markets and Hierarchies: Analysis and Antitrust Implications.* New York: Free Press, 1975.

Wirth, John D. *The Politics of Brazilian Development, 1930–1954.* Stanford: Stanford University Press, 1970.

## Periodicals

*Christian Science Monitor*

*Conjuntura Econômica*

*Diário Comércio e Indústria*

*O Estado de São Paulo*

*Exame*

*Folha de São Paulo*

*Gazeta Mercantil*

*Índice Semanal*

International Financial Statistics
Isto É
Jornal da Tarde
Jornal do Brasil
Journal of Commerce
London Times
Petrobrás News
Quarterly Economic Review of Brazil

Relatório da Gazeta Mercantil
San Francisco Chronicle
Science
Sugar and Sugar Sweetener Outlook
Veja
Visão
Wall Street Journal


## Other Published and Unpublished Materials

Brasálcool. "Relatório descritivo das condições de acesso a empreendimentos álcooleiros localizados na região do Estado de Mato Grosso." São Paulo, 1981.
Central Bank of Brazil. *Annual Report, 1981*. Brasília, 1982.
Comissão Executivo Nacional de Álcool. "Roteiro para elaboração de projetos." Brasília, 1979.
_____. *Proálcool, Relatório Anual 1980*. Brasília, 1981.
_____. "Proálcool, Relatório Mensal, April 1981." Brasília, 1981.
Conselho Nacional de Pesquisas Tecnológicas. "Availação tecnológica do álcool etílico: versão preliminar." Brasília, 1978.
Conselho Nacional de Petróleo. *Anuário Estatístico, 1979*. Brasília, 1980.
_____. *Anuário Estatístico, 1980, Complemento 1979*. Brasília, 1981.
_____. *Anuário Estatístico, 1982*. Brasília, 1983.
Copersucar. *Aspectos econômicos da produção de cana, açúcar e álcool: periódo 1978/80*. São Paulo, 1980.
International Sugar Organization. *Sugar Yearbook, 1980*. London, 1981.
Instituto Brasileira de Geografia e Estatística. *Sinopse Estatística do Brasil, 1977*. Brasília, 1977.
Lara Resende, Marcelo. "Energy Prices and the Post Oil/Energy Crisis Brazilian Inflation: An Input-Output Study." Ph.D. dissertation, Yale University, 1982.
Navarro, Lamartine. "Análise do desenvolvimento do Plano Nacional de Álcool." São Paulo, 1979.
Nunberg, Barbara. "State Intervention in the Sugar Sector in Brazil: A Study of the Institute of Sugar and Alcohol." Ph.D. dissertation, Stanford University, 1978.
*II National Development Plan, 1975–79*. Brasília, 1974.
U.S. Department of Energy. *The Potential for Energy Conservation in Nine Selected Industries*. Vol. 2. Washington, 1978.

## Interviews

Accioli, José de Lima. Secretaria de Tecnologia Industrial, Ministério da Indústria e do Comércio. Brasília, 1981.

Bacha, Edmar L. Professor of Economics, Pontifícia Universitária Católica. Rio de Janeiro, 1981.

Baer, Werner. Professor of Economics, University of Illinois. Rio de Janeiro, 1979.

de Barros, Francisco H. President, Empresa Brasileira de Álcool (Brasálcool). São Paulo, 1981.

Bash, Richard. Consul, United States Consulate, São Paulo. São Paulo, 1981.

Bresser Pereira, Luiz Carlos. Professor of Economics, Fundação Getulio Vargas. São Paulo, 1981.

Camolese, Nelson. *Usineiro*. São Paulo, 1981.

Cardoso, Fernando Henrique. Director, CEBRAP. São Paulo, 1981.

Caron, Dálcio. Faculdade de Economia e Administração, Universidade de São Paulo. São Paulo, 1979.

Castro de Barros, Armando. Instituto de Pesquisas Tecnológicas. São Paulo, 1979.

Chagas, Carlos. Brasília Bureau Chief, *O Estado de São Paulo*. Brasília, 1981.

Chaves de Mendonça, Antonio Aureliano. Vice President, Federative Republic of Brazil. Brasília, 1981.

Chaves de Mendonça, Manoel Ignácio. Comissão Nacional de Energia. Brasília, 1981.

Disch, Arne. Instituto de Pesquisas Econômicas. São Paulo, 1981.

Fizzotti, Virgílio. Dedini Metalúrgica. São Paulo, 1979, 1981.

Gall, Norman. Journalist. São Paulo, 1979.

Goldemberg, José. Instituto de Física, Universidade de São Paulo. Stanford, California, 1980, and São Paulo, 1981.

Gotlib, Márcio Diniz. Assessor-Chefe, Assessoria de Diretoria, Copersucar. São Paulo, 1979.

Gutemberg, Luiz. Editor in Chief, *Jornal da Semana Inteira*. Brasília, 1981.

Homem de Melo, Fernando. Professor of Economics, Instituto de Pesquisas Econômicas, Universidade de São Paulo. São Paulo, 1981.

Hudson de Abranches, Sergio H. Professor, Instituto Universitário de Pesquisas do Rio de Janeiro (IUPERJ). Rio de Janeiro, 1981.

Junqueira, Luiz Roberto. Director, Brasilinvest, S.A. São Paulo, 1981.

Leão, Francisco M. D. *Usineiro* and businessman. São Paulo, 1979, 1981.
de Lima Fernandes, Marcos. Secretaria Executivo, Comissão Executivo Nacional de Álcool (CENAL). Brasília, 1981.
Lins, Hilton Barreto. Mobil Oil do Brasil, S.A. São Paulo, 1979.
Lisboa, Lázaro. Banco do Brasil. São Paulo, 1979.
Mattar, Helio. Diretor, Departamento de Economia e Engenharia de Sistemas, Instituto de Pesquisas Tecnológicas. São Paulo, 1979, 1981.
Ming, Celso. Economics Editor, *O Estado de São Paulo*. São Paulo, 1981.
Mirisola Neto, Eugenio Paulo. Mobil Oil do Brasil, S.A. São Paulo, 1979, 1981.
Moraes Rego, Luiz Carlos. Brasilinvest, S.A. São Paulo, 1979.
Moura, Alkimar. Professor of Economics, Fundação Getúlio Vargas. São Paulo, 1979.
Navarro, Lamartine. Diretor, Destilaria Alcídia, S.A. São Paulo, 1979.
Naves, Sidonio. Comissão Nacional de Energia. Brasília, 1981.
Nunes de Almeida, Aloisio. Economist, Copersucar. São Paulo, 1981.
Ometto Pavan, Virgílio. Usina Santa Cruz. Araraquara, São Paulo, 1979.
Paiva, Ruy Miller. Economist, IPEA. Rio de Janeiro, 1979.
Paschkes, Mauro. Commodity Broker, FINASA-ACLI. São Paulo, 1979, 1981.
Periscinoto, Alex. Director, Alcántara Machado Periscinoto Comunicações, Ltda. São Paulo, 1981.
Pisa, Fernando Toledo. Instituto de Açúcar e do Alcool (IAA). São Paulo, 1981.
Pischinger, Georg. Manager, Technical Research, Volkswagen do Brasil, S.A. São Paulo, 1979, 1981.
Policaro, Alberto. Superintendente de Crédito, São Paulo, Banco do Brasil. São Paulo, 1979.
Rodrigues, Eduardo Celestino. Comissão Nacional de Energia. São Paulo, 1981.
Saavedra, José. Vice President, Morgan Guaranty Trust of New York. São Paulo, 1981.
Saeki, Jorge. Legal Counsel, Ford Motor do Brasil, S.A. São Paulo, 1979.
de Souza e Silva, Carlos Eduardo. Instituto de Pesquisas Tecnológicas. São Paulo, 1979.
Szmrecsányi, Tamás. Professor of Economics, Universidade Estadual de Campinas. São Paulo, 1981.

Texeira, José Carlos. Secretaria de Tecnologia Indústrial, Ministério da Indústria e do Comércio. Brasília, 1981.

Thomé, José Carlos. Energy Editor, *Gazeta Mercantil*. São Paulo, 1979.

Toledo, Candido Ribeiro. Comissão Nacional de Álcool (CNA). Rio de Janeiro, 1979.

Veras, Arnaldo Ignácio. Ministério de Agricultura. Rio de Janeiro, 1979.

Venetianer, Tomas. Vice President, Anderson Clayton, S.A. São Paulo, 1981.

Vidal, Walter Bautista. Formerly of the Secretaria de Tecnologia Industrial, later of IPEA. Stanford, California, 1980, and Brasília, 1981.

Wilson, Donald E. President, Anderson Clayton, S.A. São Paulo, 1981.

Six officials of the Banco do Brasil, Brasília, 1981; two Banco do Brasil officials, São Paulo, 1981; and one Petrobrás official, Rio de Janeiro, 1981. Names held in confidence.

# Index

Abranches, Sergio H. Hudson de, 95–96
Agricultural crops, 67–68
Akerlof, George A., 86n
Alagoas state, 129
Alcohol, anhydrous, 22, 212; in conventional automobile engines, 30, 32; demand for, 66; economic inefficiency of, 170–71; production statistics for, 42 (see also Alcohol production); social losses on, 30, 38; value of, 32, 33, 38, 41
Alcohol boom: causes of, 201 214–15, 223–27, 244; demise of first, 125, 228–33, 240–42; second, 242–45
Alcohol consumption: investment incentives for, 73–76; flexibility in, 39
Alcohol exports, 178, 231
Alcohol fuel: availability of, 123; competition for control over prices, 205–8; costs of, 75–76; demand for, 66;

efficiency in conventional gasoline engines, 22, 30; history of, 130, 136–53; and pollution, 26; price relative to gasoline, 123, 185, 191, 205–8, 227, 230, 234; retail prices for, 180, 185; supply and demand for, 240–41; supply of, 219, 227; surplus of, 237, 238, 239, 243; value of, 20–21, 32, 33, 38, 41
Alcohol, hydrated, 259; consumption of, 215; demand for, 66; in factory-made alcohol cars, 32; net social losses generated by, 38–39, 44; production statistics for, 42, 44; pump price for, 206, 207; value of, 32, 41
Alcohol-powered cars, 11, 15, 16, 48, 191; comparative fuel inefficiency of, 66, 75, 230; consumer dissatisfaction with, 230; consumer response to, 31–32, 66, 73–76, 83–84, 112, 213, 243–44; factory-made, 32; incentives for consumer purchase of, 180–81, 185,

277

Brazil: economic growth of, 6 (*see also* Economic miracle in Brazil); steered economy of, 6-9
Brazilian Central Bank. *See* Central Bank of Brazil

Calmon de Sá, Angelo, 162, 164; on alcohol-powered cars, 177; alcohol program supported by, 178
Capital: goods industry, 7, 169; of international banks, 204-5; local private, 181, 183, 184; of multinational corporations, 183, 184; private costs of, 25; social costs of, 25
Capital budgeting, 45-46; decision rules for, 60-61; model under market and strategic uncertainty, 46, 52-64
Capital markets: international, 236; state intervention in, 25
Cardoso, Fernando Henrique, 8n
Cash flows: in capital budgeting analysis, 53; estimations of, 46, 55; from investments in distilleries, 70-71; of political products, 56, 57
CDE. *See* Council for Economic Development
CENAL. *See* National Executive Commission for Alcohol
Center for Aeronautical Technology (CTA), 139
Center-South Brazil, 131-32; compared with the Northeast, 24, 137-38
Central Bank of Brazil, 12, 14; credit constrained by, 162-65, 167, 170; credit facilitated by, 203; credit policy on annexed distilleries, 88, 122-23; and diffuse policy-making authority, 97; and exchange rates, 26; macroeconomic policy of, 26; "monetary budget" of, 201n, 222-23; policy reversal by, 88; primary mission of, 87
Central control, 120-21; on alcohol production, 173; conditions for impairments of, 121; limited in policy-making, 173
Central decision makers: conflict resolution by, 114-17; defined, 13n; facing mutually exclusive jurisdictional claims, 151-52, 257; mutual adjustment with ordinary investors, 82-84; mutual adjustment with privileged in-

vestors, 78-82, 120; relative to task environment, 99-101; and state apparatus, 101-4, 114-15; variability in control over policy-making by, 88-89, 102-4
Circularity in steered economies, 253-54
CMN. *See* National Monetary Council
CNA. *See* National Alcohol Commission
CNAl. *See* National Alcohol Council
CNE. *See* National Energy Commission
CNP. *See* National Petroleum Council
Coal, 187, 189, 227
Coalitions: for private control over alcohol production, 181, 183; and privileged political products, 257-58; in state politics, 156-65
Coase, Ronald, 23n
Coffee, 67n, 108; bumper crop of, 223; exports of, 135; plantations of, 131; production of, 132
Collective action by private investors: efficacy of, 81-82; obstacles to, 83, 84
Commodity prices, 39, 243
Competition: for authority in policy-making, 104-6, 108-9, 255; for control of alcohol program, 143-44, 151-53, 170-73, 181-85; during policy implementation, 170; over control of, 205-8; over productive control, 105-6, 170, 181-85, 186, 195
Complexity of issue areas: consequences of, 111-12, 120 123-24, 197; defined, 107; role in dispersing policy-making authority, 107-8
Conflict: over alcohol sector policy, 142-44, 151-52, 170-73, 181-85, 205-8; defined, 110; in energy policy-making, 177-78; generation and resolution of, 109-10, 114-17, 118-19; in policy implementation, 170
Consumers: incentives to buy alcohol cars by, 74-76, 83-84; linked with alcohol producers, 121; as ordinary private investors, 83; political signals interpreted by, 121-22, 229-33. *See also* Alcohol-powered cars
Contradictions of rule, 10-11, 92-95, 254. *See also* Macropolitical goals
Control. *See* Competition; Productive control; Regulatory control
Cooperatives of producers, 137-38, 217. *See also* Copersucar

Raiffa, Howard, 51*n*, 60*n*
Ranchers, 49–50, 258
Raw materials, debate on, 142–43, 145
Refineries. *See* Petrobrás; Petroleum
refineries
Reformist strategy, 191–92
Regulatory control: competition for,
106, 151–53, 181, 186, 199; defined,
105; by financial bureaucracy, 200–
201
Resource allocation: patterns of, 252–
58; in a steered economy, 250
Risk: of automobile industry, 192–95;
in financing distilleries, 163–64; re-
duction of, 81–82
Risk-free assets, 53, 54, 56, 60, 62, 63
Road system, 176
Road tax, 234*n*
Ross, Stephen A., 86*n*
Rural employment, 140, 170

Saavedra, José, 205*n*
São Paulo, 23, 24, 41*n*; private invest-
ments in autonomous distilleries in,
49; Secretariat of Agriculture in, 142;
sugar industry in, 81, 131–33, 137–38
Schelling, Thomas C., 117*n*
Schumpeter, Joseph A., 105*n*
Segmentation, 95–97, 106–8; defined,
95, 107; and dispersion of authority,
107–8; political signals impaired by,
120
Serra, José, 7*n*, 10*n*
Shadow exchange rates, 26–29, 35–37
Shonfield, Andrew, 3
Shubik, Martin, 2*n*; on game theory,
47*n*
Signaling, concept of, 85. *See also* Political signals
Simon, Herbert, 98; on nearly decomposable systems, 112*n*; on "task environment," 100
Simonsen, Mario Henrique, 184, 186*n*,
200*n*; on alcohol for motor fuel, 171;
alcohol program opposed by, 160–
61, 172; energy policy of, 188–89,
190, 196, 209, 226; on finances for
alcohol production, 180
Social benefit-cost analysis, 21*n*, 22–44;
estimation of social costs in, 24–29;
social profitability in, 29–30
Social costs. *See* Costs, social

Social objectives of alcohol program,
140, 142, 169, 181
Social returns and profitability of alcohol production, 29–30, 33, 37–39;
compared with social costs of sugar
production, 41; and world oil prices,
32–34
State: conflict resolution among officials of, 114–17; mutual adjustment
with private investors, 5–6, 44, 46,
48–60, 73–76, 77–91, 249; partisan
mutual adjustment among officials
of, 91–117, 156–65
State-of-the-world approach to private
investment, 54–55, 57, 61–64; on annexed distilleries, 69–70; on consumer purchase of alcohol-powered
cars, 75
State sector-specific policies, 3–4; for
alcohol production from sugarcane,
19–44; centrality in Brazilian politics,
6–9; changes in, 50, 53, 55, 56–57;
compared with microeconomic intervention, 48; for consumer purchase of
alcohol-powered cars, 75; instruments
of, 8, 25, 75; mutual adjustment with
private investment, 5–6, 44, 46, 48–
64, 81; obstacles to effectiveness of,
9–10, 42–44, 162–65
"Statization" of the economy, 93, 183
Steel industry, 80
Steered economy: analyzed in Brazil,
6–9, 25; capital budgeting in, 45–46,
52–64; capital markets in, 25; circularity in, 253–54; compared with
other market-oriented systems, 254;
equilibrium conditions in, 58, 60,
122; game theory applied to, 51–52;
market forces in, 45–76; microeconomic foundations of, 52, 58; strategic uncertainty in, 46–50
Stepan, Alfred, 94*n*; on the Brazilian
military regime, 8*n*, 78*n*
Stobaugh, Robert, 174*n*
Storage of alcohol, 167, 180, 237
Strategic uncertainty. *See* Uncertainty,
strategic
Strike by metallurgical workers, 212–13,
214
Structured differential access, 253
Subsidized credit. *See* Credit, subsidized
Substitution possibilities, 30; between
alcohol and gasoline-powered cars,

Designer:    Janet Wood
Compositor:  Ampersand, Inc.
Text:        11/13 Baskerville
Display:     Baskerville
Printer:     Bookcrafters, Inc.
Binder:      Bookcrafters, Inc.